CHURCH, INTERRUPTED

CHURCH, INTERRUPTED

HAVOC & HOPE

THE TENDER REVOLT OF POPE FRANCIS

JOHN CORNWELL

CHRONICLE PRISM

Library of Congress Cataloging-in-Publication Data
Names: Cornwell, John, 1940– author.
Title: Church, interrupted : havoc & hope : the tender revolt of Pope
    Francis / John Cornwell.
Description: San Francisco, California : Chronicle Prism, [2021] | Includes
    bibliographical references. |
Identifiers: LCCN 2020042851 | ISBN 9781797202013 (hardcover) | ISBN
    9781797203614 (paperback) | ISBN 9781797202020 (ebook)
Subjects: LCSH: Francis, Pope, 1936– | Church renewal—Catholic
    Church—History—21st century. | Catholic Church—History—21st century.
Classification: LCC BX1378.7 .C67 2021 | DDC 282—dc23
LC record available at https://lccn.loc.gov/2020042851

Manufactured in the United States of America.

MIX
Paper from responsible sources
FSC
www.fsc.org   FSC™ C005010

Design by AJ Hansen.
Typesetting by Happenstance Type-O-Rama. Typeset in Freight Text Pro.

10 9 8 7 6 5 4 3 2 1

Chronicle books and gifts are available at special quantity discounts to corporations, professional associations, literacy programs, and other organizations. For details and discount information, please contact our premiums department at corporatesales@chroniclebooks.com or at 1-800-759-0190.

 CHRONICLE PRISM

Chronicle Prism is an imprint of Chronicle Books LLC, 680 Second Street, San Francisco, California 94107
www.chronicleprism.com

For Beatrix,
Veronica, and Giselle

CONTENTS

"*Hoping against hope! Today, amid so much darkness, we need to see the light of hope and to be men and women who bring hope to others.*"

—POPE FRANCIS AT MASS, MARCH 19, 2013

A PERSONAL PREFACE

Anyone reporting critically on the papacy and state of the Catholic Church, however objective their intent, risks being caught in the crossfire between Catholic factions. Some years ago, I was offered an explanation for these internecine quarrels while interviewing the late Cardinal Carlo Maria Martini, once thought of as a future pope. He said:

> We are not all contemporaries in a biographical sense . . . some are in the 1990s, some Catholics are still mentally in the 1960s and some in the 1940s, and some even in the nineteenth century; it's inevitable that there will be clashes of mentalities.

Here at the outset, I offer a brief account of where I'm coming from, mentally and autobiographically.

Irish on my mother's side, English on my father's, I belong to generations raised before the Second Vatican Council, that historic reforming meeting of the world's bishops in the early 1960s. The supply of priests, so plentiful in those days, relied on encouragement of vocations among boys barely out of childhood. The practice went back four hundred years to another attempt at the Church's reform, the Council of Trent. Large numbers of prepubescent boys were routinely packed off to junior seminaries for priestly formation lasting up to twelve or more years. Premature recruitment for such a drastic vocation, involving a perpetual vow of celibacy, could be absurdly casual.

At twelve years of age, in a "holy Joe" phase, I was an altar server, and I loved the dressing up, the parading around amidst billowing incense: High Mass, funerals, weddings, street processions. One morning, after serving his Mass, our Irish parish priest in London's East End asked what I hoped to be when I grew up. I suspect he already knew the answer. An interview with our local bishop followed, and I was accepted as a candidate for the priesthood, to the pride of my devout mother and the puzzlement of my agnostic father—who thought I was more in need of fresh air and football.

Aged thirteen, I was dispatched 150 miles from home to spend five years in a junior seminary, a monastic hilltop Gothic building in the Peak District. It was a cloistered life. We received an excellent classical education, taught by young priests who were stern disciplinarians. We were in and out of church all day long, and fresh air was provided in the form of cross-country runs.

At eighteen, I graduated to the senior seminary, a rambling, damp, red-brick building surrounded by screens of trees, close to the city of Birmingham. We were obliged to dress in soutanes and Roman collars, clerics in the making. Our studies in philosophy and theology were increasingly abstract, dogmatic, and defensive. The Church was supreme in its truth and holiness, triumphant: the one path to salvation. All other Christian denominations, all other faiths, were wrong: The Jews had hard hearts; the Protestants were culpably ignorant; Muslims were bloodthirsty infidels. We were reminded daily of the special status of our priesthood in prospect, a profound transformation that would descend on us with the oils of ordination.

Yet despite the long hours in prayer, the beautiful liturgical round, the friendship in community, I felt increasingly imprisoned and rebellious. To relieve my misery, I would escape in secrecy to the cinema down in the city, hiding my Roman collar with a scarf. I made little progress in the spiritual life; I was not becoming a better person. I had doubts, starting with the real presence in the Eucharist, and ending with the entire story of original sin and redemption. I slipped away one morning without farewells and without regrets. I was convinced that I would not look back.

At university, basking in unfamiliar freedoms, I became an agnostic. Yet in G. K. Chesterton's novel *The Innocence of Father Brown*, the hero priest speaks of the "unseen hook and an invisible line" long enough to let one "wander to the ends of the world, and still to bring [one] back with a twitch upon the thread." It took twenty years to feel that twitch. The faith of my wife and children was a factor: Their Catholic Christianity bore witness to something deeply missing in my life. I began to explore the power of Christian community and imagination rather than logical proofs and apologetic arguments. Christianity was what you did rather than a set of ideas in your head. There was no return to the Church of certitudes, ultimate truths, and righteousness.

The journey was slow, with bouts of skepticism and irritation. I went to Mass on Christmas Day to hear the choir sing "Happy birthday, dear Jesus" at the consecration. Where was the solemnity of the ancient liturgy? I had yet to catch up with the significance of the Second Vatican Council, its benefits and its difficulties.

Meanwhile, I was a journalist on a national newspaper. On assignment in Rome I was invited, by a chance meeting with a Vatican official, to investigate how the "smiling pope," John Paul I, met his death after barely a month in 1978. Was he poisoned by prelates in the Vatican, as the late David Yallop claimed in his world bestseller *In God's Name*? I interviewed Yallop's chief homicide suspect, Archbishop Marcinkus, head of the Vatican Bank; the papal doctor and embalmers; and many others within the Vatican; I met with John Paul II, who blessed my investigation. Yallop's accusations were based entirely on circumstantial evidence that proved to be flimsy or inaccurate. My subsequent book, *A Thief in the Night*, concluded that the pope died of a neglected embolism. Without intending it, I became something of a champion of the Church—although the editor of one Catholic paper wrote to express disappointment that Marcinkus was, after all, no murderer.

I next tackled the life of Eugenio Pacelli, the man who became Pius XII, the wartime pope. The pope of my boyhood, his austere face stared down from so many cloisters and classrooms. I set out to refute claims that he was a Nazi sympathizer, but I discovered a circumstance that seemed to me even worse in its consequences, fully justifying the book's title, *Hitler's Pope*. In 1933, as Cardinal Secretary of State, Pacelli (the future Pius XII) negotiated a treaty with Hitler that, despite good intentions, demoralized a Catholic opposition in Germany and gave Hitler credit in the eyes of the world. The issue was neither his holiness nor his intentions, but his devastating diplomacy. I was accused of the sin of calumny, of "smearing" a "saint." The book perhaps contributed to the delaying of his imminent beatification; I appeared to have fulfilled the role of "devil's advocate," which John Paul II abolished to expedite hordes of new saints. *Hitler's Pope* also prompted a stream of articles and books more rigorously academic than the hagiographies to date.

I next wrote a portrait of John Paul II. Impressive pope that he was, John Paul was reluctant to believe that priests had extensively abused young people; he was inclined to blame the malice of the media and rogue clergy in Anglophone countries. He relied on the "charism" of personal "discernment" rather than the facts, which led him to honor Father Marcial Maciel, founder of the Legionaries of Christ and the most psychopathic sexual abuser in the Church's modern period. Not satisfied with debauching many junior seminarians, Maciel fathered two children and sexually abused them too. Titled *Pontiff in Winter*, the resulting book ran counter to the generally uncritical adulation of John Paul's "greatness." I became something of an outsider as a Catholic writer, hardly at home on either side of the so-called conservative-liberal divide.

Then I experienced a second wave of doubt and disillusionment.

The clerical sexual abuse crisis was testing the faith of many Catholics. Cardinal John Henry Newman wrote a powerful essay, "The Grammar of Assent," on how one comes to religious belief; his argument is perhaps equally valid for loss of belief. We come to faith, he declared, not through an effort of the will or logical arguments but a "feeling toward," or a "yes," on encountering a religion's people, its rituals and practice, over time. As he puts it, the "popular, practical, personal evidence," backed up by the Church's "authority," the magisterium. Yet if this be true of the path to faith, then it is equally true of a resistance to assent, leading to a "feeling *against*," or a "*no!*" As for authority, the priestly abuse scandals appeared to have damaged the Church's *moral* standing, drastically, perhaps irreparably. Like many, I found my faith in Catholicism, rather than Christianity, challenged by the sickening "popular, practical, personal evidence" of the clerical sexual abuse scandals.

Then, on March 13, 2013, watching the televised appearance of Pope Francis as he first appeared on the balcony above St. Peter's, I felt the tug of another "unseen hook" and twitch of the string. It was an inclination of the heart, a sense of awakening; some might call it a moment of grace: the possibility of new beginnings, a promise of hope, for the entire Church—practicing, lapsing, and lapsed.

PRUDENZA AUDACE, OR BOLD PRUDENCE

In Pursuit of the "Francis Effect"

Many Catholics revered John Paul II and Benedict XVI as holy and outstanding popes; they hoped that Francis would perpetuate his two predecessors' papacies. Many esteemed their restraints on post-Vatican II "excesses," their insistence on the indissolubility of marriage. They applauded their refusal to allow the divorced and remarried to receive communion. Both popes had banned discussion of women priests and condemned the sin of homosexual practice. There were Catholics who hoped for more of the same.

Others, the so-called liberals, wanted substantial change. They talked of getting the spirit of the reforming Second Vatican Council back on track: a collegial Church with more local discretion for bishops, fuller participation of laypeople and especially women. The more progressive hoped for moves toward a married clergy, inclusion of the LGBT community, even the ordination of women and gay marriage.

Meanwhile, led by advocates for those who had experienced abuse, Catholics across the world were calling for full disclosure of historic cases; the ending of statutes of limitations; zero tolerance for clerical perpetrators and those who covered up for them; instant laicization of the accused; and stricter safeguarding, public contrition, and compensation. Some called for breaking the seal of Confession when a confessor had recognized a penitent priest who had confessed sexual abuse.

Francis, old as he was, overweight and stricken with sciatica, nevertheless appeared youthful and appealing: He had a big smile and a tendency to hug, he wore down-at-the-heels lace-up boots and was driven around in a Ford Focus compact. He spoke his mind: One day early in his papacy, asked about a homosexual priest, he replied, "Who am I to judge?" Those five words, albeit taken out of context, have defined his papacy, to the joy of many and the alarm of others. He appealed to Catholics and non-Catholics alike, especially in America. He was named Person of the Year by *Time* and *The Advocate* magazines. He appeared on the cover of *Rolling Stone*. *Fortune* magazine placed him at number four on its list of the world's fifty greatest leaders.

Early on, Francis signaled his hope for a more inclusive Church, embracing the doubting, lapsing, suffering faithful: "I prefer a Church which is bruised, hurting, and dirty because it has been out on the street, rather than a church which is unhealthy from being confined and from clinging to its own security." He spoke plainly.

In *The Joy of the Gospel*, his first major published address to the world, he wrote of "transforming everything" in the Church—customs, ways of doing things, language, structures—"for today's world rather than for her self-preservation." He urged the virtue of mercy as the key to conversion of hearts; he planned a Jubilee year of mercy, compassion, forgiveness, tenderness.

Before the first year was out, John Allen Jr., a respected American Vaticanologist, wrote: "The new pope has utterly changed the public narrative about the Catholic Church." Instead of the story focusing on child sexual abuse, he noted, the headline was "People's Pope Takes the World by Storm."

Gary Wills, the American academic and writer on Catholic affairs, speculated that Francis would dismantle the authoritarian, pontifical role of the papacy, allowing scope for the Catholic faithful at large to reform and run the Church. Wills concluded: "A pope who believes in *that* Church will not try to change it all by himself." In other words, the

Church was in need not of a super-pope, but a pope who encouraged the faithful to run their Church.

In those early months, Allen and Wills seemed to have predicted correctly: It promised to be a successful, popular papacy. Yet as the years came and went, despite his continuing popularity and the enthusiasm for his message of mercy and hope, Francis became an object of criticism by a small but influential conservative constituency of clergy and journalists; increasingly harsh, it reached levels of unprecedented disparagement of a living pope in modern times. The factions at first raised questions; then became increasingly emboldened, charging that he was leading the Church into heresy and breakup. Meanwhile, advocates for the sexually abused claimed that he was failing them as the scandals kept coming. Where, they asked, was the zero tolerance?

By 2018 Richard Rex, Cambridge professor of Reformation history, could assert: "It is beyond question that the Roman Catholic Church is currently in the throes of one of the greatest crises in its two-millennium history. In human terms, its future might be said to be in doubt for the first time since the Reformation."

The shock suggestion invokes echoes of historic former prophecies. Adam Smith wrote in *The Wealth of Nations* of the coming collapse of Roman Catholicism under the weight of its own contradictions; Thomas Carlyle spoke of the Church as a galvanized corpse. And yet it was Thomas Babington Macaulay who penned the famous declaration of the Church's indestructibility: that it should "still exist in undiminished vigor when some traveler from New Zealand shall, in the midst of a vast solitude, take his stand on a broken arch of London Bridge to sketch the ruins of St. Paul's."

While Catholics languished without priests in Latin America, where almost half of the faithful now lived, the sexual abuse crisis was repelling untold numbers in the affluent West, disgusted by a clergy so hard on the laity's sexual mores while hiding their own dirty secrets. In Europe and North America the conflict between conservatives and liberals was a running sore, destroying the great boast of unassailable Catholic unity; there was talk of a looming schism. And beyond these divides was the vast nominal faithful of the indifferent, the lapsed, or the barely practicing: the discouraged and the disillusioned; the abused and the scandalized. Despite its 1.3 billion baptized official membership, the Church had for years been facing a dilution of belief and shrinking Mass attendance, described by leading sociologist of religion Stephen Bullivant as the "Mass Exodus."

For Professor Rex, however, speaking for many conservative Catholics, the biggest, the most perilous crisis was Pope Francis himself: the "crisis within a crisis," he called him. Rex focused on the appeals Francis made for understanding and compassion in cases of divorce and remarriage. Should such Catholics be allowed to receive Communion? The Church taught that the remarried divorced were adulterers unless they refrained from sex.

But why the fuss over that single issue?

Rex argued that by opening a discussion on the "Catholic Church's absolute, inflexible, and perennial insistence on the indissolubility of marriage," Francis had opened the way to surrendering on "an entire alphabet of [Catholic] beliefs and practices: abortion, bisexuality, contraception, divorce, euthanasia, family, gender, homosexuality, infertility treatment. . . ."

Francis was not to alter the Church's teaching on marriage or any other belief, but many critics mistook his mercy for heresy, his paradoxes for confusion, his calculated disruptions for chaos. Either the law of God in Scripture was to hold, his conservative critics were saying, or anything goes. Francis would declare that Christians are called "from casuistry to mercy," that "in God, justice is mercy and mercy is justice."

The critics were not convinced. The outcry from their well-funded media platforms revealed the extent to which Francis disrupted devoutly held beliefs and attitudes, or perhaps comfort zones. Francis challenged and shook a dysfunctional Church that already stood in danger of failing and fragmenting.

———————

This book tells the story of Francis through seven years of a roller-coaster papacy: the difference he has made to the life of the Church; his reactions to world crises, including global poverty, the plight of migrants, racial prejudice, the coronavirus pandemic, and the far-reaching future consequences of climate change.

Francis warned that his papacy would be short-lived, a reasonable assertion as he was seventy-six years of age at his election. He set himself an impressive pace of work, travel, and administrative and pastoral labor, crisscrossing the world on more than fifty official papal trips; issuing a torrent of documents and decrees; delivering daily homilies, addresses, and interviews. At the same time, he spent many hours a day in private prayer. And he has done this while being the object of nonstop derision, hostility, and criticism mounting to loathing, from one influential wing of the Church. At times he appeared like a long-distance runner, his exhausting progress jeered and hampered by the very spectators who should support him.

Instead of attempting a comprehensive chronicle, even if that were possible, I have taken soundings across his key initiatives and reactions to events. I have focused on a consistent feature of his papacy: a capacity to hold opposites in tension, his many paradoxes giving rise to disruption. Then another kind of tension: "Hope is this living in tension, always," he preached one morning at Mass. "We cannot make a nest here: The life of the Christian is in ongoing tension. If a Christian loses this perspective, their life becomes static and things that do not move are motionless." Seeking the Church as a comfort zone, he was saying, is not an option.

I embarked on this book encouraged by an awakened impulse of personal hope from the first day of his papacy. I learned in subsequent days that many friends and acquaintances felt a similar sense of reengagement, of hope. In time I encountered people of other religions and of none who had been encouraged, heartened, initially by nothing more than his down-to-earth demeanor.

There were those who had an instant and opposite reaction. A writer on the conservative magazine *Rorate Coeli* wrote: "Horror! Of all the unthinkable candidates Bergoglio is perhaps the worst." As the months and years passed there was a mounting impression of contradiction: lenient austerity, *prudenza audace*—bold prudence, he called it. He told a young audience that it was important "to make a mess."

He was elderly, approaching his eighties, and yet capable of boundless energy. He made mistakes yet admitted them and apologized like no pope before him in the modern history of the papacy. He disliked his ring being kissed and preferred the title Bishop of Rome to Supreme Pontiff or Vicar of Christ. Asked to describe himself, he said: "I am a sinner"; he meant it, and it was no doubt true. There were fleeting moments, surreal for a pope: breaking tradition to wash the feet of two women and Muslims at a prison in Rome; the sight of him, cheek to cheek with a gay man of color and embracing a transgender visitor; the shock of him kissing the toe caps of South Sudanese leaders.

The Francis Effect, as some have called it, would prove no sweet balm of the soul. His papacy would be a rough ride of paradoxes, shocks, somersaults, great and small—a catalog of disjointed challenges that often felt like "a mess." In the Latin rite of the Mass the priest recites a verse of a Psalm before approaching the altar: . . . *Anima mea . . . quare conturbas me?* . . . Oh my soul . . . why are you disturbing me so? Francis, from the outset, had the power to shake up souls. He certainly woke up mine. But it was not to be a welcome awakening for all.

Disruption is familiar in corporate and economic strategies; therapeutic interventions are common in the treatment of destructive and self-destructive addictions and neuroses. From the outset he interrupted the authoritarian, dogmatic, self-referential clericalism; institutional corruption; scandalous internal divisions; the falling away of untold millions of the baptized. Beyond the Church he has spoken out on major issues of the global economy and society; offered new visions for the value of labor, the addressing of racism, the relief of poverty and inequality, the fate of the environment.

He altered what it means to be a pope; the papacy can never be the same again. He offered a renewed, more hopeful vision of what it means to be a Catholic Christian; the Church can never be the same again. That he has restored hope in the Church and in the world is the theme of this book.

PART ONE

———

INTERRUPTING THE CENTER

Taking the Church to the Periphery

CHAPTER ONE

WHAT POPES ARE FOR

The Tasks Facing Francis

T he Roman Catholic Church is the largest single united religious community in the world, embracing every nationality, ethnicity, language, culture, politics, ideology, and geography. No wonder James Joyce dubbed it HCE: Here Comes Everybody. Despite undeniable failings, scandals, and crises down the centuries and into the present, Holy Mother Church, as she is traditionally known, was for millennia, and remains, a formidable force for moral and spiritual flourishing in the world, the Mother Church for all Christians. Despite the shame of their minority, the majority of the clergy and sisterhoods, the parishes and collective movements, comprise countless people dedicated to the common good. Her breakup would spell catastrophe for all Christians, and for the world. That her unity depends on the papacy is an open secret.

The pope's spiritual domain reaches out across every continent; and the flow of information, back to his desk, is prodigious. It was said that John Paul I, a gentle, pastoral soul, died within a month of his election in 1978 overwhelmed by administrative pressures. He was of a nervous disposition. One day he dropped an armful of documents from his rooftop garden into the courtyard below. He retreated to his bed where his secretary found him lying in a fetal position, face to the wall, sobbing. As an American Vatican official once put it to me: "He took one look at his in-tray and freaked."

The pope is assisted by a community of more than a thousand officials, comprising cardinals, bishops, priests, and laypeople, known as the Curia. But he carries his burdens of responsibility, finally, alone. He is no chairman of a board, making collective decisions. Historic imperial protocols survived until recently. Leo XIII, pope of the late nineteenth century, required his aides to remain on their knees in his presence. Pius XII would not allow bureaucrats to ask him questions or turn their backs on him; they took phone calls from him on their knees. As recently as the reign of Paul VI in the 1960s and 1970s, popes were carried through St. Peter's Basilica on a litter, fanned by ostrich feathers. Paul was the last to wear the magnificent silver and gold papal tiara, the triple crown, signifying father of princes and kings, ruler of the world, and vicar or deputy of Christ. Paul attempted to describe the papal isolation in a private note to himself:

> I was solitary before, but now my solitariness becomes complete and awesome. Hence the dizziness, the vertigo. Like a statue on a plinth—that is how I live now . . . my duty is too plain: decide, assume every responsibility for guiding others, even when it seems illogical and perhaps absurd. And to suffer alone . . . Me and God. The colloquy must be full and endless.

The Church is a huge operation. While its 5,000 bishops administer their dioceses independently up to a point, the pope, who has nominated each one personally, exerts control over them and the half million priests and 700,000 religious sisters of the world. While the many congregations or orders of religious have their special rules and hierarchies, they are ultimately under obedience to the pope.

The Church is regulated from the center by its own legal system, canon law. For centuries the laws were a jungle of case histories. In the early twentieth century the legal system became highly regulated, modeled on the Napoleonic Code. The Holy See, the Seat and diocese of the Bishop of Rome, has a global network of papal embassies and ambassadors, nuncios, resident in more than a hundred countries.

The Church maintains thousands of schools, colleges, universities, think tanks, multiple media organizations, hospitals, clinics, international charities, global NGOs, and research institutes.

Finances of the Holy See, meaning the pope's own "seat" of his bishopric of Rome, are partly run through the Vatican Bank; and there are other central savings and investment entities. The dioceses and religious institutions across the world run their own revenue, investment, and fiscal operations, as do parishes. A measure of the Church's diocesan wealth is the extent of payouts in sexual abuse suits. By 2018 it was estimated that the crisis in the United States alone had cost dioceses $3 billion and rising. This does not count lost revenues. At least nineteen dioceses have filed for bankruptcy protection.

The Church boasts that it survives and thrives through its unchanging beliefs and practices: *semper eadem*, always the same. Yet it has yielded to many modern advances and developments, in particular the revolutions in communication that facilitate the Church's outreach. Today the digital revolution is transforming the way the Church understands, regulates, teaches, and converses with itself. Church historian Eamon Duffy writes: "Catholicism is a conversation, linking continents and cultures, and reaching backward and forward in time. The luxury of sectarianism, of renouncing whatever in the conversation cannot be squared with the perspective of one's own time and place, is not an option." And yet the Church is under threat of splintering, while vast numbers of the faithful continue to abandon her. What keeps her together, tenuously, for the time being, is the Holy Father, also known as Universal Father.

——————

In 2013, the year of Jorge Mario Bergoglio's election, the demands on a new pope in terms of reactive leadership would have daunted a prelate younger by several decades. He had worked long and tirelessly as Cardinal Archbishop of Buenos Aires, a deeply conflicted city and province numbering sixteen million inhabitants, with widespread poverty. He held senior posts of ecclesiastical responsibility at a time when Argentina was ravaged by its Dirty War of the late seventies and early eighties. At the same time, he assumed leadership responsibilities for the Church in Latin America at large.

The pressures of the papal office have increased in recent decades with the speed of communications and multiplying internal crises. Apart from the clerical abuse catastrophe and pressing Vatican financial scandals, Francis faced a host of global issues, starting with Europe, the home of Christianity. Despite repeated pleas by former popes, the European Union, from its Brussels center and participating countries, failed to acknowledge the continent's Christian roots within its institutions and culture. Francis was the first pope to admit the obvious when he delivered one of his word-bombs aimed at exploding complacency: "Christendom no longer exists!" he said at Christmas 2019.

Vocations to the priesthood and religious sisterhoods were plummeting. Parishes were closing by the week in every European country, especially in Germany, where hundreds of thousands of the faithful were relinquishing their official church membership annually, thus withdrawing their personal payments (collected in government tax returns) made under German law to a citizen's faith of choice.

When the dissident Swiss theologian Hans Küng viewed the masses pouring into Rome in April 2005 for the funeral of John Paul II, he wrote in *Der Spiegel*: "Don't be fooled by the crowds. Millions have left the Catholic Church under Pope John Paul II's leadership. The Catholic Church is in dire straits." The trend continued through the papacy of Benedict XVI and into the reign of Francis.

In the United States, according to figures published by the Pew Research Center in 2016, only 15 percent of cradle Catholics attend weekly Mass, and 35 percent of them no longer admit to Catholic identity. In the United Kingdom the figures were worse. Only 13 percent of baptized Catholics went to Mass and 37 percent no longer thought of themselves as Catholic.

Research by sociologist of religion Stephen Bullivant, in his 2019 book *Mass Exodus*, found a catalog of reasons for "disaffiliation," as he termed it, beyond the obvious reaction to clerical sexual abuse. Informants who defected in the 1970s cited the bans on contraception, sex before marriage, divorce, and homosexuality. As the decades passed, they mentioned boredom with church services, combined with skepticism about doctrine, especially the teaching on hell; dislike of particular pastors; bad experiences in the Confessional box; rejection of belief in the afterlife. A significant number of dropouts, particularly among women, Hispanics, and African Americans in the United States, include those who felt let down by the Church in their hour of need. The latter often left Catholicism for another Christian denomination, or even non-Christian religion.

A different kind of attrition was occurring in Latin America, where 43 percent of Catholics are now concentrated, and where the virtual monopoly of the Catholic Church is being eroded by Pentecostal groups. In the course of the twentieth century, and into the twenty-first, the figure of Catholic affiliation in Latin America shrunk, according to a Pew survey in 2014, from 90 percent to 70 percent. Protestant evangelicals were challenging the former Catholic near monopoly with provision of education and improved living standards financed by charities in North America. Evangelicals, moreover, unconstrained by an ordained, exclusively male, and celibate leadership, were capable of spreading and maintaining the faith with lay preachers embedded in their communities.

Christians, including many Catholics, suffered greatly in Muslim countries, starting with the invasion of Iraq in 2003, continuing with the civil war in Syria in 2011, and the violence spreading sporadically across majority Muslim communities of Asia: Indonesia, Pakistan, Bangladesh, and Malaysia. At Easter 2019 hundreds of worshipers were murdered in two Catholic churches in Colombo, Sri Lanka, by ISIS terrorists.

The fate of the Church in mainland China, which numbers up to ten million Catholics, was a problem for successive popes. A split arose between the largely underground Church and the growth of an "official" Church approved by the government. In 2010 Beijing manipulated the ordination of several bishops without sanction from Rome. The bishops were automatically excommunicated. Should Francis continue to condemn the official Church and encourage the underground?

From the outset, Francis faced novel and long-standing doctrinal issues vying for his attention: demands for female ordination, a married priesthood, challenges to papal teaching on the moral status of gays, lesbians, and transgender people; demands for same-sex marriage. Topping the list, however, was the "irregular" status of growing numbers of divorced and remarried Catholics, perhaps as many as 40 percent, officially denied the sacrament of Holy Communion.

But there was another pressure, a burden on every pope's conscience: the onus to lead the Church creatively, positively, rather than just reactively. How should he bring his own special talents and personality to bear on his mission as a world religious leader? What contributions would he make to the spiritual good of the world? How would he put a stamp on his papacy, offer views on major world events, tragedies, disasters natural and man-made? How would he relate to other Christian communions, as well as to other faiths? How would he offer religious hope in an increasingly faithless world?

A pope expresses his pastoral office with homilies at his morning Mass; addresses to special audiences—general and private; speeches on foreign trips; those special letters to the world known as encyclicals and exhortations. In addition, Francis made extensive use of spontaneous press conferences, especially on his frequent plane trips, and private interviews with journalists. Moreover, he exploited the power of visible gestures amplified by the media: the kissing of feet; the hugs and kisses; the wide-eyed ear-to-ear grin.

Then there are the encounters. A pope has a nonstop flow of visitors: heads of state, representatives of many hundreds of religious organizations; political leaders, special interest and advocacy groups, pilgrims; general audiences of tens, hundreds, and thousands; sporting teams; assorted trades and professions, the hairdressers, gynecologists, accountants. Then there are the Catholic bishops of the world coming into Rome from more than a hundred countries for their routine visits for personal and collective audiences, each seeking counsel for his own set of local problems.

At the same time, from the first day of his papacy he received invitations to make official visits to countries around the world. These grueling trips, often fraught with security problems, would require long-haul flights and loss of sleep every few weeks.

Perhaps most important of all, he is guardian of the Church's doctrinal truth handed down from the Gospels, the early Church, its councils, the writings of his predecessors. In a very real way, the pope is both the symbol and the energizer of Catholic unity, the watchman over authentic Catholicism, holding together a global community: *ut unum sint*—that they may be *one*. All this he does while subjected 24/7 to searing media scrutiny.

A pope brings his own peculiar background, skills, experience, and personal history to the task. Pius XII was a canon lawyer and a diplomat; Paul VI served Pius XII for many years within the Curia before being sent to the diocese of Milan; John Paul II was a pastor and philosopher who grew to prominence as Archbishop of Kraków in conflict with the Soviet regime. Benedict XVI was a professor of theology before taking on the role of protector of the Church's doctrinal orthodoxy.

Francis was the first pope from Latin America, the first pope in the modern period to have run a teeming metropolitan diocese afflicted by poverty during a period of violent political conflict. He is the first pope named after St. Francis, with a determination to invoke the spirituality of St. Francis during his papacy.

He is the first Jesuit pope. Joining the Society of Jesus as a young man, his formation was based on a half millennium of Jesuit history and spirituality. The Society of Jesus, as it is properly called, embodies a world community of highly disciplined priests: intellectual, famous for their obedience, teaching skills, and missionary zeal. He would bring that training and commitment to his papacy, as well as disruptive tendencies for which Jesuits had been passed over as *papabile*, potential popes, since their foundation.

When he stood on the balcony above St. Peter's Square on the night of his election, he acknowledged that the cardinals had made an extraordinary choice to meet the multiple crises afflicting the Church, a choice "from the ends of the earth." There are tales of newly elected popes suffering frayed nerves and tears on their election. Cardinal Timothy Dolan of New York says that Francis accepted his election "without hesitation." Certainly, from the outset, Francis appeared self-confident and calm. In so many ways, his life and vocation, his leadership qualities, honed during nine years as a bishop and twelve as a cardinal, prepared him for that moment.

CHAPTER TWO

TWO POPES DILEMMA

The Presence of the Emeritus Predecessor

In addition to the mammoth tasks and the many crises he faced on the day of his election, Francis began his papacy in historically exceptional circumstances. He was elected not in consequence of the death of his predecessor, Benedict, but because of his abdication: a situation that had not occurred for more than six hundred years.

Francis inherited a heavy, still unfolding legacy from his predecessor; a burden that did much to explain Benedict's action. In the months before the resignation, news of a scandal known as Vatileaks leached out of the offices of the Holy See. In May 2012 the investigative journalist Gianluigi Nuzzi published a book titled *His Holiness: The Secret Papers of Benedict XVI*. These "secret papers," stolen from Benedict's desk by his butler, Paolo Gabriele, revealed conflicts, corruption, character assassination, and financial malfeasance at the heart of the Vatican's bureaucracy, spreading out across the world to the Church's embassies, or nunciatures.

In a further blow to Pope Benedict's peace of mind, Professor Gotti Tedeschi, head of the Vatican Bank, and coauthor of Benedict's encyclical *Charity in Truth*, was sacked by the bank's directors for alleged failings in standards of governance (which he declared were linked to his efforts for greater transparency). A triumvirate of octogenarian cardinals was entrusted to write an in-depth report on the state of affairs. It was, in part at least, a consequence of their findings, delivered on December 17, 2012, that Benedict decided to resign. Amid the incompetence, corruption, and infighting, their eminences informed Benedict of the existence of "gay lobbies" involving not only Vatican clerical bureaucrats but religious orders in Rome and around the world.

When he retired, Benedict was expected to disappear from view, as if deceased, giving Francis a free hand. Instead of retiring to a remote Bavarian monastery, as some expected or recommended, Benedict stayed put, still accepting the title "His Holiness," still wearing the pectoral cross of the Bishop of Rome, publishing, massaging his record, meeting cardinals and theologians, making statements. Benedict was to remain at the very heart of the Vatican, visible, involved. If Francis was the living, reigning pope, then Benedict became his shadow, the undead pope emeritus. His very existence encouraged critics who sought to undermine Francis.

————

Since his years as Catholicism's chief doctrinal watchdog, starting in 1981, Benedict, as Cardinal Joseph Ratzinger, talked and wrote of the inevitability of a smaller Church, cleansed of imperfections. Francis's vision of the Church was diametrically opposite. He espoused a big-tent church, merciful to sinners, hospitable to the strayed and disaffiliated, not just tolerant of other faiths but seeking fellowship. He sought to encourage doubters, console the abused, and reconcile those excluded because of their orientation. He likened the Church to a place of healing for the sick and wounded in spirit.

There was a clash on an immediate matter of current affairs: Francis took no time to support migrants crossing the Mediterranean by boat. In July 2013, he traveled to the island of Lampedusa off the coast of Sicily to say Mass and encourage the large numbers of refugees. Yet it had been the policy of Benedict (and John Paul II before him) to dissuade refugees from leaving home, in the belief that wealthy nations should assist development in the migrants' countries of origin. Matteo Salvini, head of the right-wing Italian Lega Party, who as minister of the interior attempted to block the disembarkation of migrants on Italy's shores, was photographed holding up a T-shirt proclaiming "Benedict is my pope."

The mere presence of the former pope was enough to test the mettle and independence of Francis from day one. Would the jolly John XXIII have initiated the reforming Second Vatican Council had Pius XII, his autocratic predecessor, been watching lugubriously from a neighboring window? And would John Paul II have shaken the rotting tree of the Soviet Union had the anguished, hesitant Paul VI, who contemplated a Vatican accord with Moscow, been lurking at his elbow? Whatever the direction of the papacy, left or right, for better or for worse, it is always the unique, exclusive primacy of one pope at a time that lends supreme authority and power to his office. Loyalty through thick and thin to the single living Supreme Pontiff is a crucial feature of papal power: *Two popes is not an option.*

That note on his solitude, penned by Paul VI, spoke of the power of papal isolation: "Me and God." For Francis, the equation was more complicated: Me, God, and Benedict. And the intrusion was made all the more difficult by the differences between the two. As young men, Benedict and Francis made decisive moves in opposite directions.

———

Joseph Ratzinger, born in 1927 in Marktl am Inn, Bavaria, was the son of a police officer. At age fourteen, he joined the Hitler Youth, the Nazi Party's organization for indoctrinating the young: He had no choice in the matter. Later, at age sixteen, he served in the Wehrmacht; his unit operated an anti-aircraft gun guarding a factory in Munich.

After the war, he studied for the priesthood and was ordained in 1951. Academic from the outset, his theology was at first progressive. As an adviser, he advocated liberalizing policies at the Second Vatican

Council. He became a professor at Tübingen University. During a period of unrest in 1968 a gang of students rampaged through the campus and into his lecture room. He believed he had glimpsed into the abyss of a new dark age. Removing himself to the tranquil environment of the University of Regensburg, he devoted himself not to change but to permanence. If the Church was to survive the surge of relativism, socialism, anarchy, and aggressive secularism, it must restore what is unchanging. In a broadcast on German radio in 1969, he predicted a different kind of Church for the future. "She will become small and will have to start afresh more or less from the beginning."

In 1981, John Paul II appointed Ratzinger head of the Congregation for the Doctrine of the Faith. As the Church's official doctrinal watchdog, he strove to hold the strict line on Catholic teaching, especially on sexual morality, while new generations of young Catholics were living together before marriage, practicing contraception, coming out as gay and lesbian, divorcing and remarrying. John Paul and Cardinal Ratzinger, his doctrinal enforcer, refused to condone the use of condoms even for African Catholics with HIV. Meanwhile, John Paul curbed the proliferating dissidents, not least the liberation theologians of South America who argued that sin could often mean not wrongdoing by individual moral agents but the injustice of social and political structures leading to poverty and oppression. Ratzinger earned himself the sobriquet "Pope's Rottweiler." Theologians guilty of unorthodoxy were summoned to his inquisitorial office for a grilling: Some were deprived of their teaching licenses, others were ordered to stop writing.

When Joseph Ratzinger succeeded John Paul II on April 19, 2005, Catholic traditionalists had the pope they devoutly wished for. He would encourage the Latin Mass again, reduce the number of marriage annulments, and restrict ecumenism and interfaith dialogue. The call for collegiality—a greater share of authority between the pope and his bishops—was laid to rest. The Church was becoming ever more centralized, even as the center was becoming overwhelmed by crises.

Jorge Mario Bergoglio, the man who was to be Pope Francis, was the son of a migrant family of modest means from northern Italy who had emigrated to Argentina. He was at first destined to become an industrial chemist; he went out with girls, danced the tango, worked part-time as a nightclub bouncer. A chance encounter with a priest unknown to him in Confession set him on the path to the priesthood. He studied at first in the diocesan seminary, then moved over to the Jesuits, where his intelligence and leadership talents were noticed. He became the head of the Jesuit province in Argentina at the age of thirty-six. His trajectory was a reversal of Ratzinger's shift from progressive to conservative. As the Jesuit superior in 1970s Argentina responsible for student priests, he revived outmoded Latin textbooks and insisted on strict clerical dress. As a young bishop he was at first a stickler for rules and episcopal protocol; he insisted on being chauffeur-driven, even when traveling a short distance.

His experience of Argentina's Dirty War in the late 1970s and early 1980s, and pastoral work among the poor of his diocese, had a decisive influence. The ambitious, reactionary priest was becoming the pastor of compassion that the world would witness in Pope Francis. As Archbishop of Buenos Aires and a significant leader of the local Church in Latin America, he identified with the oppressed peoples of the region and the poor: what he called "the leftovers."

As pope, and without specifying, he has frequently referred to his failings and culpability: "I am a sinner." Investigations into his life and work in Buenos Aires reveal allegations of betrayal during the Dirty War that ravaged the country. In May 1976, as the military under the junta persecuted and murdered tens of thousands of the country's citizens, two of Bergoglio's fellow Jesuits, Fathers Francisco Jalics and Orlando Yorio, were arrested and tortured. They were working in slum districts of Buenos Aires, running "base communities" considered subversive projects by the regime. Francis has been accused of condemning these priests by information he supplied the junta and his failure to persuade the regime to release them. They were eventually freed (according to some versions, despite Bergoglio's inactivity), but six other parish workers, also arrested, were never seen again. Yorio in 1995 accused Bergoglio of filing a "false report to the military." More recently, the Argentine investigative journalist Horacio Verbitsky, on the basis of a single note in the state archives, charged that Bergoglio publicly asked for a favor for Father Jalics, but behind his back accused him of activities that could have led to his death.

In another incident, a twenty-three-year-old woman, Elena De La Cuadra, was five months pregnant when she was kidnapped in 1977. Her father sought Bergoglio's help, but her family claimed that he failed to mention that she was pregnant. The baby was born and given away, as was the practice with the offspring of these mothers, and Elena disappeared. In 2010, during the trial of the military responsible for torture during the Dirty War, Bergoglio, giving witness, denied that he knew anything about the regime's treatment of pregnant women. His critics state that this is not credible.

Father Yorio appears to have died believing that Francis was a liar and a traitor, but Jalics declares that "after numerous conversations, it became clear to me that Orlando Yorio and I were not denounced by Fr. Bergoglio."

In the Netflix movie *The Two Popes*, a segment of the narrative, given extra credibility by the use of actual news clips and black-and-white handheld camera reconstructions, portrays Father Bergoglio in an ambivalent light. Most early biographers give Francis the moral benefit of the doubt, just as historians are not inclined to suggest that Benedict had sympathy for the Nazi cause. The film is less fair to Benedict, who appears to confess his guilt in failing to condemn the notorious sexual abuser Father Marcial Maciel. Yet it was Benedict who, on becoming pope, acted swiftly to censure and remove him.

The savage Dirty War in Argentina clearly deepened Francis's experience of suffering and remorse, as well as his resilience, visible at times in his bodily posture and expressions. Sometimes his face would seem to sag with melancholy, cheeks flaccid, the mouth turned down.

Then, on greeting someone, or in a moment of enthusiasm, his dark eyes would light up, his face ageless, suffused with a brilliant smile. There were times when his voice would become inaudible, lips barely moving; then, as if seized by joy, he would speak emphatically, energetically, like a young man.

————————

Many popes in the modern period have chosen to work closely throughout their papacies with an assistant companion. Pius XII worked closely with his housekeeper Mother Pasqualina; Paul VI, despite his meditation on papal solitude, had Monsignor Pasquale Macchi; John Paul II was assisted by the faithful Father Stanislaw Dziwisz. Jesuits spend part of their lives in community, yet often their mission involves living and working alone. Francis, the Jesuit, decided from the outset to be a loner in the Vatican, assisted as we shall see, by temporary secretaries who had other tasks.

Benedict, both as pope and after his resignation, benefited from the services and companionship of a close aide. Georg Gänswein, a handsome archbishop, was known for his skiing, tennis playing, and sartorial *bella figura*. Nicknamed "Bel Giorgio," he was the inspiration for Donatella Versace's winter 2007–2008 "clergyman" collection. As a young man, and a fan of Cat Stevens, he wore his hair long. Popularly known as Gorgeous Georg, he remained Benedict's secretary after the resignation, and became his caregiver. He took up residence with Benedict in a renovated building behind a thick hedge and high fences in the gardens of Vatican City.

Gänswein would initially promote the idea, unique in the history of the papacy, of a papal partnership. Francis and Benedict together, he declared, in May 2016, represented a single "expanded" papal office with one "active" member and one "contemplative" one. Francis took no time to reject the notion: "There is only one Pope."

Benedict evidently laid plans for his retirement many months ahead of the announcement. In the early 1990s, John Paul II built a residence in the Vatican gardens, with a chapel attached, to house a community of twelve contemplative nuns who engaged in silent prayer to support his pontificate. In the fall of 2012 Benedict, without signaling the purpose, ordered a renovation of the convent, now cleared of the nuns, to create a suitable Vatican retirement home, office, and chapel, overseen by Gänswein. People refer to it as a "monastery."

In July 2012, moreover, Benedict appointed the conservative Bishop Gerhard Ludwig Müller as the new head of theological orthodoxy, the Congregation for the Doctrine of the Faith. Benedict must have known, even at this point, that he was planning his resignation and therefore saddling his successor with a traditionalist doctrinal watchdog who would be difficult to replace (although Francis would remove him in 2017).

In another striking pre-resignation maneuver, Benedict appointed Gänswein as both personal secretary and head of the papal household. Gänswein was to run the new pope's apartments and offices in the Apostolic Palace, where popes have resided and worked for hundreds of years. This enabled Gänswein to monitor the conversations and meetings of the new pope. This was one of Benedict's last appointments before resigning, hence difficult for Francis to countermand without seeming disrespectful. But Francis opted to live not in the papal apartments but in the Santa Marta guesthouse, a hotel for visiting prelates within the Vatican, while allowing Gänswein to arrange audiences in the papal apartments with grand figures like royalty and heads of state.

Francis bore the circumstance of living alongside the "emeritus" pope and "prefect of the household" Gänswein with evident forbearance. He told reporters that it is like "having a wise grandfather in the house."

It was widely expected that Benedict might soon die, or retreat into bedridden silence, debilitated by old age. But he was evidently in good health, active physically and mentally, alert to developments. He still had years, and he was inclined to remain active, receiving visitors, massaging his record, ready to give an opinion. There was no experience or protocol for dealing with a retired pope; Benedict made the rules for a "pope emeritus"—such as they were. As time passed, the situation was destined to become awkward and eventually problematic.

CHAPTER THREE

FRANCIS AT WORK

A Minimalist Global Office

G iven the mounting crises, Francis's lifestyle and work routine were spare and frugal from the outset. Many puzzled over how he achieved so much with such a minimal administrative operation. The offices of popes traditionally involve the presence of full-time secretaries and butlers within the ample marble spaces of the Apostolic Palace high above St. Peter's Square. Antonio Spadaro, editor of the Jesuit magazine *Civiltà Cattolica*, describes how he came to interview Francis at the Santa Marta hotel where Francis was living and working in two small rooms:

> *I emerge from the lift and I see the pope already waiting for me at the door. . . . I enter his room and the pope invites me to sit in his easy chair. He himself sits on a chair that is higher and stiffer because of his back problems. The setting is simple, austere. The workspace occupied by the desk is small. I am impressed not only by the simplicity of the furniture, but also by the objects in the room. There are only a few. These include an icon of St. Francis, a statue of Our Lady . . . a crucifix and a statue of St. Joseph sleeping. . . .*

Vatican officials talk of Francis "playing his cards close to his chest." He spends a lot of time on the telephone. He is used to putting through the calls himself rather than using an intermediary. Receiving calls is another matter. Amid official papal business, there are many pastoral phone calls: a man whose son died of Parkinson's disease; a woman "living in sin" to reassure her that she should go to Confession and then to Communion in a different parish; a philosopher to congratulate him on his new book. The list goes on to include calls in response to strangers who had merely sent a postcard or letter describing a personal problem.

He relied on two part-time priest-secretaries through the first six years of his papacy, the Argentine Father Pedacchio Leaniz and the Egyptian Father Yoannis Lahzi. It was considered significant that both bureaucrats had jobs elsewhere in the Vatican; it was assumed, moreover, that their double functions meant that Francis thereby had eyes and ears in important departments. Leaniz, for example, worked in the congregation for choosing new bishops. The priest who runs Santa Marta, Monsignor Battista Mario Salvatore Ricca, was also appointed by Francis to work in the Vatican Bank, enabling him, if necessary, to report back on the activities of the bank's governance commission and the board of directors.

An informant is quoted: "He does not want any filters. Sometimes he will tell one of his secretaries 'so and so is arriving in a few minutes' and that is the first they hear of it. Sometimes he tells one without telling the other."

In January 2020, Pope Francis appointed Father Gonzalo Aemilius, a forty-year-old Uruguayan priest, as a replacement for Father Pedacchio Leaniz. Aemilius worked with street children and drug addicts, and was known to Francis for many years. Writing in *America* magazine, Gerard O'Connell declares that "it is important to know that right from the beginning of his pontificate, Pope Francis made clear that he did not want . . . a personal secretary who would be 'the gatekeeper' to the pope, one who would consequently accumulate or exercise considerable influence or power during the pontificate."

From the first week, Francis followed a routine he established as Archbishop of Buenos Aires: rise at 4:45 a.m.; private prayer until Mass at 7 a.m., celebrated without an altar server; during the Mass a short homily, available to the world via internet; thanksgiving prayers made in the back row of the chapel; individual greetings to those invited to the Mass; breakfast, collected on a tray (same for lunch and supper), in the basement cafeteria with selected guests (he is said to eat whatever is on the Italian menu, but has a special liking for empanadas); morning given over to meetings and phone calls; siesta, one hour; rosary before supper; bed by 10 p.m.

Francis wrote longhand in large notebooks, and in 2015 admitted to a class of schoolchildren that he was a "dinosaur" when it came to machines, incapable of using a laptop or computer. He would nevertheless make use of Twitter and Instagram, operated for him, and by 2017 we see him using an iPad during his Angelus address to pilgrims. Yet despite the minimalist administrative establishment, he managed to communicate his message and mission with clarity to his heads of department, and to the entire world via judicious and skillful handling of the media.

Commenting on Francis's leadership qualities, management guru Gary Hamel, writing in *Harvard Business Review*, declared that "He understands that in a hyper-kinetic world, inward-looking and self-obsessed leaders are a liability." Getting things done, for Francis, appeared to be more about connections and encounters with people, about relevance, than about documents, administrative processes, and status. The simplicity and modesty, the outward-directed energy, have been crucial to his prodigious output. Resilient and flexible, he avoided systems, structures, protocol, formality.

———————

The papacy, with all its complexities, active and reactive, sacred and profane, resides at the center of a formidable communications hub in an era of 24/7 high-speed information. During his time as bishop and archbishop in Buenos Aires, Jorge Bergoglio avoided interviews with journalists, doubtless conscious of the hazards of media bias in his perilously troubled homeland. He would later reveal himself to be arguably the most media-savvy pope in history.

His first formal address, made three days after his election, was to the media corps assembled in Rome for the conclave. In the great audience hall of Paul VI, he welcomed 6,000 journalists from scores of countries, perhaps the largest gathering of media professionals ever assembled. His talk signaled an awareness of the new and massive potential of the digital media, with its immediacy, global outreach, interaction, and power for good despite its capacity for distortion, prejudice, and fake news. After a few uplifting remarks about journalism exemplifying, at its best, the virtues of "goodness, truth, and beauty," he gave them a scoop. He explained how and why he chose the name Francis, indicating the future trajectory of his papacy with its focus on poverty and the ethics of safeguarding the environment. He was about to change the story not only of the papacy but of the Catholic Church itself.

He said that on his election, Cardinal Cláudio Hummes of Brazil gave him a hug and a kiss, saying: "Don't forget the poor!" Francis, ad-libbing in a style that would become familiar, said:

> *And those words came to me: the poor, the poor. Then, right away, thinking of the poor, I thought of Francis of Assisi. Then I thought of all the wars, as the votes were still being counted, till the end. Francis is also the man of peace. That is how the name came into my heart: Francis of Assisi. For me, he is the man of poverty, the man of peace, the man who loves and protects creation; these days we do not have a very good relationship with creation, do we? He is the man who gives us this spirit of peace, the poor man.... How I would like a Church which is poor and for the poor!*

The story circled the globe in minutes. In the United States alone, which accounts for only 6 percent of the world's Catholic population, there are 17,651 parishes and nearly two hundred dioceses, each with its own websites and flavors of liberal or conservative bias. In addition to Eternal Word Television Network (EWTN) with its outreach to forty million viewers, there are more than one hundred Catholic newspapers and magazines, including the influential, left-leaning, Jesuit-owned *America*; the middle-of-the-road *Catholic Digest*; the left-leaning *Commonweal*; the right-leaning *First Things*; the left-leaning *National Catholic Reporter*; and the right-leaning *National Catholic Register*; all internationally accessible online.

A few weeks after that first meeting with journalists, Francis gave an impromptu press conference flying back to Rome from the World Youth celebration in Rio de Janeiro. The journalists on the flight submitted questions, as was the custom, in advance, but Francis declined to see the questions. He wanted to handle the encounters unprepared. A veteran Vatican press man confessed: "We were sitting there, really and truly, with our mouths hanging open."

From the early days of his papacy, despite former interview shyness, Francis submitted himself to an extraordinary grilling on camera. It was for a film destined for theaters, TV, Google, Netflix, YouTube, and DVD. The aim was to get his presence, personality, and message out to the widest possible audience, Catholic and non-Catholic. The choice of director was a shock—Wim Wenders, an ex-Catholic. Wenders is the five-times married director of a list of prizewinning art house movies including *Paris, Texas* and *Wings of Desire*. *Paris, Texas* tells the story of a man alienated by the breakdown of his marriage and separation from his only child. The opening sequences carry striking symbolism of desert spirituality and the dark night of the soul, as Travis, separated from wife and child, walks into the wilderness. *Wings of Desire* features a realm of guardian angels hovering over Berlin, involved and yet powerless to act, until one angel becomes incarnate.

A fiercely independent experimentalist, Wenders studied medicine, philosophy, and painting before turning to filmmaking, learning his craft in the United States. Although brought up a Catholic, he moved via agnosticism and Lutheranism to a position he called Ecumenical Christian. Remembering the day of the election, he wondered how the new pope would "blow the wind of Franciscan spirituality through the world." He was even more surprised when he received a letter from the Vatican inviting him to consider making a film about Francis. "I was so shocked that I had to walk around the block," he says.

Wenders decided that it would be a poor film, *cine povera*, low budget, in the same spirit as Francis's outreach to the poor. He was to interview Francis for two hours consecutively on four occasions spread over four years. There were no successive takes; the first take was *it*. Wenders was impressed at the way Francis would greet and speak to every member of the crew before starting.

Wenders eventually viewed for inclusion some eight hundred hours of archival footage of papal trips and other material in order to punctuate the interviews with significant moments in those early years of the pontificate. He employed a technology known as Interrotron in order to give the audience a sense of looking directly into Francis's eyes: an impression of intimate encounter.

One reviewer of the resulting film, titled *Man of His Word*, wrote that Francis "opened up the church to everyone and reached out to the world. No one is off limits. The film beautifully captures a man on a mission, to show the love of Jesus for everyone." Another opined: "I didn't know that Google marketed and sold Roman Catholic propaganda." *Man of His Word* attained an 82 percent Rotten Tomatoes approval rating.

The film showed Francis in an array of contexts: at the mass audiences in the Paul VI auditorium; in slum districts talking intimately with small groups of people; at outdoor rallies addressing hundreds of thousands; approaching the high altar in St. Peter's for complex liturgy; at the United Nations and the European Union; walking through the crowds at St. Peter's Square, limping with sciatic pain like a sailor on board a heaving deck. Francis gave the impression of using his time to the greatest effect while exploiting the media to amplify his impact, which journalists were quick to call the "Francis Effect." He understood the power of digital media to constructively disrupt the Church. He also understood the power of the media to spread damaging fake news and gossip about the Church and about himself.

CHAPTER FOUR

GOSSIPING "COPROPHAGIA"

Francis on Slander and Fake News

At an early morning Mass, six months into his papacy, Francis delivered the first of many blistering attacks on the sin of gossip and fake news, likening it to terrorism. He did not mince his words: he called it "the sickness of coprophagia," meaning "eating shit." He was also reminding the Church at large of the damaging consequences of malicious tittle-tattle and calumny in everyday life. Yet he had his sights on the besetting vice closer to home—his own offices, within the walls of the Vatican and extending out to the papal nunciatures, the embassies of the Holy See around the globe. He appeared to recognize that a major obstacle to disrupting the status quo and all that was wrong with it was a culture of cynicism, calumny, and corrosive gossip at the administrative heart of the Church. If the Curia was to be effective, the institution would have to change.

Veteran Vaticanologist Marco Politi comments that the Curia is a mix of good and bad: "a microcosm of jealousies, abnegation, lethal rumor mongering, and careerism, and the spirit of sacrifice." The enemies of Francis, he said, act and speak behind the scenes, "they blend into the atmosphere of general applause and display submissiveness to the pope . . . but in private they can be cutting."

As one Curial monsignor told me: "The Vatican is a court, a palace of gossipy eunuchs. The whole place floats on a sea of brilliant bitchery."

My informant, himself no mean gossip, enlarged on a brief anthropology of the worst types among the Vatican community:

> *They start young . . . they never consort with anyone who is not going to further their careers . . . attaching themselves to particular Cardinals, and sucking up . . . they have no outside interests . . . and if they meet up in some little trattoria with their pals their one obsession is the office: who they did down and how they triumphed in this or that petty bureaucratic dispute.*

High on the list of topics is sexual innuendo—true or false, the gossips make no distinction. Frédéric Martel's recent book, *In the Closet of the Vatican*, a veritable gossip-fest, claims that at least 80 percent of Vatican bureaucrats are gay, explicitly or in "the closet," virtually characterizing the hallowed institution as a gay brothel. The scandal-mongering he listened to, the backstabbing and insinuations, fact and fiction, are nevertheless symptomatic of a long-term sickness.

Over the years I have spent many days as a visitor within the Vatican. The atmosphere is unreal, like a permanent Sunday afternoon. The physical structure creates a sense of hothouse separation, an enclosed palace filled mostly with celibates adrift from the real world. A British diplomat once captured the atmosphere: "The stupendous architecture of St. Peter's, which is pure Michelangelo . . . is like a safety curtain that shuts out the world. The effect is a little like living in an embalmed world. . . . It is like being suspended in midair, or isolated on an island or a liner." The clerical bureaucrats, from lowly priests up to cardinal archbishops, are dressed in skirted soutanes with color-coded sashes and skull caps, purple, magenta or scarlet. There are the variegated titles to match: Your Grace . . . Your Excellency . . . Your Eminence . . . My Lord. At the major ceremonies in St. Peter's Basilica the Curia appear in force, genuflecting and bowing (there are a variety of depths to the bows depending on the honor being bestowed), parading their silks and lace amid billowing incense.

One of my informants would talk of the show-offs who love the dressing up; the lazy and demoralized who do the minimum; the "really good men, who are effective priests" among the leaders; and finally the leaders who have become "twisted and weird with a way of life they can't cope with." He quoted a comment by Cardinal Newman: "Now the Rock of St. Peter on its summit enjoys a pure and serene atmosphere but there is a great deal of Roman malaria at the foot of it." The passage describes the "light-headed" clerical gamblers, who today we might call spin doctors, "nursing" a conflagration. "Not much has changed," he said.

Francis is arguably the first pope, in the modern period at least, to lambaste the malicious tongue-wagging of the Roman prelates. "We are used to gossip, to spreading rumors, and we often transform our communities as well as our family into hell," he said, ". . . killing one's brother and sister with one's tongue." Gossip, in other words, leads to soul murder.

Writing on Vatican and papal affairs over a number of years one eventually takes for granted the prevailing, corrosive, and spiteful potential of clerical gossip, which seeps into news and commentary in the Catholic media. The Vatican whispers provide ample material for the wars between Catholic conservatives and liberals around the world, generating a style of malice and contempt to create a kind of "hell," as Francis says.

Francis would even find it necessary to criticize his diplomatic corps, the hundred or so "apostolic nuncios," clerical ambassadors of the Holy See. "It is therefore irreconcilable," he declared, "to be a pontifical representative criticizing the pope behind his back, having blogs or even joining groups hostile to him, to the Curia and to the Church of Rome."

Francis himself became a target of malicious tongues on the day of his election because of his rejection of the pomp and circumstance of the papacy: the red silk cape, the golden throne, the Merc limousine, and the marbled grandeur of the official Apostolic Palace. Yet he is not alone among modern pontiffs in being subjected to malicious gossip.

Benedict was said to have gay tendencies, with the proviso that he did not engage in gay sex. The rumors circulated for years within the Vatican, sometimes surfacing in the secular press. The Catholic commentator Andrew Sullivan, referring to Benedict, wrote in a column that it was obvious to him that "the current Pope is a gay man . . . his gayness is almost wince-inducing. The prissy fastidiousness, the effeminate voice, the fixation on liturgy and ritual, and the over-the-top clothing accessories are one thing." He was referring to Benedict's predilection for showy apparel and accessories: the gold cufflinks, the designer sunglasses, fancy headwear revived from medieval pontificates, the ruby footwear that, in the words of the Irish writer Colm Tóibín, "would take the eyes out of you."

Each pope has been the target of gossip from within his own institution. John Paul II, it was said, had a "Polish girlfriend"; they went camping "alone together" in the mountains. John Paul I, the "smiling Pope," who lasted a month, was ridiculed like no other Pope in recent history. He "waddles like a duck," one prelate told me. An archbishop, laughing in a pleasant vein, said they "made Peter Sellers a Pope"; the writer Anthony Burgess, living in Rome and befriended by many *monsignori*, told me that he was informed, on impeccable authority, that "he's a pederast." Paul VI was "a ditherer, completely controlled by his secretary, Monsignor Macchi." Pius XII was "ruled by his housekeeper, Sister Pasquelina. . . . " It was said that she burst in on a meeting between Pius and US Secretary of State John Foster Dulles to tell him that his soup was getting cold. The nun was known among the *monsignori* as *La Popessa*.

Throwing mud at one target often results in spattering another. Martel cites Archbishop Paul Marcinkus, former head of the Vatican Bank under John Paul II, as the central figure in a circuit of alleged rent boys and "cruisers" with a "hearty appetite" for gay sex and a weakness for Swiss Guards. He adds that "for mysterious reasons Marcinkus became one of John Paul II's favorites at the beginning of his pontificate. According to several sources, the pontiff had a 'genuine affection' for this controversial Vatican figure." Thus Martel insinuates that John Paul II approved not only of Marcinkus, the alleged murderer and crook, but also of his role as head of a promiscuous homosexual ring within the Vatican.

This interested me personally as I spent many days interviewing Marcinkus in 1987 and 1988, recording our conversations. I also spent many weeks and months interviewing his contemporaries inside and outside Vatican City. My investigation took me to Philadelphia, Phoenix, Montreal, and Zurich—where I interviewed a recently retired sergeant of the Swiss Guards. As opposed to the well-attested misconduct in his commercial dealing, I found, like other investigative journalists, nothing untoward in his private life; although much was made of the fact that he occasionally played tennis with his female secretary. I never once heard a suggestion that Marcinkus was gay, although I later discovered that Italian criminal investigators, attempting to build a case against him, excluded a homosexual link, despite trying hard to prove one. They then attempted to find a lead to a rumored female lover. They came up with nothing.

Martel's final shot at the allegedly sex-crazed homosexual Marcinkus, favored by John Paul II, is typical of the casual, malicious gossip circulating in the Vatican. Martel claims that Marcinkus, on retirement, took himself off to a "luxury retirement home" in Sun City, Arizona, with visions of swimming pools and high living. I visited Marcinkus before his death in 2006. He was living in a cramped, scruffy two-room bungalow, with furniture that looked fit for a fire sale. In the dusty yard out back there was a slimy plunge bath. The property was owned by an octogenarian bishop, Ernest Primeau, from Canada. Marcinkus was spending his "luxurious" retirement working pastorally as a parish assistant priest, and he chose Arizona because he suffered from emphysema.

The case of Marcinkus, who was clearly no saint and whose financial misdemeanors were more a matter of incompetence than malfeasance, reveals the power and range of Curial gossip. Ironically, he was the first to offer me, on tape, an honest, albeit roughly stated, perspective on the phenomenon of Vatican gossip:

> *If you can't find charity here in the Vatican, where will you find it? It's supposed to be a place where you find joy. You get three or four priests gathered together and they're criticizing other people. You're going to say, "What is this! I thought this was a place of love?" . . . You can get caught up in this exaggerated bureaucracy where all the bad elements of being a person can come out.*
>
> *This is what happens in this place. . . . You get a little bit here, a little bit there. . . . This is a village, excuse me if I say this, a village of washerwomen, you know, they get down in the river, wash clothes, punch 'em, dance on 'em, squeezing all the old dirt out. In normal life people get away and have other interests, but here— what else is there to talk about?*

The carping against Francis, began, as we have seen, on the evening of the election, with criticism of his rejection of pontifical accoutrements and tradition. The malign gossip would expand rapidly, eventually isolating Francis as the pressure of the crises increased. "The risk," comments Archbishop Giancarlo Bregantini of Campo-Basso, "is that, despite everyone calling him holy, good, and gifted, in the end the pontiff will be left all alone." In the summer of 2018 *The Times* of London published a blurred image of Francis walking across an open square of the Vatican, unaccompanied by security or attendants. Catherine Pepinster, a former editor of *The Tablet*, declared that the image was symbolic of his isolation: "Here is a man struggling to find allies or support from the Catholic faithful. . . ."

Yet for Francis, the worst circumstance from the very beginning was not knowing his true enemies from his friends. After the most vicious attacks and calls for his resignation in the summer of 2018, Francis told a young priest outsider: "Good. Now they are showing themselves in their true colors and we'll know how to deal with them."

Francis would be relentless in his insistence on the corrosive damage done to morale and spirituality through gossip. Talking to a group of religious he declared: "If you find yourself about to drop a gossip bomb—bite your tongue!"

Of all the malicious gossip leveled at Francis, the most insidious was the charge that his election was invalid; that he is a self-excommunicated Anti-Pope. The allegation is based on the story of the so-called St. Gallen Mafia. A group of senior prelates, including leading European cardinals, used to meet up from the late 1990s to discuss the state of the Church in the world and exchange views on the future of the papacy. The leading figure was Cardinal Carlo Maria Martini of Milan, the progressive archbishop and Jesuit I cited at the beginning of this book.

The group met in the town of St. Gallen in Switzerland. The perception that freedom of discussion was discouraged by John Paul II prompted the participants to broach wide-ranging topics. They were critical of the centralizing hard-line theology of Cardinal Joseph Ratzinger, and were unhappy with the prospect that he would be elected pope on the death of John Paul. Their favorite was Cardinal Martini, but Jorge Bergoglio was also mentioned as a potential future pope although he never joined their meetings.

In the run-up to the conclave after John Paul's death, Bergoglio heard of the moves in his favor and begged not to be considered. The group met for the last time in 2006, a year after Ratzinger was elected.

Nevertheless the rumors persisted: that following the resignation of Pope Benedict, four St. Gallen members—Cardinals Walter Kasper of Germany, Godfried Danneels of Belgium, Karl Lehmann of Germany, and Cormac Murphy-O'Connor of England—lobbied the conclave cardinals for Bergoglio, with Bergoglio's acquiescence.

The cardinals in question would expressly deny the allegation; but this has not deterred the rumormongers, whose motives would become clear. Under the rules for the valid election of a pope laid down by John Paul II, titled *Universi Dominici gregis*, it is expressly stated in Article 81:

> *The Cardinal electors shall* [...] *abstain from any form of pact, agreement, promise, or other commitment of any kind which could oblige them to give or deny their vote to a person or persons.* [...]

A circuit of conservative media platforms have consequently argued that Francis was elected through aggressive lobbying and his own involvement, and that he was therefore automatically self-excommunicated along with his coconspirators. Hence Francis is not a valid pope and the papacy remains vacant. Every trustworthy investigation into the allegation reveals that the St. Gallen group did not meet to discuss the 2013 election; nor did Francis conspire with a lobby to have himself elected.

Another tactic of the anti-Francis lobby is to suggest that Benedict was unduly pressured to quit. According to canon law, a resignation has to be freely made. Rumor has it that Benedict came under pressure from Vatican conspirators set on dismantling firm Church doctrine in order to promote a progressive papal agenda. The "Benedict is still the pope" lobby rejects Benedict's written statement that he resigned of his own free will. Others claim that Benedict was blackmailed; that there were lawyers attempting to sue him or even arrest him as the head of a "criminal organization," an employer of sexual abusers.

Francis began his papacy attempting to disrupt harmful gossip close to home by confronting the Curia in unprecedentedly blunt terms. He also attacked gossip as he traveled throughout the world, and persisted with his campaign when talking with special groups. He saw in harmful gossip a feature of an underlying cynicism and failure in charity that was undermining the mission of the Church at every level. The vehemence and depth of his preoccupation with the problem was evident in the images he employed. It was a kind "terrorism," a "diabolical cancer," "it tears people apart," "to gossip is to kill." It was a sign, he believed of a deep spiritual malaise. It destroys, he said, "the Holy Spirit's gift of peace."

Francis was well aware that the relentless criticisms leveled at him via the Catholic conservative media were both wounding and self-wounding in their flagrant insults and attempts to demonize him, making him an object of ridicule and contempt in the eyes of the faithful. As in the secular media, the tenuous line between cool, evidence-based, well-argued criticism of authority and violence by other means had been transgressed. Criticism of a reigning pope was degenerating into vilification and unrestrained character assassination. As a writer who dared to criticize Pope Pius XII's diplomacy, forty years after his death, on the basis of amply sourced documentation in four hundred pages of argument, I have been accused routinely of calumny and detraction to this day. Some of those same critics think nothing of casually destroying the reputation of a living pope on a daily basis.

In the meantime, there was the wider problem of combating media bias and fake news within competing Catholic platforms, as well as in the secular press globally. To get his message across to the world, Francis had been laying plans to reorganize and exploit the digital media revolution in a way not seen since the introduction of Vatican Radio by Pius XI back in 1931.

PART TWO

CHANGING THE STORY

Francis Disrupts the Systems

CHAPTER FIVE

DIGITAL DISRUPTION

A Revolution in Communication

I n March 2020, as the coronavirus epidemic spread across the world, Pope Francis announced that the Holy Week ceremonies in St. Peter's—the high point of the Church's liturgical year—would be broadcast to the world from a virtually empty basilica. Already he had instituted the livestreaming of his Sunday morning Mass in the Santa Marta chapel, his weekly general audience, and the Sunday Angelus homily and prayer for pilgrims in St. Peter's Square. Now his early morning weekday Mass would be livestreamed, attracting half a million worshipers a day.

In most parts of the world Mass was available in every language, offering church services in real time for many millions of Catholics now in isolation. Catholics who had not attended Mass for years rediscovered the service at a time of spiritual, physical, and often psychological isolation. Francis commented that he was against "virtualizing" the Church, but he counseled prudent obedience to the government's decree for lockdown. He added: "It's true that right now we should build this familiarity with the Lord this way . . . but in order to get through the tunnel, not to stay here."

He was conscious not only of the Catholic media's partisanships, antagonisms, and divisions, broadcast and amplified by online providers, the wealthier without paywalls, but also the positive extent to which he could exploit the digital revolution. Among the first to grasp what he was doing, albeit from its own perspective, was the business community. The recognition was as significant as it was novel.

Just one year into his papacy, in the spring of 2014, Pope Francis received two prizes at the Tribeca Disruptive Innovation Awards: the Adam Smith Prize, presented by the *Harvard Business Review*, and the Tribeca Book of the Year Award for his first encyclical, *The Joy of the Gospel*. According to the business magazine *MIT Sloan Management Review*, "... disruptive innovation has gripped business consciousness like few other management theories." In a review of enduring business books, *The Economist* characterized disruptive innovation as "one of the most influential modern business ideas." Other commentators have noted that the theory is so widely accepted "that its predictive power is rarely questioned. The theory's influence has spread far beyond the business world."

Albeit with little finesse, the American business community was the first to identify the parallels between Francis's evangelization and new management theory. Business experts began to talk and write about Francis's "disruptive" style of management. Writing in *Forbes* magazine, journalists Irwin Kula and Craig Hatkoff hailed Francis as an "epic innovator"; he was like an "incoming CEO" confronted by a "raft of challenges." Francis might well have found their excitable reactions queasily toe-curling if well meaning.

The pope, they declared, was like a new boss facing shrinking margins, loss of market share, and hemorrhaging personnel. From day one of his reign he addressed the big question, "What are the jobs to get done?" His goal, they wrote, was evidently to serve "society's most vulnerable"; and he changed the Church's "brand" in one strike from "institutional self-preservation" back to its core mission: to minister to the poor. In the parlance of disruptive innovation theory, they went on, he

> *... had focused on the products and services not only from the point of view of the decreasing number of existing consumers of*

*Catholicism, particularly in the West, but also the much larger
market of non-consumers—the non-practicing Catholics and
non-Catholics.*

The writers warned, however, that while Francis's disruption created excitement and energy, it also prompted "anxiety and resistance
from incumbent management and conservative laity."

Disruptive innovation classically involves a challenge to the current provider of a service or product: landline telephony overtaken by
cell phones; Uber undermining taxicabs. Another notable feature in
the journalists' view was Francis's ability to lead by example. "Rather
than changing any creed, dogma, or theology—that would inevitably
create unnecessary tension and resistance—the Pope's actions and
practices simply embody the genuine mission of the church." The idea,
they wrote, is that theology follows practice: "Lead by example and live
the change you want to see in your company. Be like the Pope and stop
pontificating."

While Francis might well have been amused by the brashness of
this analysis, he was acutely conscious of what he called the "epochal
changes in culture and communications." He was set on a path to
destabilize papal norms, and the digital revolution was to be a key.

Among his many modes of infotech encounter, Francis was to
exploit Twitter (@Pontifex) in nine languages, and a prodigious
range of TV and podcast opportunities—from addressing astro-
nauts in space, to delivering a TED talk via podcast at a conference
in Vancouver. Among the variety of his available smartphone initiatives was an app available in six languages that connects callers to a
"Worldwide Network of Prayer with the Pope"—"Click to Pray"—
through smartphones and tablets. According to one news agency, AFP,
Francis, with fourteen million followers, has "more clout on Twitter
than any other world leader because he is so widely retweeted." He is
reportedly retweeted on average more than 10,000 times in Spanish
and 6,400 times in English.

Kevin Systrom, cofounder of Instagram, tells how he paid two visits to Francis in 2016, first to talk about the power of the platform, and second to get him started. Systrom says that he explained to Francis that "no matter who you are, if you have something to say, Instagram's the place to do it."

On his second visit, he said, "We had just flown in. We were bleary-eyed. He walked in, and he turned the corner, and he goes, 'Kevin!' It was like seeing an old friend from your basketball team or something. . . . We had an iPad, and it was all set up. The name was filled out. So, literally, all he had to do was click 'sign up'." Under the username @franciscus, he posted his first photo in March 2016. By 2020 he sanctioned a joint venture called VatiVision, an on-demand streaming service of television series, movies, and documentaries with a Christian flavor: a religious version of Netflix.

Francis appointed a group of digitally savvy clerics and laypeople and sanctioned a range of meetings to bring theologians and ethicists up to speed on the infotech future. In 2016 he hosted a conference, Power and Limits of Artificial Intelligence, which included the late Stephen Hawking, Demis Hassabis—joint founder and CEO of Google DeepMind—and Yann LeCun of Facebook. Through 2019 the Vatican sponsored a series of meetings and seminars on robotics, AI, and big data. In November a group of media heads and university ethicists explored digital regulation and ethics at a meeting titled The Common Good in a Digital Age; speakers included figures from NATO, Mozilla, and Facebook. The Holy See partnered with Microsoft to offer an international prize in ethics and artificial intelligence after a meeting between Pope Francis and Microsoft's president, Brad Smith.

On a more entertaining level, an example of the enthusiasm Francis sparked among Vatican personnel for digital initiatives, a Jesuit created the first-ever *Minecraft* server at the Vatican. The DigitalJesuit server was inspired by Niantic's top-rated *Pokémon Go*, where players build an eTeam, or evangelization team, by capturing Catholic saints.

———————

Back in 1996, the Jesuit Thomas Reese, at that time editor of *America* magazine, wrote: " . . . the next century will see a paper-less Vatican at the center of a church connected by computers and telecommunications . . . the Vatican will probably find it impossible to control the flow of information and ideas as communications technology allows more people to have access to a variety of views."

Early in his papacy, Francis took steps to revolutionize the entire Vatican media, technologically and managerially. He inherited three big communications baronetcies that were often at loggerheads or in confusing overlap: the Vatican Press Office, the Pontifical Council for Social Communications, and the Vatican Information Services. Among these enterprises, and with clashing responsibilities and governance, were the Vatican Radio and the Vatican Television Center (CTV); the Holy See's daily newspaper, *L'Osservatore Romano*; photographic services, including valuable syndication rights; printing presses; publishing houses; and the various libraries and archives, including the Archivio Segreto (in 2013 Digita Vaticana was established to raise funds to digitize the Apostolic Library, formerly known as the Secret Archive—no longer "secret" under Francis). By 2020, the Jesuit journal *La Civiltà Cattolica*, overseen by the Vatican's secretariat of state, launched a Chinese digital edition with an accompanying WeChat, the Chinese media and messaging app.

Among his advisers was Chris Patten (Lord Patten), devout Catholic and former Conservative MP, who led the negotiations on behalf of Britain with China over the future of Hong Kong. He was at that time chancellor of Oxford University and chair of the BBC Trust, which monitors ethics and regulation within the corporation.

Francis planned to merge the overarching departments, numbering 650 personnel from forty different national backgrounds. Much of the material disseminated by the Vatican in previous papacies, apart from Vatican Radio, had been in hard copy. The plan was to go entirely digital; and to be "of service" to the proliferating Catholic media in dioceses and parishes throughout the world, including commentary websites, TV and radio stations, magazines and newspapers. The Vatican's media services under Francis would no longer end at lunchtime and cease to function on holy days; the operations would be open until ten at night, seven days a week. The merged Vatican information services would now form a single department, or dicastery, called the Secretariat for Communication. The new operational head was to be fifty-year-old Monsignor Dario Viganò, who specialized practically and academically in media craft (Monsignor Viganò is not to be confused with Archbishop Carlo Maria Viganò, who accused Francis of hypocrisy and called for his resignation in September 2018). Dario Viganò's declared intention, he said, was to build "a central content hub . . . after the Disney business model."

The idea of comparing the global Catholic Church to Disney's range of fantasy productions and projects—movies, theme parks, TV, books, comics, toys, computer games—may well have struck both liberals and conservatives as the final consummation of the abomination of desolation. Yet the "model" offered a crude comparison. Duncan Wardle, who ran innovation and creativity at Disney for twenty-five years, comments: "It's now about disrupt or die . . . it's not about iteration anymore, it's about innovation. . . ." An essential feature, he goes on, involves the use of interactive media to respond, as a flexible service, to the needs of consumers right out to the peripheries, rather than expect consumers to look to the center for guidance and choice of content.

The disruption is reminiscent of the shift in BBC policy in recent decades. At the founding of the corporation, Lord Reith established the ideal that a national broadcaster should provide programs that it considers culturally worthy and improving for listeners; today the corporation listens and is informed by its audiences to a degree unknown in the past. Analyst Jason Moser, writing in the *Los Angeles Times* in 2018, says the key to the Disney business model is "direct-to-consumer offerings," meaning that that the providers take more control in partnership with the consumer. How this was to work out in relation to the Church in the world was increasingly obvious as Francis talked constantly of decentering from the "self-referential" Church. The Vatican center was to become a responder rather than a pontificator, a service rather than a magisterial head office.

Awareness of the powerful, universal influence of the digital media within religious communities revealed many dangers, not least how the faithful could be "acted upon" as target consumers in promotion and marketing strategies. An example of this is the phenomenon of so-called geofencing, whereby a constituency or community is exploited by a marketer through knowledge of their digital profiles. Geofencing first came to notice through the practice of retailers tracking shoppers via their cell phones as they made their way through malls and supermarkets. The system can be used equally by political marketers tracking parishioners at Sunday Mass. According to Heidi Schlumpf at the *National Catholic Reporter*, it works like this: "Politically minded geofencers capture data from the cell phones of churchgoers, and then purchase ads targeting those devices." The data can then be matched with other databases, ". . . including voter profiles, which give marketers identifying information such as names, addresses and voter registration status."

The lobbying organization CatholicVote.org, which runs the largest Catholic voter mobilization program, boasts that geofencing of Catholics can win presidential elections. For example, it has identified some 200,000 regular Mass-goers in Wisconsin, a key battleground state that Donald Trump won by only 22,748 votes in 2016. In 2020 CatholicVote announced plans to use geofencing in Wisconsin, Michigan, Pennsylvania, Arizona, and Florida. The group used geofencing in Missouri in 2018 to help defeat Democratic Senator Claire McCaskill by denouncing her as "anti-Catholic" for her policy on abortion.

Recognition of the changes in information technology, local regulation, and "intelligent automation" led to the Vatican procuring appropriate software. An example of this is the Bizagi software system that enables the Vatican center to cope speedily with local situations, whether they be legal circumstances with consequences for abuse cases, or revenues and investment patterns with significance for traditional policies at the Holy See's center for local banking regulations and charity laws. According to the company's promotions:

> When operating in the real world of legacy systems and complex global operations, the digital world can seem unreachable. Change can't happen fast enough, yet conventional roads to transformation result in lost time and unpredictable returns. Bizagi wraps around existing legacy systems to transform today's organizations and digital businesses.

Viganò talked of the move to the periphery in terms of Thomistic political philosophy, "adhering to the concept of subsidiarity," meaning management at the apex of hierarchy surrendering control over matters that can be handled lower down, or locally. "The local churches," he says, "have developed their own communication structures, and we must interact with them in a subsidiary way and never substitute for them. We must assist them in whatever way we can so they can do their work well." The vision also appeals to a theological insight invoked by St. Augustine of Hippo, the *sensus fidelium*, the "feel" of all the faithful, and the importance of attending to the "echo" of the faithful to the Church's teaching: a *listening* Church. (Not long after getting the digital revolution under way Dario Viganò was himself disrupted, after using a routine digital editing process to redact a piece of copy exploiting a quote by Emeritus Pope Benedict in a book promotion blurb. He was exposed and resigned, but Francis retained him in an advisory capacity.)

It remains to be seen whether new information technology will aid the conundrum of the twenty-first-century Church: how to achieve a balance between the bishops and the papacy; the laity and the clergy; the periphery and the center. At the very least, Francis decided to follow the principle of "disrupt or die."

"Catholicism," as Church historian Eamon Duffy has written, as quoted above, "is a conversation, linking continents and cultures, and reaching backward and forward in time." Francis clearly understood the virtual impossibility of keeping the Church together, or initiating change, without skillful management of the complex new forces of communication. And yet those forces had extensive positive potentials. One of the ancient titles of popes, Pontifex, or Pontiff, means a maker or builder of bridges. It is clear that Francis saw the digital revolution as an epochal new means of building bridges, of reaching out in new ways, as well as receiving.

CHAPTER SIX

FRANCIS AND MAMMON

Reforming the Vatican Money Changers

I f Francis had swiftly set in motion an infotech revolution, he would face seemingly insuperable difficulties when he attempted to disrupt the Vatican's complex financial affairs. Vatican finance has long been a riddle wrapped up in an enigma, as Winston Churchill once said of the Soviet Union. By taking the name Francis, he signaled his priority of serving the needs of the poor, in apparent contrast to the Vatican's reputation in recent decades for wealth and corrupt money dealings. The problems were deep and historic.

On the morning of June 18, 1982, more than thirty years before the election of Pope Francis, the Italian banker Roberto Calvi was found hanging by the neck from a builders' scaffold below Blackfriars Bridge, which spans the Thames in central London. A half brick and pieces of rock were found in his pockets. It was reported by journalists (my newspaper office was a hundred yards away) that Blackfriars, *Fratelli neri,* is an Italian nickname for the Freemasons. It was also recalled that the ancient Masonic oath acknowledges that a traitor to the brotherhood should be roped and weighed down with masonry where the tide rises. Had Calvi committed suicide? Or had he been executed?

Despite a variety of inquests, it is uncertain to this day how he died. Yet it became increasingly clear in subsequent months and years that the Vatican was deeply involved in Calvi's business dealings in the person of the president of the Vatican Bank, Archbishop Paul Casimir Marcinkus, a tough-looking, rough-speaking, Chicago-born canon lawyer. What was an archbishop doing running a bank? Marcinkus allegedly once said: "You can't run the Church on Hail Marys...."

Religious movements need money, but an operation like the Catholic Church needs money on a global scale, as does the papacy. Separate from Vatican money are the independent finances of major dioceses around the world, some of which are extremely wealthy, particularly in the United States and in Germany, where the dioceses' income amounts to six billion euros a year. Then there are the independent funds and properties of the great religious orders—the Jesuits, the Franciscans, the larger missionary societies.

In 2014, Brother Michael Perry, head of the Franciscan order of Friars Minor, announced that the group, numbering fourteen thousand members, was on the verge of bankruptcy after the discovery of embezzlement by members of the order. Swiss prosecutors seized Franciscan bank accounts because of alleged illegal operations. The losses to the order, according to the statement, amounted to tens of millions of dollars. A Vatican source told me that Francis said to Brother Michael: "What surprises me is not so much how you came to lose the money, but why, and how on earth you had it in the first place!"

In previous centuries money played a crucial, at times shameful, part in the papacy's survival. In the mid-nineteenth century, Pius IX fled into exile after the Eternal City was seized by a republican mob. His return a year later, protected by French troops, was paid for with a loan from the Rothschilds, New York bankers. The Jews of the city, given freedom by the republicans, were forced back into Rome's ghetto and made to pay the interest on the debt.

Back in the late Middle Ages, the sale of indulgences and trade in relics was a notable ingredient in the corruption that led to the Reformation. Earlier still, the Franciscans, famous for their strict ideals of poverty, were instrumental in overturning the moral ban on usury. They created the first banks in our modern understanding of the term, known as *Montes Pietatis*, perfecting double-entry bookkeeping and promoting the possibility of development through microcredit to craftsmen, small farmers, and other small and medium businesses.

The Jesuit community at Salamanca of the late sixteenth century can claim to have established modern financial markets, exploring anew the ethics of usury under Christian auspices. They believed that lending money in a developing economy was a way of spreading risk in a start-up business. Interest, they argued, was a legitimate means of compensating risk.

Within the Vatican a principal financial center is known as APSA, the Administration of the Patrimony of the Holy See. It serves as a treasury and financial investment operation mainly run by lay professionals, although members of the Curia, the Vatican bureaucracy, have discretionary control. APSA also manages Peter's Pence, for the pope's almsgiving around the world. The center administers a portfolio of stocks, bonds, and real estate, originally purchased with the settlement paid by Mussolini's regime in 1929 to compensate Italy's sequestration of the Papal States in the mid- to late nineteenth century. The original figure was 750 million Italian lire in cash and a billion lire in bonds, at today's value about $1.5 billion. The value of the "patrimony" fund is now estimated at $800 million, mostly in property and land.

APSA has not been without controversy: In the 1960s it was a major investor in the Watergate complex in Washington, DC, with rumors that the Vatican used its influence to lift zoning restrictions. As recently as 2019, APSA was involved in the ownership of a luxury apartment scheme in London's affluent Chelsea, prompting headlines questioning Vatican financial dealings.

Then there is the so-called Vatican Bank, known as IOR—*Istituto per le Opere di Religione*—or the Institute for Religious Works—founded by Pius XII in the depths of the Second World War when currency transactions were an essential part of relief aid across borders. The ownership of the bank is in the name of the reigning pope. It is situated in a former dungeon; a service elevator rises directly into the pope's official apartments. It is basically a savings-and-loan house. There are deposits held by the pope himself for the special purposes of his mission.

The Vatican Bank was not to escape scandal in the immediate postwar era. According to US intelligence reports, some two hundred million gold coins, stolen by the Ustaše allies of Hitler, and valued today at $500 million, came into the Vatican for "safekeeping," after which the trail ends. It is said that John Paul II transferred $30 million to the Solidarity movement in Poland during the 1980s. The pope is the only shareholder. Account holders are principally Vatican employees and religious congregations enjoying modest interest. Money is lent out at a paltry rate to missionary projects, dioceses, and religious societies throughout the world. It makes money by depositing revenues in government bonds and securities, and accounts in other banks.

———————————

The bank came under the spotlight again due to Archbishop Marcinkus's involvement with the controversial banker Roberto Calvi. Early in the 1970s, Marcinkus bought shares in Calvi's Ambrosiano Bank and made large deposits at high interest rates. Marcinkus had a cleric's view, a disdainful view, of the integrity of all business. By taking on the bank, he evidently expected to get his hands dirty. He claimed in an interview with me in 1987 that he had only undergone five days' instruction in banking. Naïveté bordering on kleptocracy has often been the hallmark of the Vatican's financial dealings.

Calvi was involved in setting up dodgy offshore shell companies, money laundering, and rigging of the Milan stock market. Via a holding company in Luxembourg, he set up ten shell companies nominally controlled by the Vatican Bank. In 1980 the Ambrosiano collapsed with debts of more than a billion dollars, mostly owed by the shell companies. In 1982, Calvi disappeared; then he was found dead under Blackfriars Bridge.

The Vatican was found liable in the consequent fallout and ordered by the Italian state to pay $250 million in compensation for "moral" culpability. In a recorded interview in January 1988, Marcinkus told me that he would have been sacked had he not "found the money" to pay the figure. He admitted that he had raided the Vatican pension fund to make good the amount and saw nothing wrong with the decision.

————————

At a discussion among cardinals in the run-up to the 2013 conclave that elected Francis, the phrase *niente piu Calvi* echoed around the room: "no more Calvi."

On the day of his election Francis inherited a Vatican financial mess, riddled with intrigue, mismanagement, and cronyism; and with alleged links to gay cliques and dubious characters and practices outside the Vatican. Among the typical stories breaking that summer was the arrest in June 2013 of Monsignor Nunzio Scarano, nicknamed Monsignor Cinquecento (Monsignor Five Hundred), for his rumored habit of carrying wads of five hundred–euro notes around in his pocket. Monsignor Scarano had worked for twenty years as the senior accountant to APSA. The allegations involved conspiracies to launder money on a grand scale via the Vatican Bank. He would eventually be acquitted of a scam involving the laundering and transfer of twenty million euros via private jet between Switzerland and Italy, but he remained on trial for money laundering in a separate proceeding, and of making false accusations for which he received a suspended two-year sentence. In another trial, Rome-based Monsignor Bronislaw Morawiec, who managed the finances of the Basilica of St. Mary Major, was given a four-year sentence for embezzling 230,000 euros.

Anybody tracking headlines on Vatican finance through the previous two decades could not fail to be shocked by its abysmal, scandal-prone record. At the turn of the new century the Vatican was listed by the UN as a top money-laundering operation. Ten years on, the Cardinal Archbishop of Naples, Crescenzio Sepe, was cited

by Italian prosecutors for alleged corruption in public works con-
tracts while he was a senior Vatican official from 2001 to 2006. It was
alleged that Sepe charged public officials cheap rents on Church-
owned properties while, as quid pro quo, large sums of state funds
were awarded for renovation of Vatican properties. Sepe denied
wrongdoing and was never charged, but the case remains open. In a
commentary on the story, the Vaticanologist John Allen Jr. remarked:
". . . even if he was guilty as charged, there was probably no knowing
intent to do wrong, because this was simply how things had always
been done."

The chaotic, opaque, morally ambivalent culture of Vatican finance
led to a situation by 2009 in which Italian fiscal authorities froze $30
million of the IOR's funds until the bank conformed to internationally agreed controls. In response, Pope Benedict approved an internal
watchdog body, the Vatican Financial Information Authority: AIF.
Three years later, in 2012, Moneyval, the Council of Europe's fiscal regulator, complained that the Vatican's financial transparency had not
improved; that if anything it had declined.

That was the year the journalist Gianluigi Nuzzi published his
exposé of Vatican corruption, based on leaked memos and the confi-
dential correspondence of Benedict. The material told of fraudulent
contract prices costing the Holy See millions and allegations of the
blackmailing of homosexual clergy. The disclosures were made with
involvement of Benedict's personal butler, Paolo Gabriele, who
had been leaking the material to Nuzzi. The affair became known as
Vatileaks for its parallels with Wikileaks.

Against this background, Archbishop Carlo Maria Viganò, deputy
governor of the Vatican City-State, sought a private audience with
Benedict to inform him of malpractice within APSA. He was specifically critical of Cardinal Secretary of State Tarcisio Bertone, who in
turn denied all allegations and accused Viganò of treachery. Viganò,
who will return later to this narrative as the 2018 "whistleblower"
demanding Francis's resignation, was dispatched from Rome in a

promotion-demotion as papal nuncio in Washington, DC, where he no doubt proceeded to nurse his grievances.

In January 2013 Italy's central bank shut down credit card transactions in the Vatican until such time as the city-state could comply with European money-laundering rules. It coincided with the results of an investigation into the state of the Holy See's finances and administration commissioned by Benedict. Conducted by three senior cardinals, it told a story of powerful "lobbies" within the Vatican, furthering the careers and financial self-interest of key individuals. Benedict handed over the three-hundred-page document to Francis shortly after he was elected.

Francis declared his determination to identify the Church with the poor of the world. He lambasted clerical love of luxury, calling out "peacock priests" and "entrepreneur priests." "The court," he told Eugenio Scalfari of the newspaper *La Repubblica*, "is the leprosy of the papacy." When a cardinal admitted that he had spent $3,000 on his apartment kitchen (after all, not an exorbitant figure by today's standards), Francis, according to a member of the Curia, who overheard it, rebuked him: "What! Is it gold-plated?" We are not told of his precise reaction (except reports that he was "furious") on learning of the $500,000 spent on "remodeling" the Vatican apartment of the former secretary of state, Cardinal Bertone. Worse still, the money, it was revealed, came from the misuse of the charitable funds of Rome's children's hospital. The charity and Cardinal Bertone deny wrongdoing.

Yet the bigger questions of wealth concerned the state and culture of financial conduct within the Holy See and Vatican City. Amid myriad calls upon his time and energies in the first year of his papacy, Francis strove to initiate proper governance and good practice. He established an audit team, COSEA—or Commission for Reference on the Organization of the Economic-Administrative Structure of the Holy See—which had the power to commission outside accountants from firms with international reputations, such as Deloitte and KPMG. In what seemed a bold and sensible move at the time, he appointed the abrasive Cardinal Archbishop George Pell to head an oversight committee, SPE (Secretariat for the Economy). Then he asked the head of the Vatican Bank, Ernst von Freyberg, to write a report demonstrating why a pope should own a bank in the first place. Von Freyberg responded by inviting a team of inspectors from the New York–based Promontory Financial Group to investigate each of the bank's 13,700 individual accounts, as well as some 5,000 corporate accounts. A third of them would eventually be closed. Meanwhile he appointed René Brülhart, a Swiss lawyer and anti-money-laundering wizard, to head the AIF overall watchdog.

A measure of the long-term success of his initiatives, by 2017 Italy would place the Vatican on its "white list" of states with "cooperative" financial institutions. That year Moneyval, the financial regulator of the Council of Europe, awarded the Vatican a favorable assessment. By 2019, the AIF could report that suspicious financial activity in the Vatican had reached a six-year low in the previous year, demonstrating that Francis's disruption was working. The report revealed that fifty-six suspicious activities had been filed in 2018, down from 544 in 2015.

Nevertheless, in an unforeseen reversal, Cardinal Pell had by 2019 returned to Australia, where he was tried and convicted of historical sexual abuse, despite his protestations of innocence. On April 7, 2020, Australia's highest court would acquit Pell of all charges, followed by his release from prison. Pell was not to return to his Vatican job. Among the reactions of outraged advocacy groups and relieved supporters, the Church Militant website suggested that Pell was the victim of a Vatican-linked conspiracy because of his economic whistle-blowing within the Holy See.

The previous year had seen another headline-grabbing scandal, cited earlier, involving the Chelsea property deal in London made in 2013 by the Secretariat of State. On October 13, 2019, the *Financial Times* trumpeted: "Vatican Police Investigate Holy See's Bet on Chelsea Property." The secretariat had apparently spent $200 million purchasing a share of a warehouse with planning permission for luxury apartments in London's affluent West End. When the United Kingdom's Brexit vote lowered property values and the deal went sour, the secretariat asked the Vatican Bank for a $150 million loan to purchase the property outright in the hope of retrieving the situation at a later date. The transaction was a bid to escape a joint ownership arrangement with Athena Capital Global fund, administered by the Italian businessman Raffaele Mincione. Internal Vatican auditors were querying payments to middlemen. The Vatican Bank not only refused to lend the money but reported the situation to the Vatican's Promoter of Justice. In the subsequent internal probe, Vatican gendarmes raided the Secretariat of State and AIF offices, hauling away files and computers. At least five Vatican employees were suspended, as well as Italian businessman Gianluigi Torzi, accused of extortion, embezzlement, fraud, and money laundering. Torzi was the Vatican's trustee in the deal.

The story went viral, prompting reports that nothing had changed in the Vatican despite Francis's best efforts, while raising an obvious, valid question: Why is the Vatican risking money on luxury property investments? The media claimed fresh evidence of Vatican financial corruption, adding the widespread rumor that the Vatican was heading for bankruptcy through mishandling of finances, unwise investments, and a sharp fall in revenues—a situation that would deteriorate further during the coronavirus pandemic.

On the flight after his trip to Japan in the last week of November 2019, journalists questioned Francis about the London deal and the investigations. The tone and gist of the questions appeared to probe whether the Holy Father had entirely lost his grip on Vatican finances.

Francis answered with bouncy assurance: "This is the first time the lids have been taken off the pots by someone inside and not outside." People should not be worried by the fact that the Vatican makes investments, he said. "The sum of Peter's Pence arrives and what do I do? Put it in a drawer? No, that's bad administration. I try to make an investment."

He went on to defend ethical portfolio investments: "If you make an investment with Peter's Pence in a weapons factory, the offering is no longer an offering," he said. "And, yes, you can buy a building and rent it and then sell it," provided, he added, "that it is sound investment, and that the people who benefit are those Peter's Pence is intended to help." This should have allayed fears that Francis was an anti-capitalist, unreconstructed Marxist.

He said that the London deal seemed to have involved "things that don't seem clean." The auditor, according to Francis, asked what he should do, and "I told him to go to the Vatican prosecutor with the information. I'm content with that because it shows the Vatican administration has the resources to report and investigate suspicious activity. . . . I signed the authorizations myself."

Francis replaced Cardinal Pell with Juan Antonio Guerrero Alves, a Spanish Jesuit with a degree in economics and a background in administration. A Vatican source claims that Pope Francis had been looking for someone to ensure "transparency" and uphold the rules of "international standards" in Vatican finances; someone, ideally, who could turn around the deficits and show how the money was being used in service of the poor.

The Vatican clearly had a long way to go before its finances were beyond reproach. A principal difficulty for Francis was the labyrinthine, entrenched nature of competing interests and responsibilities within the Vatican city-state, combined with the culture of internecine rivalry aided by corrosive gossip and rumormongering. Christopher Lamb, *The Tablet*'s Rome correspondent, writes: "Targeted leaks, vicious infighting, and petty power games reveal a pattern of self-destructive behavior that threatens the hard work done to bring economic credibility to the Holy See. It reveals that the changes that the Pope has to implement in the Roman Curia are cultural, as well as structural."

Meanwhile there were lawyers hard at work attempting to hold the Vatican liable for sexual abuse cases. Before Christmas 2019, the Associated Press reported that attorneys in fifteen American states were "scrambling to file a new wave of lawsuits alleging sexual abuse by clergy" thanks to new rules that either extended or suspended the statute of limitations on claims going back decades. AP quoted reports claiming that the lawsuits, involving 5,000 new cases, could cost more than $4 billion.

At the same time, Britain's prominent human rights lawyer Geoffrey Robertson was urging national and international lawmakers to set aside the Holy See's claim to be a sovereign state. Statehood was the major impediment to efforts to sue the pope in person for "crimes against humanity" in respect to clerical abuse of children. If Francis really yearned for a poorer Church, surrender of its wealth for the crimes of its priests would be the swiftest route.

Meanwhile Francis was faced with the more mundane task of imposing proper governance and regulation on a set of financial entities over which he had ultimate responsibility yet limited control. The financial bureaucracy, or bureaucracies, of the Vatican, based on the decayed traditions of an imperial court, combined with a civil service that once administered an entire country—the Papal States—were not fit for the purpose. Hidden funds, ancient usages, jealously guarded privileges, and an addiction to secrecy created a self-protecting web of intrigue. While financial control spelled power, the clerical executives of that power, as I discovered in the case of Marcinkus, invariably lacked a grasp of business ethics, or even of good business regulatory practice. Disruption of this state of affairs would take time; meanwhile, a series of smaller disruptions would make progress.

On September 25, 2020, Francis demoted one of the most powerful princes of the Church, Cardinal Giovanni Becciu. From 2011 to 2018, Becciu had headed the secretariat of state, a prelate close in seniority to the pope himself. The secretariat had handled the controversial Chelsea property deal. Francis not only sacked him from his new post, as prefect of the Causes of Saints, but rescinded his rights as a cardinal. Accountability, Francis was demonstrating radically and effectively, went to the very top. Becciu would insist that he had done nothing wrong.

CHAPTER SEVEN

FRANCIS SPEAKS OUT

A Poor Church for the Poor

E ven as Francis prepared in 2013 to clean up the financial mess in the Vatican, he was completing a sermon to the world, an apostolic exhortation, in which he would discuss economics, globalization, wealth, and poverty. His life in Argentina as man and boy inevitably shaped his long-term thinking, his spiritual and political views about poverty. The migrant memories of his parents and grandparents, as well as life in a country founded on immigration, explained his intense feelings for the predicament of migrants during his papacy.

Jorge Mario Bergoglio was born in 1936, the eldest son of Italian emigrants from northwest Italy who moved to Argentina. When his grandparents landed with their six children in 1927, his grandmother, Rosa, in the heat of the Argentine summer, was wearing a fur coat into which were stitched the proceeds in cash of the sale of her husband's Italian business—a coffee shop in Turin. They escaped an Italy economically devastated by the First World War, and arrived in Argentina, one of the most prosperous countries in the world at that time. Grandfather Bergoglio joined two brothers who had migrated earlier and were building a paving company. But the business went under when the Great Depression of 1929 hit. The family moved to Buenos Aires where Jorge's father, Mario, who had now trained as an accountant, eventually married into another family of Piedmont immigrants.

Jorge's family was comfortable but far from wealthy. Through the war years the Argentine economy grew modestly until General Juan Domingo Perón became president in 1946. Perón, who identified with the *pueblo*, the people, led a program of widespread nationalization, with strong links between government and unions. While boasting socialist credentials, Peronism resembled fascist corporatism. Perón favored selection over election, and fostered state-run associations in every aspect of civic life. The Perón years saw the growth of leadership adulation and populism. He encouraged an "us against them" rhetoric; workers against the elite. Foreign investors, especially American and British, were seen as exploiters.

Perón was ousted in a military coup in 1955. There was a massive flight of foreign currency and investment, rampant inflation. As the economy continued to fail, the belief persisted that poverty was best eliminated by wealth distribution rather than wealth creation. Despite the absence of Perón, his leading ideal survived: that the state should represent the interests of the *pueblo*, the have-nots.

In June 1973 Perón, now 77, returned to Buenos Aires from exile in Franco's Spain after an absence of eighteen years. That same year Father Jorge Bergoglio, only three years after making his final vows, became head of the Jesuits of the Argentine province. (I arrived in Buenos Aires on assignment that summer to cover Perón's reelection, returning again in 1975.) Perón died in 1974 after a few months in power. Argentina descended into a long-running military dictatorship and a cruel Dirty War. Father Bergoglio was obliged to steer his priests through dangerous crosscurrents.

The conflict involved a lethal cocktail of ideological clashes—political and economic—in which Marxist-Leninism, Maoism, Guevarism, anarchy, and forms of corporatism, socialism, and capitalism were in violent contention. Guerrillas, notably identified with the groups known as Montoneros, carried out bombings, kidnappings, and assassinations on state and private institutions; the military waged firefights and arrested thousands of innocent people suspected of

fellow traveling, including priests. The military death squads imprisoned, tortured, and killed an estimated 30,000 people, often taking
their children and "gifting" them to officers' families. The junta, led by
General Leopoldo Galtieri, would eventually fall apart following the
loss of the Falklands War in 1982.

Beginning in the late 1980s the country attempted a Reaganomic-
like free-market liberalization under the presidency of Carlos Menem.
State-run industries were privatized, subsidies and tariffs dismantled.
But the benefits of this sudden free-market apotheosis were accompanied by closures, layoffs, and a rise in poverty in Buenos Aires to about
35 percent of the population. Devaluation was resisted to combat inflation; borrowing became difficult. The free market, known in Latin
American left-wing parlance as *neoliberalismo*, was judged the cause of
the country's economic woes.

Father Bergoglio shared a detestation of *neoliberalismo* as he
climbed the Catholic hierarchy, increasingly identifying himself with
the "option for the poor." After an initial period of standing on ceremony, he began to cook his own meals, took the bus, looked scruffy,
and spent time in the expanding shanty suburbs. Friday nights he
would go out to the red-light districts seeking to help the city's many
prostitutes.

He nevertheless rejected the liberation theology movements associated with "Marxist Jesuits" elsewhere in Latin America. Had he not
done so, he would never have been made bishop under John Paul II.
Yet he was still politically and economically left of center. In 1998,
following John Paul II's visit to Cuba, he contributed to a pamphlet,
Dialogos entre Juan Pablo II y Fidel Castro (1998). He wrote that "no
one can accept the precepts of neoliberalism and consider themselves
Christian."

While clearly affected by the Argentine experience under Menem,
he was also looking back to the ideals of Peronism. His lingering attachment to Peronism was evident in his oft-quoted nostalgic mantra
Techo, Tierra, Trabajo, Roof, Soil, Work—Home, Land, Job: the basis, in

his view, of all human dignity. These ideals, harking back to Leo XIII's *Rerum Novarum*, echoed Catholic social teaching of the late nineteenth century, although the aspiration for "soil," *tierra*, was unrealistic in a densely populated city like Buenos Aires.

In May 2007, Cardinal Bergoglio was the final editor of a document produced by the meeting of two hundred bishops, representing some of the poorest regions of the world, at Aparecida, site of Brazil's national shrine to the Virgin Mary. Bergoglio gave a speech in which he talked of the poor as the *sobrantes*, the "leftovers," the marginalized groups who find themselves redundant—migrants, the homeless, the unemployed, the sick, and the elderly.

Back in Buenos Aires, in a series of conversations with his friend Rabbi Abraham Skorka, later published as *Heaven and Earth* in 2010, Cardinal Bergoglio revealed his open approval of the long dead Perón: "The Church," he said, "did not confront Perón, who was close to certain members of the clergy" and who drew on "social Doctrine of the Church." He went on to criticize lay and clerical Catholics who were not satisfied with being "shoulder to shoulder with the needy" but "fell into the trap of becoming ideological." They became "estranged from the Church's healthy development and suffered repression."

Considering the Church at large, Bergoglio declared that "hedonistic, consumerist, and narcissistic cultures have infiltrated Catholicism." He said, "It is necessary to engage the world, but always from the religious experience." He praised Franciscan spirituality, the idea of poverty as a virtue—a life choice. "Francis of Assisi," he said, "contributed an entire concept about poverty to Christianity in the face of the wealth and pride and vanity of the civil and ecclesial powers of the time."

On November 24, 2013, eight months after his election, Francis published *Evangelii Gaudium, The Joy of the Gospel.* The text had been started by Benedict, but there was a bold section on economics, twenty pages long, obviously the work of Francis. It was a clear statement of his "option for the poor," echoing aspects of Latin America liberation theology. He starts by declaring that it is not the task of a pope to offer a "detailed and complete analysis of contemporary reality"—by which he evidently meant economics, with its social and political undertones. And yet, unlike his predecessors, he proceeds to call on all Christians to get involved in concrete and practical responses to economic injustice: "It is no longer possible to claim that religion should be restricted to the private sphere and that it exists only to prepare souls for heaven."

He is plain in his rejection of "trickle-down theories," which are not "confirmed by the facts" and show a "crude and naïve trust in those wielding economic power." He denounces the domination of market forces over human beings, everything coming under the law of competition and the survival of the fittest. "Human beings are themselves considered consumer goods to be used and then discarded."

He contradicts the belief that economic growth, encouraged by a free market, will result inevitably in justice and inclusiveness. He advocates the welfare state, saying that injustice follows when people reject "the right of states, charged with vigilance for the common good, to exercise any form of control."

He repeats his warnings on the coming environmental calamity in a world of unrestrained capitalism. A system that devours anything in the way of increased profits, including the environment, "is defenseless before the interests of a deified market."

There were world-class economists who shared Francis's views, not least Joseph E. Stiglitz, a former academic economist who had been senior vice president and chief economist at the World Bank. Not only was Stiglitz a critic of neoliberalism but he slammed the globalization policies of the World Bank and the International Monetary Fund. In 2003 Stiglitz was appointed to the Pontifical Academy of Social Sciences, where he was said to have a strong influence over Monsignor Marcelo Sánchez Sorondo, the academy's chancellor.

French economist Thomas Piketty appeared to agree with Pope Francis on the relationship between unchecked capitalism and a rise in global inequality. In his *Capital in the Twenty-First Century* (published that same year, 2013) Piketty called for more wealth redistribution through taxation to combat globalization's contribution to economic inequality.

Yet Francis suffered immediate and sharp criticism from the likes of Rush Limbaugh, who declared that Francis "doesn't know what he's talking about . . . this is Marxism." To which Francis's defenders responded—No, this is Christianity! But there was stern criticism too from experts within the Church, an example of which was an essay by Catholic economist Philip Booth, program director at the UK Institute of Economic Affairs. The pope, he wrote in the pages of the *The Tablet*, employed the rhetorical trick of "knocking down straw men." Nobody, Booth insisted, believed in the "absolute autonomy of markets." Markets, he went on, involve cooperation between people in the context of institutions. They can be restrained by the moral and ethical behavior of those involved, by institutions that develop within markets themselves, by civil society, culture, and governments. Commenting on the "complete autonomy of a market" he declared, is "like talking about the complete autonomy of a brothel without reference to any of the people operating within it." What's more, "it is meaningless in the context of Christian anthropology."

Booth was not alone among economic commentators, including Catholic ones, in claiming that globalization had brought a billion people out of poverty since 1980: "The fall is staggering, and the main cause is globalization," wrote Booth, " . . . just consider how the mobile phone—which is a technology produced by multinationals but harnessed by smallholders, fisherman and stallholders in Africa—has changed the lives of millions of previously poor people."

R. R. Reno, editor of the Catholic periodical *First Things*, wrote a similarly abrasive criticism of Francis's "sweeping generalizations about economics." Francis ignores, he wrote, the corruption in state-dominated economies, while singling out trickle-down theories. His rhetoric, he concluded "contributes to our already degraded political culture."

And yet, Reno appears to concede a point with a backhanded compliment. He tells his readers that they should treat Francis's "provocations" as a challenge to triumphant capitalism "rather than a call for its overthrow." He goes on: The challenge is "something we need, especially those of us who benefit from the wealth-creating power of capitalism . . . we're often blind to its negative consequences, sometimes willfully so." Which could be taken as the very point of Francis's disruptive "provocation."

It remained for Francis to demonstrate in action what he meant by "concrete" support of people trapped by unjust economics. He began to do this in a dramatic, public fashion during a trip to Bolivia and Ecuador in July 2015. It would become a familiar feature of his visits to developing countries where exploitation by large corporations was everywhere visible. His audiences were gatherings of street vendors, poor small farmers, truckers, people who made a living sifting through mountains of garbage. He encouraged his listeners to challenge the global economic system that "has imposed the mentality of profit at any price, with no concern for social exclusion or the destruction of nature. . . ." They should fight, he said, "for change, real change, structural change." It was time, he went on, to combat "new colonialism" responsible for inequality and exploitation.

At the same time, he offered an apology for the sins of the Church: "Some may rightly say, 'When the pope speaks of colonialism, he overlooks certain actions of the Church.' I say this to you with regret: Many grave sins were committed against the native people of America in the name of God."

Earlier that year, he preached against exploitation in a slum area of Naples afflicted by drug dealing, violence, and an absence of policing.

He had a message for corrupt politicians and the Camorra gangs that control trafficking of every kind. He told the people "to resist criminals and their accomplices. I today, humbly and as a brother repeat: Convert yourselves to love and justice." After celebrating Mass, he ate with male and female inmates in a local prison where there were also transsexuals and AIDS sufferers.

His disruptive approach to the problems of poverty, racism, and xenophobia, and their solutions, were from the periphery, the poor themselves. It was as if he did not seek change by addressing businesspeople, managers, investors. His strategy was bottom-up, from the people, the workers. Nor was he advocating state-controlled industries and businesses. Yet as often as he stressed that he was not anti-business, nor against wealth creation, but against exploitation and injustice, his critics grumbled and carped. He had done much to interrupt complacent attitudes toward Vatican finance, and signaled the direction in which he wanted the Church to go—to identify itself with the poor and with poverty. Yet he was about to surprise the world with a Christian vision of a parallel and related kind of impoverishment: the destruction of the environment.

PART THREE

THE QUALITIES OF MERCY

Francis Teaches Tenderness

CHAPTER EIGHT

"BE PRAISED!"

Francis on Our Common Home

On May 24, 2015, Francis signed off on a document entitled *Laudato Si'*, a phrase in early medieval Italian, "Be Praised," taken from the poems of St. Francis in praise of nature as sister and mother.

> *Praised be You my Lord through our Sister,*
> *Mother Earth*
> *who sustains and governs us,*
> *producing varied fruits with colored flowers and herbs.*

Subtitled "Care of our common home," the document is a meditation on our relationship with God the Creator, human beings, nature, and the planet. The small book, known as an encyclical or letter, is addressed not just to the Catholic faithful but to the entire world. In the midst of the torrent of scientific and social warnings, assertions, and denials, Francis was delivering a wake-up call, and he was emphatic: The world faces a climate catastrophe; it is man-made and inextricably linked to fossil fuel consumption. It was unprecedented for a pope to teach so explicitly on such an issue, and signified that as pope he was leading the Church into a wider set of moral concerns over a wider set of evils.

Yet ancient spiritual insights lie at the heart of that extended moral vision, principally the spirituality of St. Francis of Assisi. It was timely in a secular sense, since it was issued ahead of the bid to agree to a climate change treaty following the United Nations Paris conference that year. *Laudato Si'* nevertheless shocked and angered the constituency of conservatives in climate change denial, including Catholics. George Neumayr, veteran journalist of the Catholic Right and author of *The Political Pope*, declared: "The document is riddled with half-truths and scattershot generalizations, many of which come from deep-seated prejudices against capitalism." The Vatican was being controlled by a "nest of extreme environmentalists." And there were other, more serious criticisms. Vatican correspondent Edward Pentin commented: "Critics have warned that by falling in with proponents of climate change science, the Pope risks getting too close to other key supporters of the theory who support population control and abortion."

Yet secular opinion was widely in favor, enthusiastic even, of Francis's intervention. The London *Guardian*, generally reserved toward Catholicism and religion in general, declared that it was "perhaps the most ambitious papal document of the past 100 years. . . . It sets out a programme for change rooted in human needs." Writing in the *New York Times,* the Catholic journalist Paul Vallely stated: "*Laudato Si'* turns out to be one of the shrewdest documents issued by the Vatican during the past century."

The nub of the document is the equivalence between human poverty and the impoverishment of nature. As Francis told film director Wim Wenders: "The poorest, of the poorest, of the poorest of the poor . . . is nature because of the way in which we rob her and abuse her." And yet, he goes on: "She is our sister, and our mother." Nature, or the environment, is not something separate or "other," he is saying. We are inextricably linked, related, and integrated with her. Francis is employing the term "integral ecology" to describe a Christian perspective on the relationship between the creator and the entirety of creation.

Some two hundred specialists and experts assisted in the research and writing of the encyclical. His standpoint, moreover, reflected the views cited in the November 2014 report of the UN Intergovernmental Panel on Climate Change. The report was endorsed almost 100 percent by the climate scientists involved.

Even if he failed to carry the entire Church with him, the document had the power to disturb the recalcitrant. Writing in *First Things*, R. R. Reno declared: "I still don't like the heated rhetoric or agree with his particular assessments, but the Bergoglian word-bombs have jarred me out of my complacency." Francis could have asked for nothing more from a staunch, caustic conservative than evidence that his disruptive word-bombs were having an explosive effect.

Six years ahead of teenager Greta Thunberg's campaign to raise consciousness about global warming, Francis was focusing on the younger generation, which will inherit a stricken planet. Young people demand change, he insists. "They wonder how anyone can claim to be building a better future without thinking of the environmental crisis and the sufferings of the excluded." Again, he was linking environmental destruction with the "leftover people," the poor, the exploited: "The earth, our home, is beginning to look more and more like an immense pile of filth."

He inveighs against the throwaway culture, combined with the greed of overextraction, overproduction, and overconsumption, with insufficient recycling leading to polluting waste. "We have not yet managed to adopt a circular model of production capable of preserving resources for present and future generations." On the concentration of greenhouse gases, and consequent global warming, he writes of the threat of rising sea levels and extreme weather events. The link between human activity and these developments is backed up, he asserts, by a "very solid scientific consensus," thus opposing the deniers and issuing a challenge to Donald Trump, who would be elected president the following year. Again, he links the "unprecedented destruction" to the consequences for people's lives.

In his catalog of polluting environments he betrays his hatred for Latin America's megacities. "We were not meant to be inundated by cement, asphalt, glass, and metal, and deprived of physical contact with nature." At the same time, despite a press conference comment earlier in the year, that Catholics shouldn't "breed like rabbits," he criticized those who blame population growth instead of extreme and selective consumerism.

It was typical of Francis to send messages containing apparent paradoxes. He would not support irresponsible parenthood, but he was not going to make an easy link between global warming and "overpopulation." It was widely recognized after all that some of the most impoverished areas of the world, sub-Saharan Africa, for example, have high population growth but low carbon emissions. Conservative Catholics, meanwhile, would continue to link the encyclical with advocacy for abortion.

Turning to the spiritual dimension, he writes: "We are not God. The earth was here before us and it has been given to us." He denies that Judeo-Christianity, in readings of the Genesis account, allows us dominion over the earth, encouraging "unbridled exploitation of Nature." The Bible tells us to till and keep the garden of the world, he writes. "'Tilling,'" he goes on, "refers to cultivating, ploughing or working, while 'keeping' means caring, protecting, overseeing, and preserving. This implies a relationship of mutual responsibility between human beings and Nature."

He rejects the notion that technology alone can solve all the problems, stressing that it is a global *moral* problem that finds its origin in a "politics concerned with immediate results, supported by consumerist sectors of the population." In response to electoral pressures, he continues, governments are "reluctant to upset the public with measures which could affect the level of consumption or create risks for foreign investment." Short-termism, he writes, "delays the inclusion of a farsighted environmental agenda within the overall agenda of governments."

He calls on local and national governments to think long-term for the "common good." And he advocates grassroots communitarian action to alter government priorities. "Unless citizens control political power—national, regional, and municipal—it will not be possible to control damage to the environment."

He points back to the 1960s, comparing the current crisis with the threat of nuclear war. In this sense *Laudato Si'* makes connections with the great plea of John XXIII's encyclical, *Pacem in Terra*—Peace on Earth—written fifty years earlier when the world stood on the brink of nuclear war. But the circumstance now, he argues, involves the injustice of "ecological debt" whereby the poor are paying for the indulgence of the rich, and our children and grandchildren will pay dearly in the future. Those who suffer most from environmental devastation, he is saying, are those least likely to benefit materially from the consumerist impulse that is causing the devastation.

In a final section Francis takes up the theme of "ecological spirituality" to be found in the rich heritage of twenty centuries of religious experience, encouraging "a more passionate concern for the protection of our world." This is not a matter of doctrine, he insists, but of "an interior impulse which encourages, motivates, nourishes, and gives meaning to our individual and communal activity." This, he goes on, has not always been the case. Christians have not always drawn on the spiritual treasures available to them. Hence a "conversion" is necessary, an "ecological conversion" that is also a "community conversion" in which people begin to live out their "vocation to be protectors of God's handiwork."

He calls for a "spirit of generous care, full of tenderness" that arises from gratitude, "a recognition that the world is God's loving gift, and that we are called quietly to imitate his generosity in self-sacrifice and good works." This gratitude and generosity, he goes on, entails a "loving awareness that we are not disconnected from the rest of creatures, but joined in a splendid universal communion."

An "ecological conversion" includes an awareness that "each creature reflects something of God and has a message to convey to us." Christ has taken into himself this material world, he goes on, "and now, risen, is intimately present to each being, surrounding it with his affection and penetrating it with his light." He writes of the need to recognize that "God created the world, writing into it an order and a dynamism that human beings have no right to ignore.... Jesus says of the birds of the air that 'not one of them is forgotten before God.' . . . How then can we possibly mistreat them or cause them harm?"

Christian spirituality, he declares, proposes "an alternative understanding of the quality of life, and encourages a prophetic and contemplative lifestyle, one capable of deep enjoyment free of obsession with consumption." This is Francis on poverty as a virtue: ". . . that simplicity which allows us to stop and appreciate the small things . . . avoiding the dynamic of dominion and the mere accumulation of pleasures." Failure to learn how to "live on little" is part of the environmental crisis, he declares.

He writes of St. Therese of Lisieux and her little way of love, not to miss out on a kind word, a smile, or any small gesture that sows peace and friendship. Integral ecology, he goes on, is made up of simple daily gestures, which break the logic of violence, exploitation, and selfishness. An integral ecology includes taking time to recover a serene harmony with creation reflecting on lifestyle and ideals, contemplating the creator who lives among us and surrounds us.

He refers to a range of spiritualities and traditions and quotes the ninth-century Muslim Sufi Ali al-Khawas, who counsels not to put a distance between the creatures of the world and the interior experience of God. The Sufi writes: "There is a subtle mystery in each of the movements and sounds of this world. The flies buzz, doors creak, birds sing, or in the sound of strings or flutes, the sighs of the sick the groans of the afflicted." Francis quotes the Franciscan philosopher

Bonaventure who declared that "contemplation deepens the more we feel the working of God's grace within our hearts, and the better we learn to encounter God in creatures outside ourselves."

He cites the Carmelite mystic John of the Cross, who teaches that goodness in the world "is present in God eminently and infinitely, or more properly, in each of these sublime realities is God." Skirting the heresy of pantheism or panentheism, the idea that God *is* all things, he adds: "This is not because finite things of this world are really divine, but because the mystic experiences the intimate connection between God and all beings, and thus feels that 'all things are in God.'" It is an exercise of the religious imagination.

He ends by quoting the "Spiritual Canticle" of John of the Cross, "these mountains are what my beloved is to me," then contemplating the connections between the sacramentals of water, oil, bread, wine, and fire, the mystery of the Incarnation, and the sacrament of the Eucharist. Since the Eucharist "joins heaven and earth; it penetrates all creation. . . . Thus the Eucharist is also a source of light and motivation for our concerns for the environment, directing us to be stewards of all creation."

Francis would move on to other issues in his busy papacy, but his climate change campaign did not end with the encyclical—it was a beginning and a continuing impetus. On the night of December 8, 2015, the Feast of the Immaculate Conception, while world leaders were in intense talks in Paris on the climate change treaty, Francis sanctioned a striking initiative—a three-hour-long slideshow entitled *Fiat Lux* projected onto the façade of St. Peter's Basilica. Images taken by eminent photographers featured hideous landfill sites swarming with ragpickers; polluted seas, mountains of dead animals, burning forests; floods, droughts, and vast overcrowded favelas.

Francis broadened the moral concerns of Catholics to understand that the ecology of the planet and human societies are interdependent; that the environment is the common home of all plants, creatures, and people; and that the entire planet shares a common relationship with the creator. He was the first pope in history to make such strong moral and theological statement, and it would prove prophetic as the environmental threats multiplied.

CHAPTER NINE

WOMEN IN THE CHURCH

Francis Attacks Misogyny

During the homily at his early morning Mass on June 15, 2018, Pope Francis spoke against misogyny. He was commenting on the text in Matthew 5:28— "... whoever looks at women with lust has already committed adultery with her in his heart." It was an admirable tirade but peculiar, with echoes of his pastoral life in Buenos Aires when he cared for prostitutes in the sprawling red-light district.

He started by declaring, "There is a rage against women, terrible rage." He invited his congregation to consider how many women have become "slaves of the throwaway mentality." Jesus, he said "changed history" in the way he respected women, who up to that point did not enjoy freedom. Women, he went on, end up exploited, enslaved, because men exploit them as objects: "This is a sin against God the creator," as men and women are created "in the image of God."

Francis expressed an early determination to alter the status of women in the Church. He said at one of his unscheduled press conferences at the back of an airplane: "Women in the Church are more important than bishops and priests." Yet to do something about it, to make it true, he had to struggle with his own generation and background.

It was to take seven years for him to bring women to a higher level than bishops and priests—at least from the perspective of promotion in the Curia. In mid-January 2020, Francis made Vatican history when he appointed a laywoman, Francesca di Giovanni, to a post within the Secretariat of State normally restricted to a prelate at the level of archbishop or cardinal. Born in Palermo, Sicily, in 1953, di Giovanni would run the Section for the Relations with States, an important multilateral division dealing with intergovernmental organizations and a network of international treaties. Di Giovanni told the Vatican media, "The Holy Father has taken an innovative decision, certainly, which—beyond my person—represents a sign of attention toward women."

Over the past decade under Francis, according to the Vatican's own figures, the number and the percentage of women working in the Vatican has increased. In 2010, under Benedict, 4,053 people worked for the pope, 697 of whom were women: about 17 percent. In 2019, the total number of papal employees rose to 4,618, of which 22 percent (1,016) were women. Among these, Francis promoted a number of women to high rank, including Barbara Jatta, head of Vatican museums, and Cristiane Murray, deputy head of the press office. There were, besides, four women appointed as councillors for the Synod of Bishops, the undersecretary at the congregation for religious orders, and two undersecretaries in the office for laity.

Francis would be criticized every day of his pontificate for failing to bring women forward in the Church; but the extent of his interruption was unprecedented. His initiatives would offer a significant alteration and hope for the future.

Within a few weeks of his election Francis appointed women as consultants to the General Secretariat for the Synod of Bishops on Young People, Faith, and Vocational Discernment. Next, he appointed a seventy-one-year-old British grandmother, Margaret Archer, to head the Pontifical Academy of Social Sciences. This international body of some thirty economists and sociologists meets in the Vatican to offer advice on justice and peace issues. Archer's role was to advise the pope in his campaign to combat human trafficking.

Francis made another key female appointment when he took on Francesca Chaouqui as an adviser in his attempt to combat financial corruption in the city-state. She was given a role in the financial audit team—Commission for Reference on the Organization of the Economic-Administrative Structure of the Holy See (COSEA). She was a public relations specialist employed by the Ernst & Young financial consultancy with a background in digital communications. Self-possessed, still in her early thirties, she appeared a token of the radical change Francis was seeking, but her appointment was also indicative of the risks he was taking and his inability to check appointments in depth. Unfortunately, her appointment was short-lived. In 2016 she left her Vatican job after being charged with leaking papers about alleged financial mismanagement. She denies the charges.

The hazards, less indicative of Francis's flexibility than of the recalcitrance of the institution, were evident in a series of appointments aimed at bringing clerical abuse of children to an end and delivering justice to victims. Known officially as the Pontifical Commission for the Protection of Minors, it was intended as a policy-making body—reporting directly to Francis. The women commissioners, from Poland, France, Britain, and Ireland, embodied leadership qualities, specialist knowledge, and life experience that no celibate male prelate could bring to the task. They were to investigate the relationship between the Church and civil authorities in reporting abusers, priestly recruitment, seminary training, and the pressures of celibate life. I interviewed the four women for the magazine *Newsweek* at the time of their appointments. They could not have been more different from the usual clerical *monsignori* recruited as Vatican committee members.

Marie Collins, age sixty-seven, who had been abused by a priest herself while hospitalized in Dublin at eleven, was head of a survivors' charity. Originally reluctant to join the commission for fear of appearing cozy with the Church, Collins says that she changed her mind in order to alter the way the Church treats survivors. Next came a world-class expert on child and adolescent psychiatry with extensive knowledge of child sexual abuse. Dr. Catherine Bonnet, a sixty-nine-year-old practitioner based in Paris, was a renowned expert in the diagnosis and treatment of child abuse. Twenty years earlier she had found herself in the eye of a storm over her refusal to believe that many cases of recollected parental child abuse were the result of false memory syndrome.

The third commissioner was a sixty-nine-year-old British mother of four, Sheila Hollins. She brought wide experience as a general medical practitioner and consultant psychiatrist specializing in learning disabilities. The fourth member was the sixty-eight-year-old former Polish premier, Hanna Suchocka. A formidable veteran politician and diplomat, she had once been dubbed "the Polish Thatcher" by the late William Safire—as much for her ability to outclass men as for her hairstyle.

Whatever difficulties lay ahead, involving the early resignation of Marie Collins due to frustration with certain officials and the Curia, Catholic women would see these commissioners as an advance guard for further lay female involvement in the running of the Church.

————————

In the Church of my boyhood, women lay and religious were regarded almost as a separate species; laywomen who married and gave birth were even seen as impure, unclean. Nuns who took vows of poverty, chastity, and obedience mainly worked as nurses, teachers, and carers; many were no more than maidservants to priests. The Catholic theological perception of women was that they aspired to the virtues of the Virgin Mary, essentially obedient, acquiescent, in need of protection. The purity of Mary, the Immaculate, signaled the imperfection of women as spouses and mothers. The ancient notion that the hymen of Mary had not broken in giving birth has continued to the present day. Even in the mid-1960s mothers of the newly born were expected to undergo a ritual of cleansing, known as Churching, indicating that childbirth was unclean. Women were not allowed onto the sanctuary of the church where Mass is celebrated without special dispensation; an element of the ban was a belief that menstruating women would pollute the sacred space.

Down the centuries, there were examples of women accepted as extraordinary in the eyes of the clergy: Catherine of Genoa in the fifteenth century, a laywoman who cared for the sick and poor; Teresa of Avila, the great mystic member of the Carmelite order of the sixteenth century; the many founders of women's religious orders. But nuns were entirely subservient to the male clergy, and laywomen, especially when they were married, were barred from any role in Church governance. Women who claimed to have experienced visions of the Virgin Mary, like Bernadette of Lourdes and Catherine Labouré, were not believed unless they took the veil, entered a cloister, and submitted themselves to the clergy. As Cardinal Martini remarked in my interview with him in 1993, Catholics experienced "from a young age . . . the segregation of and humiliation of women religious."

In my junior seminary the cooking, cleaning, and laundry was done by a team of cloistered nuns who had taken a vow of silence. I did not exchange a word with any of them in the course of five years. We sometimes caught sight of these women through an open doorway, usually on their knees, soapsuds up to their elbows, scrubbing, scrubbing. We called them "the witches," as did our priest teachers.

After the Council, religious women united to improve their status. Yet even as feminist theology began to flourish in universities throughout the world, nuns were rarely given the opportunity to pursue such studies. Missionary nuns attempting to encourage safe sex and family planning were strongly disciplined. Yet there were saintly nuns who colluded with the most insidious forms of attack on women: Mother Teresa of Calcutta, canonized by Francis in September 2016, shockingly declared at the World Conference on Women in Beijing in 1995: "Those who want to make women and men the same are all in favor of abortion."

The treatment of women at the very heart of the Church in Rome had been generally scandalous down the years, despite the liberalizing initiatives of the Second Vatican Council. In January 1989 I interviewed a woman who claimed to be the first lay female employee hired in an administrative capacity within the Vatican:

> These people were terrible to me when I first came; they wouldn't talk to me, even on the phone. There were priests and monsignori who would come and stand at the door and just stare at me in silence. Even the lay staff were difficult; after the first day they had me banned from the canteen. Later on, big deal, they changed their minds and said I would be welcome. I never set foot there again.

She introduced me to another secretary appointed in the 1980s, the personal assistant to a top theologian. She said: "I wasn't allowed to speak to anyone in the Vatican. When he went out of the office for a while he would lock me in."

Secretaries in the Vatican are one thing; women national leaders are another. Speaking in March 2020 at an Irish-American event in Boston, former President of Ireland Mary McAleese told how Pope John Paul II refused to shake her hand when they first met, and shook her husband's hand instead, asking him: "Would you not prefer to be the president of Ireland instead of your wife?" Mrs. McAleese said she responded: "You would never have done that to a male president. I'm the elected president of Ireland whether you like it or not." She has consistently spoken of her impression of the Catholic Church as an "empire of misogyny."

Pope Benedict, similarly lagging in his octogenarian clerical attitudes towards women, criticized in 2012 the Leadership Conference of Women Religious (LCWR), representing 57,000 nuns, which comprised 80 percent of the religious sisters in the United States. He denounced the LCWR group for its "radical feminism" and for distorting the teaching of the Church. They were ordered to rewrite their statutes under supervision of a disciplinary committee of bishops. The order was inherited by Francis and the process dragged on until 2015, when it was satisfactorily resolved.

———————

On his election, Francis promised a fresh start in the Church's attitudes toward women, although he betrayed occasional blinkered clerical attitudes from the outset. Asked whether he would ever appoint a woman to head a Vatican department, he quipped: "Well, pastors often wind up under the authority of their housekeepers." Although he was to appoint women to senior Vatican posts, there was evidently a recalcitrant cultural perspective lurking in Francis's nature, perhaps pointing back to attitudes in Buenos Aires.

Although Francis worked pastorally among the prostitutes of Buenos Aires and deplored male sexism, something of the Argentine machismo seemed to have rubbed off on him. In the book of conversations with Rabbi Abraham Skorka, published in 2010, he remarked that "a constant feminist philosophy does not give women the dignity that they deserve. . . . I would say that it runs the risk of becoming *machismo with skirts*." It was probably not the first time he used that phrase, and it was not to be the last. The Catholic ethicist Jamie Mason wrote that Francis's comment portrayed the feminist struggle for equality as "vindictive macho men in female drag." Even when Francis was attempting to champion women in the Church, he could be clumsy. In 2014 he remarked that some leading women theologians were "strawberries on the cake" of theology.

Such remarks served to obscure the striking changes he brought to the Vatican: "The feminine genius," he said, "is needed wherever we make important decisions." In October 2013, addressing a hundred women from Catholic organizations, he said that he deplored the spectacle of *servidumbre* (Spanish for "servitude") inflicted on women.

At an in-flight press conference, he said:

> *The role of women in the church must not be limited to being*
> *mothers, workers, a limited role . . . No! It is something else. . . . All*
> *we say is: They can do this, they can do that, now they are altar*
> *servers, now they do the readings, they are in charge of* Caritas.
> *But there is more! . . . profoundly more, even mystically more . . .*
> *Women, in the Church, are more important than bishops and*
> *priests; how, this is something we have to try to explain better,*
> *because I believe that we lack a theological explanation of this.*

We can see in this a progressive spirit striving to understand not only what women theologians were telling him, but what his heart was telling him. But then, too much can be expected of a pope. In his characteristic habit of holding opposites in tension, he was firm on male and female difference, as one would expect; yet he opened up the possibility of a measure of fluidity without getting too deeply into the transgender controversy. "Masculinity and femininity are not rigid categories," he counseled. And he warned against rigidity in gender stereotypes, arguing that it can "hinder the development of an individual's abilities, to the point of leading him or her to think, for example, that it is not . . . feminine to exercise leadership."

At his first Holy Week ceremony, he shocked Catholic traditionalists when he went on his knees to wash and kiss the feet of two women. According to traditionalists no priest, let alone a pope, should stoop to touch female feet. The following year he asked the Vatican department handling liturgy to prepare to issue a decree allowing the foot washing of "all members of the people of God," including women. It was formally issued in 2016.

Meanwhile there was the question of a women priesthood, or at least diaconate. The official tone and message against women in priestly roles had been set by John Paul II in his 1994 letter on the priesthood, *Ordinatio Sacerdotalis*, which banned even discussion of the subject for all time: Many priests came to believe that it was a sin, constituting "grave matter," even to ask questions on the issue, let alone answer them. The following year, to mark the World Conference on Women in Beijing in June 1995, John Paul at least went some way toward apologizing for the wrongs inflicted on women in the Catholic Church, while making a "heartfelt appeal that everyone in a special way, states and international institutions, should make every effort to ensure that women regain full respect for their dignity and role." Yet as he stressed repeatedly, the role of women was to emulate the Virgin Mary.

Jackie Hawkins, executive editor of the Jesuit-based journal of spiritualty *The Way*, found John Paul's statement of apology a devious mix of flattery and reassertion of patriarchal attitudes. "Give me a self-confessed, fully paid-up male chauvinist any day," she wrote, "rather than a man who, with however much goodwill mistakenly believes that he understands women—and feels bound to tell them so":

> *Then, presumably when we are meant to be totally disarmed and breathless with anticipation, the manacles snap shut.... Only men can be icons of Christ, Mary is modeled, unrecognizable as a real woman.... We are, still, simply human props of various designs. Words of flattery and support have proved hollow.*

John Paul II made it a matter of virtually infallible doctrine that women could never be priests, but the campaigns could not be suppressed. I had raised women's ordination during my interview with Cardinal Martini in Milan in 1993. "The problems, the questions raised by women's issues," he said, "should be taken seriously by both sides." He went on:

> *As for the issue itself, I think we should come to it little by little, to gradual solutions that will satisfy not only the most progressive but the majority, while remaining true to the tradition and within the*

*bounds of common sense. . . . But I can foresee that we'll have some
decades of struggle ahead. When people ask me, and it's usually
Americans: "Will we have women priests?" I answer: "Not in this
millennium."*

His eyes sparkled with amusement, since our conversation was
still in the twentieth century, with only seven years to go to the new
millennium.

Francis was questioned frequently about the possibility of women's
ordination; he responded firmly in the negative. Whatever he might
have pondered privately on the question, he realized that any step—
even to open up an investigation, study, or debate—could prompt
schism.

Yet if there is to be any change in the decades ahead, a first step, as
occurred in the Anglican and Episcopalian churches, must be to invite
women into the diaconate. The role of deacon in the Catholic Church
is regarded as an entry into the clerical estate. Deacons cannot celebrate Mass, but they can express the ministry in a range of activities:
baptism, marriage, funeral services. Until Francis was elected, a female
diaconate was out of the question.

Six years into his papacy, in October 2019, Pope Francis said of a
women's diaconate: "I am going to take up the challenge . . . that you
have put forward, that women be heard." A report by the International
Union of Superiors General had come to a "partial result on what the
reality of the women's diaconate was like during the first centuries of
the church and its implications today." This enabled Francis at least
to reconvene the commission at a later stage since the report "falls
short of what the woman is; in the transmission of faith. . . ."

The papal historian, former Jesuit, and Catholic commentator
Peter Hebblethwaite used to say that the Anglican and Episcopalian
churches are laboratories in which the future of the Catholic Church
is worked out. A women priesthood was greeted with much debate
and bitterness in the Church of England: In time both Protestant

denominations sanctioned not only women priests but women bishops. A first step was women deacons.

The example of the non-Catholic churches showed that should a women's diaconate be accepted within the Catholic Church, it would open the way, eventually, to a Catholic female priesthood. To begin with, the sight of women dressed in clerical garb, including Roman collars, as would be their right if they became deacons, would certainly prepare the laity for the idea of female priestly ordination. Cardinal Müller, Benedict's head of doctrinal orthodoxy, said in 2002: ". . . it would be real discrimination of woman if she is considered as apt for the diaconate but not for the [priesthood] . . . the unity of the sacrament would be torn at its root."

In the event, Francis was to disappoint expectations of an early decision on women deacons, but he had disrupted the intransigent position of his predecessors and his initiative is there to be picked up in the course of a future papacy. As with so many of his advances, he was opening the way across broad fronts.

CHAPTER TEN

THE DILEMMA OF DIVORCE AND REMARRIAGE

From Casuistry to Mercy

I n the fall of 2013, Jacquelina Lisbona, an Argentine woman living in San Lorenzo, a town in the northwest of the country, wrote a letter to Francis posing a personal moral dilemma. Her husband, Julio Sabetta, had previously been married and divorced without an annulment. So her parish priest told her not to receive Communion because her marriage was not recognized by the Church: It was "irregular," and both husband and wife were "adulterers."

But in April 2014, she received a surprise telephone call from Francis himself, rebuking her parish priest. "Some priests are more papist than the pope," he allegedly said. He advised her to go to Confession and receive Communion in another parish. The story came out via Julio's Facebook page and was picked up by a local radio station before going viral. The program prompted widespread consternation across the Catholic world, especially among the traditionalists who claimed that Francis was creating moral confusion. Yet Francis began to teach that it was the traditionalists who were confused—about justice and mercy, spirit and letter.

Francis would frequently raise the passage in Mark's Gospel chapter ten where the Pharisees try to catch out Jesus on the prohibition against divorce. Was it lawful, they asked, for a husband to put away his wife? Francis would comment frequently on the way Jesus refused to answer such questions, "because they thought of the faith only in terms of yes you can, or no you can't."

The issue of the "adulterers," those Catholics who had divorced and remarried, was to become a catalyst for his constant message of mercy as a crucial path to healing for individuals and the entire Church. His central message was that mercy did not alter fundamental moral truths, nor the requirements of justice. Justice and mercy, he preached "are not two things but a single one, only one thing. In God, justice is mercy and mercy is justice." The paradox was to prompt hope among people who felt cut off from the Church; it was also to cause much disruption and anger.

The significance of the coming disputes over divorce, remarriage, and adultery was the inference to be drawn for other sexual and moral issues. To the conservative mind, to transgress the red line of indissolubility of marriage would open up the possibility of allowing sex before marriage, gay sex, same-sex marriage, many divorces, even polygamy. Moreover, it would make a mockery of those countless generations that had, with suffering and hardship, kept to the Church's strict matrimonial rules.

The problem of the divorced and remarried had evidently been on Francis's mind for some years. Returning from Brazil in 2013, he fielded a wide range of questions before somebody asked whether divorced and remarried people could receive Communion.

He started by talking about mercy. Divorce and marriage, he was saying, is just one of many wounds suffered by the faithful—especially, he said, the effects of clericalism, abusing priests, and corruption in the Church. He went on: ". . . the Church is Mother . . . she must go to heal the wounds with mercy. But if the Lord does not tire of forgiving, we have no other choice than this: first of all, to cure the wounds." He cited the Prodigal Son, whose father ordered a feast, not a punishment. Mercy means "going out to find the wounded . . . not just waiting for them to come to you." He could have been talking of any of the gamut of sexual and relational problems facing Catholics.

Instead of reiterating the clear teaching, in the manner of John Paul II, he engaged in a verbal balancing act. He went on to make a passing reference, without explanation, to "the theology of *economy,* as we call it." Of which more below. Next, he said that he was due to discuss the matter with his Council of Cardinals, and that it would be a topic for the future Synod of Bishops: a signal that he was going to reopen the marriage and divorce question, which everybody thought had been definitively settled by his predecessors. Moreover, he and the bishops would now explore it from the perspective of "matrimonial ministry," then the problem of marriages that were null from the beginning, and then "anthropology . . . speaking and speaking again, going and returning . . . we are on the way for a somewhat profound matrimonial ministry. And this is everyone's problem, because there are so many, no?"

As if to back up the "so many," he cited his home diocese of Buenos Aires, and a remark made by his predecessor, Cardinal Antonio Quarracino, who reckoned that half the marriages in the province were null and void.

Based on his pastoral years in Buenos Aires, Francis was convinced that incalculable numbers of Catholics were suffering because of their "irregular" marital status. He was looking for ways in which these excluded Catholics could be brought back, based on his belief that doctrine must be tempered with compassion, casuistry with mercy.

It is widely accepted that in common with non-Catholics, some 50 percent of Catholic marriages end in divorce. The figures are complicated by the fact that not all Catholics marry in church, and some divorce more than once. Many second unions are partnerships rather than marriages. A further complication is distinguishing between Catholics, cultural Catholics (who no longer practice), and ex-Catholics (who neither believe nor practice). CARA, the Catholic statistics organization, argues that a truer picture of divorce among practicing Catholics is closer to 28 percent.

Many divorced and remarried Catholics ignore Church teaching and receive Communion. But many more have left the Church because they no longer feel welcome. They are told by priests and lay Catholics of an orthodox tendency, and following Christ's words in the Gospel, that they are "adulterers"; it is hard for friends, family members, and children to accept such a label. Within my own close family, we had experience of the ban on divorce and remarriage over many years.

My late mother was typical of Catholics of the previous generation in this dilemma. She came from a large, poor Irish family; my father became a Catholic in order to wed. They married young during the Depression of the 1930s and raised five children during the Second World War and the austerities of the late 1940s. They were incompatible, unhappy for twenty years before separating and eventually divorcing. My father married again. Then my mother fell in love with a widower; they married in a registrar office. She hoped to secure a Church annulment. In the meantime, on the instruction of the parish priest, she ceased to receive Communion. It was breaking her heart.

A Catholic annulment is the judgment of a tribunal of canon lawyers that the original marriage was invalid. Before the election of Francis, it required the decision of two courts and a final decision in Rome. It could take years, and it was expensive. A variety of reasons could be cited: pressure to marry on one or both of the couple; insanity at the time of the marriage; impotence; close familial affinity; failure to understand the vows and commitments. Rarely, nowadays, a partner argues that the marriage was never consummated.

In the case of my mother, I was called to give witness under oath to a canon lawyer at London's Westminster Cathedral. Aunts and uncles on both sides of the family had also been called. He was an elderly priest, probably in his eighties, and hard of hearing. He wrote out my testimony slowly, in longhand, in a school exercise book. He focused on the possibility that my father was mentally deranged before he married. I could not state under oath that my father was mentally ill before the marriage. Her annulment was turned down after five years.

In 1922 only twenty Catholic annulments throughout the entire world were allowed by Rome, including two from insanity, one from impotence, and the largest number, nine, because one at least of the partners felt compelled. Annulments became more numerous after the Second Vatican Council. They swelled rapidly in the United States from fewer than four hundred a year in the late 1960s to the tens of thousands after Pope Paul VI allowed the American bishops to apply a swifter process: The American Church came to be called an "annulment factory."

Following the years of the "sexual revolution," couples were splitting more easily and frequently; the United States led the way. Under John Paul II, however, the rules were tightened, leading to a fall in applications; there was also a reduction in the number of church weddings. Today annulments in the United States still account for half of those allowed by the Church worldwide, although the US Catholic population is only 6 percent of the Catholic population globally. Because it is by far the wealthiest of the Churches, there are sufficient numbers of canon lawyers to process all comers.

In other Western countries, where annulments are a fraction of the American figures, pastors often relate that divorced and remarried Catholics simply flout the ban and go to Communion anyway. They are following the well-worn path of those Catholics who not only ignore the teaching on contraception, but don't believe in it (according to CARA, 76 percent of Catholics in the United States don't believe in the teaching). The doctrine that declares contraception a sin has not changed, but it is no longer taught, no longer widely observed, and seldom confessed.

Catholic doctrine on marriage is scripturally grounded. In Matthew's Gospel, Jesus is being tested by the Pharisees on the Mosaic law that allows divorce. He hearkens back to the book of Exodus: "For your hardness of heart Moses allowed you to divorce your wives, but from the beginning it was not so. And I say to you: whoever divorces his wife, except for unchastity, and marries another, commits adultery; and he who marries a divorced woman, commits adultery." Given Jesus's tendency to irony the passage might well have been aimed at those Pharisees who manipulated the law to dump their wives. Yet it has been taken as absolute and definitive by the Catholic Church, although not by the Eastern Orthodox Churches, which are fully Apostolic (descended from the Apostles); their sacraments are recognized by Rome, but allow up to three divorces and remarriages.

The Roman Catholic teaching on the indissolubility of marriage has held fast down the centuries until the most recent ruling by John Paul II, following a synod on marriage and the family in 1981: ". . . The Church reaffirms her practice, which is based upon Sacred Scripture, of not admitting to Eucharistic Communion divorced persons who have remarried." Marriage, he went on, is a symbol of something greater and higher than their human union: It reflects the ". . . union of love between Christ and the Church. . . ."

John Paul granted, however, that remarried couples could receive Communion if they "live in complete continence." And to make doubly sure he was clearly understood: ". . . that is, by abstinence from acts proper to married couples." At the same time he insisted that the Church "forbids any pastor, for whatever reason or pretext even of a pastoral nature, to perform ceremonies of any kind for divorced people who remarry." That would put paid even to a simple blessing in church (a blessing by his parish priest was denied one of my brothers who divorced after his wife left him, and remarried in a registrar office after seven years; our family, Catholics all, assembled in the local Anglican church, whose priest was only too happy to oblige).

Yet Francis's suggestion in his 2013 press conference that he would reopen the issue demonstrated his determination to disrupt the firm ruling of his predecessor within weeks of his election. There was no concerted outcry at the time, but in the fall of 2013 the chief of the Congregation for the Doctrine of the Faith, Cardinal Gerhard Müller, published a piece in the Vatican's newspaper, *L'Osservatore Romano*, emphatically repeating the Church's strict teaching on the question. The article prompted a riposte from Cardinal Óscar Rodríguez Maradiaga, one of Francis's close advisers, telling Müller not to be so dogmatic: "The world isn't like that, my brother." Such public fraternal clashes between cardinals were rare, but it was a sign of things to come. When Francis finally dismissed Müller in 2017, it would be remembered how the doctrinal supremo made an early challenge to the papal remarks on marriage.

In the meantime, few picked up on Francis's reference to the "theology of economy," which traditionally—and mainly in the practices of Eastern Orthodox Churches—explores extenuating circumstances within moral problems such as poverty, external pressures, and ignorance. "Economy," practiced in Eastern Orthodox Christianity, comes from the Greek οικονόμια, *economia*, meaning "handling," "managing" a situation, assuming prudent management. There are two kinds of management: that of God in the fallenness of human nature, and pastoral management—how the Church should handle moral problems in particular circumstances, in the here and now. The latter implies a discretionary power granted to pastors by Jesus with the power to "bind and to loose" (Matthew 16:19, 18:18), an authority passed on to the bishops for all time. In the Eastern Churches this "economy" involves discretionary power to make dispensations, recognizing that the Church's rules cannot account for every situation that arises. It allows for the spirit rather than the letter in the interest of souls and puts love and mercy above absolute law.

A leading advocate of this kind of compassionate "economy" was an outspoken, eighty-year-old former professor of theology, Cardinal Walter Kasper. Just four days after his election, Francis praised Kasper publicly as "a clever theologian, a good theologian," whose book on mercy had done him, Francis, "a lot of good."

On February 21 the following year, Kasper was assigned to give a keynote address to his brother cardinals. He restated the Church's teaching on marriage in uncompromising terms, but he went on to sketch out an argument for a position between "extremes of rigorism and laxity" so as to allow some divorced and remarried Catholics to receive Communion subsequent to the individuals involved taking a "penitential path . . . a narrow path . . ." This was classic Francis think-ing, the maintenance of opposites. Those familiar with Kasper's views back in the mid-1990s noted that he was a champion of special "adap-tations" to local circumstances: economy. Yet one did not have to be an arch-traditionalist to see the danger of doctrinal differences spring-ing up across the world, with a potential for conflict between national groups of bishops. Meanwhile conservatives challenged the inference that Church teaching on divorce was responsible for the increased fig-ures of Catholic disaffiliation in Germany. They argued that despite laxity on issues of divorce, the Protestants lapsed at an even greater rate than Catholics.

The columnist and author Ross Douthat, pondering the issue sev-eral years later, concluded that conservatives suspected that "Kasper's proposal was designed to be a depth charge, released to shatter the edifice of Catholic moral teaching on sexuality and allowing creative rebuilding in the rubble." The explosive sentence could be applied equally to the Francis Effect.

As Francis encouraged compassion for people suffering marital breakdown (like my mother in her day), he had been preparing a world-wide campaign of spiritual reconciliation. While the focus remained on the remarried, he was creating the broadest possible climate for understanding, healing, and hope.

He was calling for a yearlong celebration of the virtue of mercy that would embrace the many moral and spiritual dilemmas that disaffili-ated many of the faithful who longed to return but despaired of being accepted. It was aimed at disrupting clericalism's tendency to empha-size the letter rather than the spirit of the law.

On the second anniversary of his election, March 13, 2015, he announced an Extraordinary Jubilee, or Holy Year, proclaimed for-mally a month later in a document titled *The Face of Mercy*. It was to start officially on a special feast of the Virgin Mary, the Immaculate Conception, December 8, and to finish twelve months later. Usually during such jubilees a "holy door" would be opened at the entrance to

St. Peter's Basilica. Francis called for "holy doors" to be established in cathedrals throughout the world, as if encouraging a universal "welcome home" symbol for prodigal children. He opened the first such door on a papal visit to Bangui, the capital of the Central African Republic, on November 29, 2015. He requested that the local events should involve the poor, the sick, the imprisoned, migrants, and people suffering from conflict. It was a local, physical example of Francis's bid to locate the world Church at its peripheries.

He declared that the year was an opportunity for the faithful to experience in a vivid fashion God's mercy and to bestow it in actual, concrete ways, practicing the spiritual and corporal works of mercy within their parishes and communities. Francis had already shown the way, assisting numbers of poor and homeless in Rome and around Italy, especially the migrants who entered the country after crossing the Mediterranean. He installed showers for the homeless under the colonnades in St. Peter's Square and provided overnight beds in a hostel. He paid visits to prisons in Italy and jails around the world on papal trips and initiated a campaign for the abolition of capital punishment. He regularly visited hospitals, giving most attention to sick children. He pleaded for every parish in Europe to harbor at least one refugee family.

Francis was urging that the corporal works of mercy went in parallel with the spiritual. Healing the broken in spirit, reconciliation of the disillusioned and despairing, was a counterpart to sustaining the hungry, the homeless, the sick. If reconciliation and mercy was a prelude to new hope, the Church had to rediscover its special mission of mercy at every level, setting aside total dependence on the law, and finger-wagging moralism. Mercy embraced a cluster of virtues, he insisted: love, compassion, tenderness, closeness. In *The Face of Mercy* he declared that love "by its very nature indicates something concrete: intentions, attitudes, and behaviors that are shown in daily living . . . this is the path which the merciful love of Christians must also travel. As the Father loves, so do his children." Mercy in practice, he was saying, reflected the mercy of Jesus in the Gospels.

The problem, however, was how to establish the principle of mercy in action as a matter of official Church teaching in relation to an urgent and widespread problem within Catholic families across the world. He was to steer the question of divorce and remarriage through two synods—those advisory meetings of bishops and varied "experts"—leading to an authoritative papal statement known as an "apostolic exhortation." Much was expected on the part of liberals who hoped for a clear directive allowing remarried Catholics to receive Communion. For ultraconservatives, any such leniency was tantamount to heresy.

CHAPTER ELEVEN

THE JOY OF LOVE

The "Economy" of Mercy Without Heresy

T he tradition of synods to solve arguments over doctrine goes back to the early Church, yet these meetings, their conduct and consequences, have had an uneven history. Paul VI revived the practice after Vatican II, but liberals complained that John Paul II, who followed Paul VI, wrote exhortations that ignored the synods' recommendations. There were stories that he fell asleep or read his breviary while the bishops spoke.

As the first synod, scheduled for October 2014, approached, the bishops were instructed to concentrate on divorce, remarriage, and admission to Communion. Philip F. Lawler, editor of *Catholic World News*, who described Francis as "predictably unpredictable," published a book preponderantly and eloquently devoted to his distress over the marriage synods. He charged that the synod paid "disproportionate attention" to the isolated issue of the remarried, which he saw as a serious imbalance when marriage and the family were under unprecedented attack. "Bishops of the Catholic world appeared fixated on a nicety of Church law," he wrote. There were progressives, however, who would have been only too happy to broaden the issues to include cohabitation, promiscuity, contraception, abortion, the legalizing of same-sex unions, and other LGBT issues.

As the bishops gathered in early October there were grievances over reporting restrictions. The Vatican press office explained that this would enable the delegates to speak freely. Cardinal Müller was ordered not to promote a volume of scholarly essays, *Remaining in the Truth of Christ*, to which he himself contributed, arguing that the relaxation proposed by Kasper ran counter to the magisterium. The publisher, St. Ignatius Press, attempted to get the book to as many of the synod bishops as possible, but a large batch went missing, prompting rumors of a liberal conspiracy to quash it. By the same token, there were counter-complaints that the distribution of the book amounted to an attempt to sway the synod in the traditional direction.

Despite the ban on reporting, there were leaks. A story was circulating that some bishops were about to propose that homosexuality is God's "gift" to the Church. Then it was rumored that "gay unions" would be endorsed. In fact, out of 250 talks during plenary sessions of the synod, only one addressed homosexuality, briefly. It was given short shrift. Cardinal Robert Sarah, prefect of the Congregation for Divine Worship, told correspondents that what had been published by the media about homosexual unions was an attempt to exert pressure from outside the synod for a change in the Church's teaching: "The Church has never judged homosexual persons but homosexual behavior and homosexual unions are grave deviations of sexuality."

Then the impression of a tension between North and South arose among the delegates. Why was the synod preoccupied with resolving a problem for the privileged minority within the Churches of Europe and North America, to the neglect of the growing Church of Africa?

Finally it was the turn of Francis to comment on what appeared an unholy wrangle. He said that since the synod was "a journey of human beings, with the consolations there were also moments of desolation, and temptations, of which a few possibilities could be mentioned." He spoke of holding in tension the doctrine on marriage and the realities of sexual unions in contemporary life. He asked the conservatives to avoid the "temptation to hostile inflexibility," and the liberals to shun "a deceptive mercy that binds the wounds without first curing them."

———————

A year later, October 4, 2015, the bishops were back in Rome for the synod proper. In advance of the meeting, Francis declared that changes would be made to the Code of Canon Law to speed up the process of annulments, easing their accessibility by eliminating the expense, and canceling the second tribunal judgment. This clarified and set aside one vexing aspect of the marriage and divorce problem, the complexity and delays of annulment bureaucracy, although countries that lacked sufficient numbers of canon lawyers would still encounter difficulties in administering a new streamlined policy.

The meeting was marked by renewed conflicts between conservative and liberal delegates, exacerbated by social media and the usual leaks. The nub of the antagonism was mutual indignation over alleged demonization. Amid a Twitter storm, conservatives complained that they were being denounced as rigid "mummified" Pharisees. Liberals complained that they were being depicted as permissive manipulators. One liberal Jesuit complained that homosexuals were being compared to Nazis. Feelings rose to such a height that Francis intervened, asking the delegates not to engage in conspiracy theories. To little avail; shortly after the papal intervention, Sandro Magister, *L'Espresso*'s special Vatican correspondent, published a letter addressed to Francis and allegedly signed by a list of senior delegates including high-ranking cardinals. It complained that the synod's procedures were dominated by liberals to "facilitate predetermined results." It pointed out, moreover, that the collapse of "liberal Protestant churches" in the interest of "pastoral adaptation" was a warning of the need for "great caution in our own synodal discussions." If it was intended to torpedo the maneuvering of the liberals, it proved a dud. Some of the leading alleged signatories denied that they had signed. Some conservatives sniffed yet another conspiracy. *Cui Bono?* Was this not a charade per-petrated by liberals themselves?

Finally, at October's end, the delegates published an agreed set of proposals. On the vexed issue of the divorced remarried and Communion, the delegates passed a proposal, recommending pasto-ral counseling (with just one vote more than the two-thirds required majority). Catholics in this irregular situation should seek the advice of a priest in order to discern obstacles to "fuller participation in the life of the Church." So disagreements now started up over how this might be interpreted. Some argued that the synod definitively ruled that people in irregular situations could not receive Communion; others that it would be allowed for some, subject to the "discernment" of a pastor. It now remained to Francis to resolve the matter in his "apostolic exhortation."

———————————

Francis published his exhortation, officially titled in Latin *Amoris Laetitia* (*The Joy of Love*), in April 2016. Described by his critics as "puzzling" and "prolix," it was written so as to lead to potentially opposite conclusions simultaneously. For the main part, the 205-page document confirmed orthodox Catholic teaching and extolled the beauty of committed marital love, including St. Paul's hymn to love in 1 Corinthians 13: "If I give all my possessions to the poor, or even give my body to be burnt, but have not love, I gain nothing. . . ." But what had he to say about the remarried divorced and recep-tion of Communion? Such difficulties, he commented, cannot be resolved entirely by rules. Pastors, he counseled, should guide cou-ples through "discernment" of their circumstances so that they may "grow in the life of grace and charity, while receiving the Church's help to this end." Moreover, a pastor should not feel that it is enough simply to quote the Church's laws to people living in "irregular" sit-uations, "as if they were stones to throw at people's lives." It was after all possible, he went on, that while a person is objectively living in sin, they might also be living in God's grace, capable of growing "in the life of grace and charity while receiving the Church's help to this end." Which could be interpreted as receiving the sacraments of Reconciliation and the Eucharist, an interpretation reinforced by a footnote (351) that would become notable, or perhaps notorious: to the effect that some people could benefit from "the help of the sacraments."

Without altering the doctrine, he was advocating individual responsibility—conscience and discernment—on the part of the pastor and the "penitents" themselves. Moreover, without mentioning specifics, the same principle surely could be extended to other moral circumstances, including homosexuality, cohabitation outside of marriage, and the unresolved, yet seldom mentioned, "sin" of contraception. And therein lay the disruption: Douthat's Kasper "depth charge."

"I understand," Francis wrote, "those who prefer a more rigorous pastoral care which leaves no room for confusion. But I sincerely believe that Jesus wants a Church attentive to the goodness which the Holy Spirit sows in the midst of human weakness."

In a further footnote (329), we find a reflection on the idea that remarried couples could avoid adultery by forgoing sex: The ideal is "not at all easy," but with the help of grace it might be practiced. On the other hand, there are "complex situations where the choice of living 'as brothers and sisters' becomes humanly impossible. And give rise to greater harm."

The Joy of Love is a classic instance of Francis, once again, holding two opposites in tension without resolution. Without giving the green light to Communion for "adulterers" he is nevertheless saying to pastors—don't be too hard on people in irregular marital situations; and he is saying to the people in irregular marital situations—don't be too hard on yourselves! He is coming close to stating that the teachings on sex and marriage are ideals rather than strict imperatives: yet not quite. The document is not a defined reform, yet it asked the faithful at large to take responsibility for their moral lives, partly encouraged by the clergy. The long and sorry exercise, which came to look, from the outsider point of view, as so much navel-gazing, was in fact a profound lesson across the Catholic moral landscape. It was asking the faithful to exercise their consciences as much as their appeals to authority and, by the same token, to cease making harsh judgments of others.

Among the cardinals who felt deeply disturbed by the document were four who wrote to Francis declaring that he had raised "uncertainty, confusion, and disorientation among many of the faithful"—a fair enough description of a Bergoglio disruption. They were Cardinals Walter Brandmüller (German, and a professor of Church history), Raymond Burke (American traditionalist), Carlo Caffarra (Italian moral theologian), and Joachim Meisner (retired German Archbishop of Cologne), all claiming to speak with authority on the Church's teachings on the matter in hand, including the authoritative writings of John Paul II. Meisner, a close friend of both John Paul II and Benedict, had also been the founder of the Pontifical John Paul II Institute for Studies on Marriage and Family, established to foster and defend the very ideas and teachings Francis now appeared to have challenged. (The following year, the head of the institute would be sacked, its focus altered to include the thinking of Francis; the adoption of a more academically pluralist approach would include non-Catholic perspectives.)

The tone of the four ruffled cardinals was formal, theologically careful, lethally polite. Their so-called *dubia*, doubts, raised five questions "to resolve the uncertainties and bring clarity." In summary they were asking whether it was possible to "admit to Holy Communion a person who, while bound by a valid marital bond, lives together with a different person *more uxorio* [having sexual relations]?"

Specifically, they were asking whether he was overturning the teaching of his predecessor "St. John Paul II" on the issue. For example: "Does one still need to regard as valid the teaching of St. John Paul II's encyclical *Veritatis Splendor* [*Splendor of the Truth*] . . . that conscience can never be authorized to legitimate exceptions to absolute moral norms that prohibit intrinsically evil acts by virtue of their object?"

Weeks passed and they received no response, so their next step was to go public, declaring that the pope's silence legitimized a decision to invite the Church at large to discuss their *dubia*. Various sectors of the conservative-liberal divide quarreled at first over the motives and the propriety of questioning the pontiff, but given the senior status of its authors, their challenge created a serious circumstance, just as this living pope was challenging the authority of a recently deceased one. Yet to question this pope's authority would legitimize questioning any other pope's authority. An obvious conclusion could be drawn: Perhaps this disruptive questioning of papal authority was precisely what Francis intended.

As the heated arguments went to and fro in subsequent months and years, it would become increasingly clear that the pope's silence was in fact his *answer*: that there *was* no answer. His message: Work it out for yourselves! He severely interrupted those who wanted clarity, yes or no, black or white. *The Joy of Love* confirmed the strict teaching of the Church in principle, but real life involved situations requiring compassion, understanding, patience, mercy, and that sense of economy long and widely exercised by the Eastern Churches.

Living, observing, and discussing the dilemma, I could not help thinking of my mother and the sacrifice she made, or was told to make, back in the 1960s: to abstain from Communion after she married my stepfather. Had she lived to witness divorced and remarried couples in the age of Francis receiving Communion, would she have resented the heartbreak she and others in her predicament had endured? A plea to recognize this circumstance was made by Professor Richard Rex of Cambridge University in his eloquent article in *First Things*:

> *If, after all, marriage is not a divine union of male and female in one flesh, dissolved only by the inevitable dissolution of that flesh in death, then the Catholic Church has, in the name of Christ,*

needlessly tormented the consciences of untold numbers of the faith-
ful for twenty centuries. . . . A church which could be so wrong, for
so long, on a matter so fundamental to human welfare and happi-
ness could hardly lay claim to decency, let alone infallibility.

Francis, and those who support him, might well say that a Church that could harbor large numbers of abusing priests and the bishops who protected them had long ago forfeited its claim to "decency." But knowing my mother, she would have said: "Thank God for a pope who is talking sense at last!"

———————

Francis ended the Year of Mercy on November 20, 2016, with an "apostolic letter to the world" titled *Mercy and Misery*—in Latin, *Misericordia et Misera*—a phrase employed by St. Augustine of Hippo as he told the story of Jesus meeting with the woman taken in adultery in John's Gospel. After her accusers, dropping their stones, have left one by one, only Jesus and the woman are left. Augustine writes, "The two of them alone remained: mercy and misery." Francis adds a simple sentence, indicating that mercy is the threshold to new beginnings and hope: "Jesus helps the woman to look to the future with hope and to make a new start in life."

The following week, Francis embarked on a series of homilies addressed to the public every Wednesday on the theme of hope for people who find themselves in difficult moral circumstances. Drawing on the Scriptures, instances from his own journey in life, and the teachings of the Church, he was intent on showing how the virtue of mercy, as he had attempted to portray it in the previous year, was the foundation of hope.

His homilies on hope week after week, from Christmas until Easter of the following year, form a remarkable cycle of meditations. Citing the Old and New Testaments, he spoke of hope as a never-ending journey through life; continuous new horizons "dreaming what is not even imaginable"; that to inspire hope requires sharing the desperation of those in despair; hope in the Lord means becoming like him; to pray is to hope; hope does not set conditions on God; hope needs a humble heart, patience, the ability to *wait*. On February 1, 2017, he invoked an arresting metaphor. Hope was expectation, like the expectancy of a pregnant woman who lives in hope of seeing the "gaze of her child that is to come." In this way too "we must live and learn from these human expectations and live in the expectation."

Even as Francis was sharing his meditations on the multiple dimensions of the virtue of hope, he was about to experience one of the worst passages of his papacy, in which he would be attacked, accused, and undermined, at times by those closest to him. He would be much in need of the virtue of that hope and patience he had preached in the preceding year.

PART FOUR

ANNUS HORRIBILIS

A Year of Trials and Fading Popularity

CHAPTER TWELVE

TROUBLE IN CHILE

Francis Embroiled in the Sexual Abuse Scandal

As fresh reports of sexual abuse continued to flood the media, Francis was attempting in many homilies and addresses to sympathize with the pain of victims; but he could not alleviate the suffering and indignation by words alone. Moreover, his insistence on the exercise of mercy conflicted at times with calls for action involving a "zero option"—immediate, irrevocable laicization without investigation and evidence. His oft-expressed views about rumor and calumny and the damage it does, and his tendency to give the benefit of the doubt, especially in the absence of what he tended, ill-advisedly, to call "proof," was to clash with the demands for justice and reparation.

January 2018 found Francis in a somber mood. As the New Year dawned, he focused on the suffering of children, victims of war, refugees, and Catholic young people at the hands of abusing priests. He issued a greeting card: A boy carries a dead younger brother on his back, waiting for the body to be cremated. Francis wrote on the card: ". . . the sadness of the child is expressed only by his lips, bitten and oozing blood."

In this fifth year of his papacy, which from the beginning he thought might be his last, Francis was to be engulfed in accusations and confrontations, mostly in relation to the sexual abuse of minors by priests and the cover-ups. It would continue unabated into 2019, as fresh revelations unfolded, and he attempted to make disruptive forays in many directions. His popularity ratings were set to plummet. A Yugov popularity poll would put him at fifteen, below President Trump. Yet the story of this year, his travels, encounters, words, and reactions, continued to reveal his wide-ranging priorities and mission in action.

On January 15, 2018, he arrived in Santiago, Chile, to face the country's own home-based clerical sexual abuse scandal. Some hundred priests stood accused. The focus of the media was on a single, sinister case: that of a sleazy prelate called Monsignor Fernando Karadima, all the more poisonous as he nurtured an unctuous "holy" exterior.

Karadima, known for his misdeeds and hypocrisy as "The Lord of Hell," was described as "an aristocratic figure, appealing to both young and old in Chile's elite." His seductions took place mainly during the Pinochet era. Politically, he was a leading light in Catholic Action, a lay right-leaning religious group that was reportedly supportive of the junta.

It had been more than forty years since General Augusto Pinochet's coup ended President Salvador Allende's brief period of Marxist rule. The regime lasted until 1990, when it lost a referendum on the restoration of democracy. Military rule was succeeded first by a center-left coalition government, then by a rightist coalition in 2010; since 2013, a second leftist government had been in power under Michelle Bachelet. The darkness of the Pinochet era, which left 3,000 dead, still haunted the country into the twenty-first century. But the anger of many that January was directed against Francis, who stood accused of tardiness in punishing the priestly abusers and their cover-up bishops.

Churches were firebombed, flyers urging his assassination were circulated; a group of demonstrators occupied the Apostolic Nunciature. Seldom had a pope faced such open threats in recent history. President Bachelet went on television to plead for calm. A former medical doctor and internationally recognized human rights advocate, Bachelet had led a coalition of socialist and left-leaning parties, including the Communists. She described herself as a religious agnostic.

In the previous twenty years, the number of those professing to be Catholic in the country had declined from 74 to 45 percent; while those identifying as "no religion" increased from 7 to 35 percent. Socialist movements in Chile had not been inspired by Catholic liberation theology in other regions of Latin America. At the same time, the Church of Francis's predecessors, especially John Paul II, was seen as antagonistic to calls for sexual freedoms as represented, for example, by LGBT supporters. Against this background, Francis was confronting, perhaps for the first time in his papacy, the limits of his message and personal appeal.

———————

Monsignor Karadima, the focus of widespread fury in the country, was accused of sexually abusing adolescents through the 1980s while enticing his victims with sanctimonious spiritual direction, targeting in particular those who were emotionally disturbed or alienated from their families. He encouraged many young men to train for the priesthood, and it was suspected that most of them were aware of his behavior. In 2010 his misdeeds were exposed by a group of laypeople in the parish of El Bosque, a fashionable suburb of Santiago; but he escaped criminal conviction due to the statute of limitations. The following year, after a Church investigation, Karadima was dismissed from the ministry and ordered to live a "hidden life of penance and prayer."

By 2018, the year of the papal visit, four of Karadima's favorite seminarians had become bishops. One of his notable protégés, although not a victim himself, was Juan Barros, nominated bishop of a small Chilean diocese by Pope Francis in January 2015. Accused of having known of Karadima's behavior, being present at his abuse, and remaining silent, Barros faced an angry group of protestors in his cathedral as he processed to the high altar on the day of his inauguration. Convinced by trusted informants that Barros was innocent, Francis had defended him back in 2015. Francis was recorded as saying that a group of extreme leftist politicians condemned the bishop "with no proof whatsoever." The story of Karadima and the pope's continuing refusal to condemn Bishop Barros dominated headlines and newscasts as he arrived in the country.

During his first address at La Moneda Palace before the president, politicians, and dignitaries, Francis spoke of his sorrow for clerical abuse in general terms. "I cannot help but express the pain and shame that I feel over the irreparable harm caused to children by church ministers," he said. But he mixed his apologies with other issues, including a critique of powerful commercial interests that undermine "natural ecosystems and consequently the common good of our peoples."

After an open-air Mass attended by 400,000 faithful in Santiago's O'Higgins Park (Bishop Barros was a co-celebrant, and Francis embraced him at the Kiss of Peace), he went on to the Metropolitan Cathedral, where he spoke to clergy and religious. "I know the pain resulting from cases of abuse of minors," he said, "and I am attentive to what you are doing to respond to this great and painful evil."

He counseled his listeners to consider the example of St. Peter's sense of guilt after the Crucifixion; how Christ's love prevented Peter from obsession with his failure and betrayals. "A Church with wounds can understand the wounds of today's world and make them her own, suffering with them."

His final official act before leaving Chile was an outdoor Mass at Iquique, a seaport near the border with Peru. On the way there by plane from Santiago, Francis performed an unscheduled marriage between cabin crew members: Paula Podest, 39, and Carlos Ciuffardi, 41. They had been wed in 2010 in a quick civil ceremony after their church marriage was canceled due to an earthquake. They now had two children. They asked Francis if he would bless their partnership; he surprised them by asking: "Do you want me to marry you?" So he performed the ceremony in the front of the plane with an airline manager as witness. Afterward Francis gave them rosaries as wedding presents.

The story went viral before the plane touched down in Iquique. So did the reactions among traditionalists who charged that the marriage had possibly been invalid since the couple had not undergone pastoral counseling, and that the pope had not required evidence of their baptismal certificates. The episode illustrates the petty antagonism of a small but media-powerful segment of Catholic opinion—to attack Francis over a small gesture of pastoral tenderness, even as he was embattled with an entire country over the sex abuse crisis.

Before departing for Peru, he found himself questioned by a group of journalists. They were standing on the opposite side of a wire fence at an air base where he was about to board a plane. One demanded why he was still supporting Bishop Barros in the light of accusations that he was aware of the abuse of his mentor Monsignor Karadima. Evidently exhausted, Francis was indignant and abrupt:

"The day they bring me proof against Bishop Barros," he said, "I will speak. There's not one piece of evidence against him. It's calumny."

Earlier that afternoon, he had witnessed an accident when a policewoman protecting his motorcade had been thrown from her horse and seriously injured. He alighted from his Popemobile and crouched over her, offering comfort until an ambulance arrived. Given the nonstop series of encounters, including visits to prison and addresses to a variety of special groups, he was probably overtired. The journalist's question about Karadima probably exasperated him.

It was ill-advised of him to employ the word "proof," for it could be construed that he was labeling Karadima's victims as possible liars. The remark circled the world within minutes. He was going to pay for that comment; in the meantime the busy schedule continued, and there were other major issues on his mind beside sexual abuse.

On the last leg of his visit, in Peru, Francis spent time in Puerto Maldonado, a city on the Madre de Dios River that leads to a tributary of the Amazon amid tropical rain forests. Speaking to indigenous Amazonian people, he returned to a major theme of his papacy. He denounced the plunder of the forests and the bribes paid by politicians to multinational logging companies. He went on to excoriate the crime of human trafficking in the region; the dangers of people being "ensnared by ideological forms of colonialism, disguised as progress, that slowly but surely dissipate cultural identities and establish a uniform, single, and weak way of thinking."

In another talk, speaking of the "motherless" power of consumerism, the exploitation of the poor and the earth, he invoked the Franciscan ideal of getting close to the poor, the need to identify with the Church at its margins.

In Lima, speaking to the bishops on a theme that he believed inseparable from all the wrongs within the Church, he pleaded with them to avoid a self-serving, inflexible, neo-traditionalist hierarchy of abstractions. Conscious of the division between them over liberation theology, he appealed to them to avoid cliques that "hamper our vocation to be a sacrament of communion." At the Government Palace in Lima, Francis talked of the "social virus" of corruption that infected not only Peru but much of Latin America. But the sex abuse issue continued to plague him.

On his final day in the country more than a million faithful attended his Mass at the air base outside the capital. But before he left for Rome, he received a visit from the bearded Franciscan Cardinal Sean O'Malley, Archbishop of Boston and chair of the Pontifical Commission for the Protection of Minors. The pope's statement that there was no "proof" against Bishop Barros was creating a new crisis not only for Francis personally but also for the Vatican's attempts to resolve the ever-expanding clerical abuse catastrophe.

Two members of O'Malley's commission had already resigned in protest over lack of progress. In an evident move to avoid damaging his own position, the cardinal gave journalists a blunt appraisal of the situation and a sharp criticism of the pope's remarks. He said: "Words that convey the message 'if you cannot prove your claims, then you will not be believed' abandon those who have suffered reprehensible criminal violations of their human dignity and relegate survivors to discredited exile." He added that he could not "address why the Holy Father chose the particular words he used at that time" but that Pope Francis "fully recognizes the egregious failures of the Church and its clergy who abused children and the devastating impact those crimes have had on survivors and their loved ones."

On the journey back to Rome, Francis was interrogated by journalists during an in-flight press conference about Barros and Cardinal O'Malley's intervention. But he was still unwilling to accuse the bishop. He said: "No one has come forward, they haven't provided any evidence for a judgment . . . anyone who accuses without evidence, pertinaciously, this is slander." Yet he admitted that he had been wrong to ask for *proof* instead of *evidence*. "The Barros case," he went on, "was examined and re-examined, but there is no evidence. That is what I wanted to say. I don't have the evidence needed to convict. And if I were to convict without evidence and without moral certitude, I would myself commit the offense of judicial misconduct." Sometime later, members of the Pontifical Commission for the Protection of Minors told reporters that Cardinal O'Malley, on his own admission, while in Lima, had given Francis an eight-page letter of allegations against Barros written by Juan Carlos Cruz, a victim of Karadima. Giving Francis the benefit of the doubt, in the midst of a high-speed foreign visit, he perhaps failed to read it or gave it only a cursory glance.

On his arrival in Rome, however, Francis sent two prelates back to Chile to investigate Barros anew as well as the wider circumstances of abuse in the country. Archbishop Charles Scicluna, a canon lawyer originally from Malta, was the lead investigator. He was accompanied by a Spanish priest, Father Jordi Bertomeu, from the Congregation of the Doctrine of the Faith. Scicluna, short and rotund with a disarming baby face, was an unblinking inquisitor. Having processed the case of the clerical sexual psychopath Marcial Maciel (guilty of multiple sexual attacks on minors, including his own love children), he was under no illusions as to what clergy could perpetrate, nor the extent of episcopal "omertà." The result of his probes in Chile was a

2,300-page report that told a story of widespread cover-up—cases dismissed, records suppressed and erased, offending priests moved on to reoffend; victims brushed off, disbelieved, humiliated. It was clear that Francis had been deceived, and perhaps had deceived himself, about Bishop Barros.

Francis made a public apology, unprecedented in any modern pope: "I have made serious mistakes in the assessment and my perception of the situation," he wrote, "especially due to a lack of truthful and balanced information. . . . I now beg the forgiveness of all those whom I have offended." Anybody who has studied the culture and behavior of the papacy in the modern period will realize the astounding disruption of this admission. While papal infallibility has always been hedged around with subtle qualifications, the very notion of a pope saying "sorry, I got it wrong" has been unthinkable. The day Francis made that admission a mystique evaporated. It may take some years, and several papacies more for it to sink in; but the papacy could never be the same again.

Summoning the Chilean bishops to Rome, he spent, in advance of those meetings, many hours with three principal witnesses against Karadima and Barros at Santa Marta: James Hamilton, Juan Carlos Cruz, and Andres Murillo, men who had been characterized by the Chilean hierarchy as liars and slanderers.

Two weeks later, Francis met with thirty-four of Chile's bishops. In an address that defined the fundamental problem of clericalism in the Church, he spoke of a "psychology of the elite" that creates "division, separation, closed circles that result in a narcissistic and authoritarian spirituality . . . elitism and clericalism are all symptoms of this perversion in a way of being church." Before leaving the Vatican, all the active bishops in the group submitted their resignations. By September, Francis would accept seven of them, including that of Bishop Barros.

September also saw a raft of actions against clergy and bishops in Chile, including the final defrocking of Karadima. The following month, the archdiocese of Santiago was ordered by Chile's Court of Appeals to pay $147,000 for "moral damages" to each of Karadima's victims: Cruz, Murillo, and Hamilton. The lifting of the statute of limitations on cases of sexual abuse would lead to the revival of a number of retrospective cases of "historic" abuse, the removal of the papal nuncio Archbishop Ivo Scapulo, and the acceptance of the resignation of the Archbishop of Santiago, Ricardo Ezzati Andrello.

Francis was acting decisively; yet dissatisfaction with him was mounting. By the summer of 2018, when it seemed that things could not possibly have gotten worse on the sexual abuse front, verdicts on his papacy were settling into a steady stream of criticism, even condemnation and vilification. The open criticism, at first isolated and uttered by individuals who themselves could be dismissed as conservative extremists, had become widespread and inexorable.

The attacks on Francis, along with his increasing isolation, were foretold by veteran Vatican watcher Marco Politi in his book *Francis Among the Wolves*. Politi quoted Cardinal Raymond Burke as saying: "At this very critical moment there is a strong sense that the Church is like a ship without a rudder." It was customary for liberals to poke fun at Burke for his love of billowing layers of scarlet silk. By 2017, however, even Pope Emeritus Benedict, watching events from his redoubt in the Vatican Gardens, would echo the thought and the imagery. In July of that year Archbishop Gänswein read a letter from Benedict at the funeral of Joachim Meisner, the Archbishop Emeritus of Cologne. It contained the stunning line that Meisner was one of those who was convinced that the "Lord does not abandon his Church, even if the boat has taken on so much water as to be on the verge of capsizing." The imagery of the barque of St. Peter, and the Supreme Pontiff as his successor and pilot of the Church, runs deep in Catholic consciousness: The insult to Francis, as captain of a sinking ship, intended or otherwise, was palpable.

A constituency of conservatives, lay and clerical, was accusing Francis of apostasy and heresy; meanwhile liberals found fault because he failed to follow through with progressive reforms, especially on sexual freedoms.

While the *National Catholic Register*, *First Things*, the Catholic broadcaster EWTN, and *Church Militant* kept up a nonstop barrage of criticism and condemnation, LifeSiteNews successfully corralled a group of cardinals and bishops ready to lend their names to the view that Francis was guilty of sowing confusion for its own sake. Cardinal Joachim Meisner: "We live in a time of *confusion* not only in society but also in the Church." Cardinal Carlo Caffarra: "Only a blind man could deny there's a great *confusion,* uncertainty, and insecurity in the Church." Cardinal Robert Sarah: "I suffer so much from seeing the Church torn apart and in great *confusion.*" Bishop Athanasius Schneider: "The Church today faces a crisis of faith that is only comparable to the great *confusion* of the Arian crisis of the 4th century." Cardinal Walter Brandmüller went one further: "Inasmuch as ever the fact of Divine Revelation is here being questioned, or misunderstood one also now has to speak additionally of apostasy."

Even as these prelates complained of the grand confusion, and now apostasy, a circumstance deemed to have been created by Francis, the cause of the Church's greatest crisis began to assume an even graver impetus. On August 14, 2018, a nine-hundred-page text was published detailing clerical sexual abuse in the state of Pennsylvania. It comprised crimes and cover-ups within the hundreds of parishes of the state's dioceses: Scranton, Allentown, Harrisburg, Greensburg, Erie, and Pittsburgh. More than a thousand acts of abuse were cited, involving three hundred "predator priests," over a period of eighty years. An Investigating Grand Jury, having read a million pages of documentation, concluded that while credible allegations were made by a thousand victims, the "real number . . . is in the thousands." At a press conference in Harrisburg, Attorney General Josh Shapiro said: "The pattern was abuse, deny, and cover up." The report told stories of unbridled debauchery. A priest in Harrisburg diocese sexually abused five daughters of one family. In Greensburg diocese, a pastor got a seventeen-year-old girl pregnant, married her, then divorced her. In Erie diocese, a priest assaulted twelve boys; he was later praised by his bishop for "all that you have done for God's people."

The report accused high-ranking individuals, monsignors, auxiliary bishops, bishops, archbishops, and cardinals, of escaping public accountability. Children were being raped by priests who were then protected or even promoted. The report listed forty-one "predator priests" in Erie, thirty-seven in Allentown, twenty in Greensburg, forty-five in Harrisburg, ninety-nine in Pittsburgh, and fifty-nine in Scranton. The members of the grand jury, signatories on the report, declared: "We know some of you have heard some of it before. There have been other reports about child sex abuse within the Catholic Church. But never on this scale. For many of us, those earlier stories happened someplace else, someplace away. Now we know the truth: It happened everywhere." Among the prominent names in the report was that of Cardinal Donald Wuerl, Archbishop of Washington, DC, Bishop of Pittsburgh, 1988–2006. The report accused Wuerl of moving abusive priests to other parishes and of failing to inform officials in those locations of the reasons for the removals. Cardinal Wuerl has denied any wrongdoing.

The grand jury stated collectively: "We saw these victims; they are marked for life. Many of them wind up addicted, or impaired, or dead before their time."

————————

It was a tribute to his faith and resilience that Francis could speak to the faithful about hope, while he took on his soul and conscience the crimes of generations of the abuses of priests and the cover-ups of bishops. At the same time a constituency of prelates and the conservative media were accusing him of heresy and the destruction of the Church.

At his morning Mass at Santa Marta's in early June he gave a homily encouraging the faithful to employ memory in order to stimulate the virtue of hope. To go forward, he said, we must think back to cherish our earliest true encounters with Jesus, remembering also those who first stimulated in us the gift of faith. He was speaking to the liturgical reading in which St. Paul urges Timothy to "*remember* our earliest encounters with Jesus." Memory, said Francis, is the salt of life.

We should retrieve through our imaginations our first meetings with the Lord, and relive them, "so as to find strength to be able to continue walking forward." Meeting Jesus is an act of Christian memory, and without memory it is impossible to continue. "When we meet forgetful Christians, we realize that they have lost the true flavor of Christian life. They have ended up being people who obey the Commandments, but without memory cannot go on. When we encounter 'forgetful' Christians, we can immediately see that they have lost the flavor of Christian life and have ended up being people who obey the Commandments without spirituality."

There are moments in the life of every Christian, he went on, when Jesus approached and showed himself. "Do not forget these moments: Think back and relive them because they are moments of inspiration, of meeting with Christ," he said. "Each of us has moments such as these: When we got to know Jesus, when he changed our lives, when the Lord showed us our vocations, when the Lord visited us at a difficult time. . . . We all have these moments in our hearts. Let's contemplate them."

Quoting Paul's second letter to Timothy, Francis said: "Remember your mother and grandmother as they have transmitted the faith to you . . . you don't receive faith through a letter in the mail, but through those who passed it on to you . . . take your strength from them."

When the water of life becomes a bit cloudy, he said, "It is important to go to the source and find in it, the strength to go on."

Francis himself had great need of strength to go on. Even as the revelations of victims in the United States and elsewhere in the world multiplied, Francis had become the visible, ultimately responsible superior of thousands of guilty priests going back decades. At the same time his critics were becoming ever bolder and more contemptuous in their criticism. Just as it seemed that his situation could get no worse, he embarked on a plane bound for Ireland, traditionally a country fiercely loyal to Church and pope, but currently in a state of collective antagonism toward the papacy and its current pontiff.

CHAPTER THIRTEEN

RESIGN!

Francis Accused of Cover-up

Back in 2015, there had been talk of Francis holding the coming World Family Day, scheduled for August 2018, in Ireland. He was conscious of the deep wounds there as a result of sexual clerical abuse, and the fact that religious devotion was in steep decline. In May 2015, a referendum legalized same-sex marriage. A further referendum voted with a two-thirds majority to end the ban on abortion. Ireland was a country where strictly Catholic views on sexual behavior, gender, and the indissolubility of marriage no longer held sway. Seminaries were closing in a country that had supplied missionaries to the world.

Anger and indignation against the Church, moreover, was everywhere evident as new abuse cases and their cover-ups continued to come to light. Then there were the stories of the Magdalene laundries run by nuns, where pregnant unmarried women worked as virtual slaves before being separated from their offspring for adoption. Many of the children died at or before birth. There were stories of the stillborn babies being thrown without identification into pits. In a population where 78 percent still admitted to Catholic identity, fewer than one in five of the "faithful" now attended Mass weekly. At St. Patrick's College, Maynooth, in its 1950s heyday housing five hundred seminarians, there were only thirty-five candidates for the priesthood in 2018.

I spent time in Dublin during 2013–14 conducting a joint seminar between the Cambridge college where I work and University College, Dublin, on sex abuse and Confession with Marie Keenan, author of *Child Sexual Abuse and the Catholic Church*. Priests told me how they were spat at in the street when wearing the Roman collar; how demonstrators would enter churches during Mass to hurl insults and missiles at the celebrants on the altar.

———————————

Francis was driven in an open Popemobile with maximum security, police facing inward every few yards along the thinly lined streets. At Dublin Castle, before a subdued audience of politicians, dignitaries, and representatives of different religions, Francis was formally greeted by Leo Varadkar, the thirty-nine-year-old Taoiseach, or Prime Minister, of Ireland since the previous year. He declared himself gay in 2015; his partner was a hospital doctor.

The Taoiseach delivered a frank speech, including condemnation of clerical sexual abuse and the Magdalene laundries. He talked of the dramatic social changes in Ireland: all manner of diversity, a decline in religion, new laws on divorce, contraception, abortion, same-sex marriage, an acceptance "that families come in many different, wonderful forms, including those headed by a grandparent, lone parent, or same-sex parents, or parents who are divorced." The circumstance of a pope being obliged to listen to a lecture on such "wonderful forms" of family life that, in strict Catholic terms, represented the negation of all the Church stood for, was surreal. Francis responded briefly in Italian. He condemned the long history of sex abuse by Catholic clergy in Ireland and acknowledged that the church's lack of action was a "grave scandal."

In the evening Francis met with a group of abuse survivors headed by Marie Collins, former member of the Vatican committee charged with addressing protection of children. Collins focused on the Magdalene laundry homes and the many thousands of mothers separated from their babies. She told him that nuns in charge of these institutions assured the mothers that it would be a mortal sin to attempt to make contact with their children in later years.

The substance of that meeting was to create subsequent problems. A heated dispute would arise over Francis's remarks on the plane back to Rome about the Magdalene crimes. He appeared to tell journalists that he had never heard about the Magdalene institutions, leading James Carroll, the distinguished American Catholic writer and former priest, whom I count as a friend, to assert that Pope Francis was either a dotard or a deliberate liar. Carroll announced a few days later that he was renouncing reception of Communion and was calling for the disbanding of the Catholic priesthood.

I later obtained a transcript of the recording of what Pope Francis actually said. It seems that Francis was admitting not to ignorance of the existence of the Magdalene institutions but of the story told by Collins that mothers who attempted contact with their children were committing mortal sins:

> And there were children at that time, who tried to find their mothers to know if they were alive, they did not know . . . and they told them it was a mortal sin to do this; and also to mothers who were looking for their children; they also told them that it was a mortal sin. So I ended today by saying that it is not a mortal sin; it is [about] the fourth commandment. And some of the things I have said today I did not know beforehand, and it was painful for me, but with the consolation of being able to help clarify these things.

He had clearly been astonished by the "mortal sin" aspect of the Magdalene story, used to warn off mothers from seeking their children. This was unknown to many people—including myself.

Francis referred to the "mortal sin" threat the day after hearing it— on Sunday morning while speaking at Mass in Dublin's Phoenix Park. He said that he placed "before the mercy of the Lord these crimes, asking for forgiveness of them," crimes that included slave work by minors and the cruel separation of children from their mothers. He emphasized that it was not a mortal sin for mothers to look for their children.

He was speaking before a comparatively thin crowd at the Mass. Half a million tickets had been disbursed but only 130,000 turned up. When John Paul II said Mass in Dublin on his visit in 1979 some 1.2 million attended.

—————

Leaving Dublin, Francis flew by helicopter to the Marian shrine at Knock in the west of Ireland. On his way he learned of a 7,000-word letter issued overnight by Archbishop Carlo Maria Viganò, former papal nuncio to Washington, DC (2012–2016). The archbishop accused the pope in person of turning a blind eye to sexual abuse. He was calling for Francis to resign. The letter, edited by a lay Italian journalist and launched simultaneously via a number of conservative media platforms, had gone global. The journalist was Marco Tosatti, veteran Vaticanologist for *La Stampa* in Turin and a conservative Catholic.

A strong feature of the letter's message was its apparently homophobic tendency. Jason Horowitz, Rome correspondent of the *New York Times*, claimed that Tosatti told him how the "enraged archbishop brought no evidence" but supplied "the flair, condemning the homosexual networks inside the Church."

Viganò's most serious charge was that Francis lifted sanctions that Benedict had placed on the American cardinal Theodore McCarrick, accused of sexually abusing adult seminarians as well as an altar boy. McCarrick, who denies having sex with a minor, was inaugurated as Archbishop of Washington, DC, in 2000 and made a cardinal the following year by John Paul II. McCarrick has since been laicized by Francis. The saga of Archbishop Viganò demonstrates the deplorable antagonism within the Church today if ever further proof were needed.

Viganò was a disgruntled prelate, struggling with a sense of betrayal and humiliation. As we saw earlier in this narrative, before his posting as papal nuncio in Washington, DC, he served as secretary-general of the Vatican *Governarate*, similar to being mayor of the Vatican City-State (2009–2011). Originally trained as a canon lawyer, he climbed the diplomatic ladder of the Holy See from the mid-1970s, with postings in Iraq, the United Kingdom, and Nigeria. Recalled to Rome in 2009, he set up accounting procedures that saved, according to his own estimate, millions of dollars a year.

He believed that he had witnessed despicable goings-on in the Vatican, including the existence of gay liaisons and conspiracies. In 2011, he addressed a letter directly to Pope Benedict on these matters, copied to Secretary of State Tarcisio Bertone. The correspondence was leaked. By going straight to Benedict, he made powerful enemies of his immediate superiors. Far from being hailed and rewarded as a brave whistleblower, he saw his subsequent removal from his position and appointment as nuncio in Washington, DC, as a posting into exile. His hopes for being elevated to cardinal status were evidently at an end.

The principal target of Viganò's letter was Francis's dealings with Cardinal McCarrick. Benedict had ruled that McCarrick should retire to a house of prayer and that he should not say Mass while he awaited the findings of a canon law trial. Viganò charged that back in 2000, the Vatican had been informed of McCarrick's "gravely immoral behavior with seminarians and priests." Despite further high-level allegations, including a denunciation by Viganò himself, no action was taken until after Benedict was elected Pope. Viganò claimed that in 2007 he sent another memorandum, prompting Benedict to place restrictions on McCarrick's activities and movements. But Francis, he alleged, lifted those restrictions and adopted McCarrick as a "trusted counselor," even though he "knew from at least June 23, 2013, that McCarrick was a serial predator." He asserted: "[Francis] knew that he was a corrupt man, he covered for him to the bitter end." In consequence, Viganò concluded, Francis must acknowledge his mistakes, in keeping with the principle of zero tolerance. He must be the first to set a good example to cardinals and bishops who covered up McCarrick's abuses *"and resign along with all of them."* He added that unless the conspiracy of silence is torn down, the Church would look like a sect with a culture "not so dissimilar from the one that prevails in the mafia."

The letter cited the guilt of three past Vatican secretaries of state—Cardinal Angelo Sodano (Viganò charges that Sodano "notoriously favored promoting homosexuals"), Cardinal Tarcisio Bertone, and Cardinal Pietro Parolin, all accused of failure to discipline McCarrick. Others equally guilty of knowing about McCarrick's behavior as an abuser of seminarians, he claims, were Cardinals Donald Wuerl, William Levada, and a clutch of high-ranking figures within the Curia, although he does not claim that they knew about abuse of a minor.

Viganò timed the publication of his letter with assistance of several conservative media platforms, so that Francis would need to respond to journalists' questions on the plane home, without consultation or preparation. Standing with a microphone, he delayed answering for a while, requesting that they ask questions first about the Ireland trip. Finally, he came back to Viganò's letter: "I read the statement this morning," he began, "and I must tell you sincerely that, I must say this, to you and all those who are interested. . . . Read the statement carefully and make your own judgment. I will not say a single word about this."

The statement, he said, spoke for itself and as journalists they should draw their own conclusions.

There were those who praised Francis's silence as a noble stance comparable to Christ's silence in the face of the Grand Inquisitor in Dostoyevsky's *Brothers Karamazov*. Others interpreted the silence as an admission of guilt. Was not Francis himself, one blogger asked, perhaps more like the Grand Inquisitor than the Christ figure?

———

Prelates began to react in short order, some predictably showing their hands. Cardinal Daniel DiNardo, president of the United States

Conference of Catholic Bishops, declared that Viganò's letter raised questions that "deserve answers that may be tainted by false accusation and the guilty may be left to repeat sins of the past." Archbishop Charles Chaput of Philadelphia vouched for Viganò's integrity. One American bishop, Joseph Strickland of Tyler, Texas, supported Viganò to the extent of instructing parish priests to read the letter to their congregations. He issued a statement declaring that he found Viganò's allegations credible.

Two weeks later, without reference to any of Viganò's "facts," Francis finally threw a wrench into the works by delivering a spiritual verdict on the matter, invoking powers of darkness. The occasion was his homily during Mass at Santa Marta. "The Great Accuser has been unchained and [is] attacking bishops," he said. "He tries to uncover sins, so they are visible in order to scandalize the people."

The mention of the Great Accuser, Satan, invoked of course further references, of which any priest of a certain era is all too aware: Pope Leo XIII's prayer to Archangel Michael against the "snares of the Devil" who "wanders through the world for the ruin of souls," or the Devil in the First Epistle of Peter who "like the lion wanders about seeking whom he may devour," repeated in the prayers of Compline each night. It was an unfortunate reflection, however, since it looked as if Francis was accusing Viganò of acting on behalf of Satan, and that the bishops he had accused were victims rather than possible perpetrators.

Meanwhile, Cardinal Joseph Tobin of Newark declared that enemies of Francis were using Viganò to push a conservative agenda. "I do think it's about limiting the days of this pope, and short of that neutering his voice or casting ambiguity around him. And it's part of a larger upheaval both within and without the Church."

According to Michael Sean Winters, regular columnist on the *National Catholic Reporter*, "This is a coordinated attack on Pope Francis. A putsch is afoot and if the US bishops do not, as a body, stand up to defend the Holy Father in the next 24 hours, we shall be slipping towards schism. . . . The enemies of Francis have declared war."

Winters argued that it was not true that Francis lifted sanctions against McCarrick: "Francis did act. He is the one who removed McCarrick from ministry in June." While accepting that Benedict issued sanctions against McCarrick, the sanctions were not enforced, he went on: "With my own eyes I witnessed McCarrick celebrate Mass in public, participate in meetings, travel, etc. More importantly, so did Pope Benedict! If Benedict imposed these penalties, he certainly did not apply them." McCarrick celebrated Mass in the Vatican, "even concelebrating with Benedict at events like consistories. . . . But, as Viganò tells it, it is all Pope Francis's fault." Viganò's testimony, concluded Winters, was the unreliable vengeance of a disgruntled former employee.

Eventually, six weeks after the letter, a senior Vatican official, the prefect of the Congregation of Bishops, Canadian Cardinal Marc Ouellet, published an open letter in French, addressed to Viganò. "I cannot begin to understand how you let yourself be convinced of this monstrous accusation, which does not stand up," he wrote. The charges were "blasphemous . . . absolutely abhorrent . . . politically motivated." He went on: "Come out of hiding, repent for your revolt and return to better feelings toward the Holy Father instead of worsening hostility against him." As to the facts of the matter, there was no record of sanctions against Cardinal McCarrick; he had, however, been "exhorted" to live a hidden life of prayer.

Cardinal Ouellet ended his letter with a suggested motive: "Dear Viganò, in response to your unjust and unjustified attack, I can only conclude that the accusation is a political plot that lacks any real basis that could incriminate the Pope and that profoundly harms the communion of the Church."

The response from the conservative Catholic media demonstrated the toxic consequences of the original letter. Writing in LifeSiteNews, the lay theologian Peter Kwasniewski of Wyoming Catholic College declared Ouellet's letter "over-the-top, sycophantic, even papolatrous.

He undermines his credibility by speaking of the Holy Father as of a veritable Messiah. . . ."

The epithet "papolatrous" was to become a routine adjective for those who defended Francis. Meanwhile, criticisms of Francis were characterized by liberal commentators as "hysterical," "fuming," "fevered." Dr. Kwasniewski certainly fumed when he reported an incident during the papal visit in November 2019 when Francis greeted the Buddhist Supreme Patriarch in Thailand. "One wonders what a pope is doing paying a personal visit to a Buddhist leader and requesting *his* blessing, as if he has something to give that Christ and His Church do not already have in a more perfect way."

Meanwhile Archbishop Viganò, having released his damaging letter to the world, was now in hiding and apparently scared. His collaborator Tosatti reported that the archbishop had been convinced that he was a victim of phone taps and on the lists of hit men.

Francis weathered the *annus horribilis* with remarkable resilience, maintaining his long hours of daily prayer, spiritual counseling, and public preaching. Not long after Viganò's attack, he gave yet another homily on hope at his early morning Mass in Santa Marta's. Speaking of hope, again, as similar to a mother awaiting the birth of her baby, he expanded the image with telling further details: "She goes to the doctor, she sees the ultrasound. Is she different? Does she say, 'Oh look, a baby, okay.' No! She rejoices! And every day she touches her belly to caress that child, in anticipation. . . ."

Hope, he went on, is concrete, "an everyday thing," an encounter with Jesus in the Eucharist, in prayer, in the Gospel, in the poor, in the life of the community, "every time we take another step toward this definitive encounter . . . preparing for that definitive encounter." Ask yourselves, he said, how you live out your identity as Christians, "whether you are expecting an inheritance in heaven that is somewhat abstract—or whether you are really hoping for an encounter with the Lord."

Despite the battering he had taken through the previous year, Francis showed day by day that he maintained a space of peace and inspiration in which he continued to meditate creatively and to teach.

CHAPTER FOURTEEN

ORIGINS OF CLERICAL ABUSE

Priests, Gay Priests, and Abusers

When Francis uttered that phrase, "Who am I to judge," during a trans-Atlantic flight in 2013, he was referring to a gay person in words that contrasted starkly with previous papal descriptions of homosexuality as an "intrinsic moral evil."

Francis's words are simple and powerful, but taken out of context by commentators on both sides of the Catholic divide who assume it means that Francis is giving his blessing to homosexuality; not that Francis has ever attempted to explain or apologize for the unadorned, unqualified way in which the phrase has been exploited. Francis was in fact speaking about mercy, while referring to a specific individual, a priest who had been accused of homosexual behavior in the past. Francis's actual words were: "If someone is gay and is searching for the Lord and has a good will, then who am I to judge him?"

Francis was affirming Catholic doctrine that a sexual tendency does not indicate sin. Contrary to the explosion of commentary, for and against the five words—Who am I to judge?—it did not sanction gay sex; nor gay marriage. That very tension, however, was taken by his critics to indicate that Francis routinely and deliberately caused ambiguity. Dan Hitchens, a nephew of Christopher Hitchens and a convert to Catholicism writing in *First Things,* judged Francis to be in moral error: "... the pope's words—combined with his actions and his conspicuous silences—are frequently, needlessly, seriously misleading about Catholic doctrine. Some of the most glaring examples relate to contraception, hell, theoretical legitimacy of the death penalty, but the list grows practically every month."

Yet there was another controversy raging at the time, over the supposed link between homosexuality and priestly abuse. A large constituency, mainly of conservative lay and clerical Catholics, were arguing that the root cause of priestly sexual abuse of minors was the existence of gays in the priesthood.

At my junior seminary in the late 1950s, I was sexually propositioned during Confession by a priest who used the sacrament as a seduction tactic. I had chosen him to be my confessor and spiritual director because, unlike most of our priests, he had an extroverted, relaxed personality. He was fun. Confessions held in his private quarters became a treat and a privilege, the religious auspices nevertheless creating an atmosphere of unquestioning trust. He had a record player and a collection of Elvis Presley LPs. Although I told him that I preferred to kneel to make my Confession, this priest, Father Leslie McCallum, who died in the 1960s, insisted that I relax in a comfortable armchair and accept a glass of Madeira. He offered a cigarette, too, which I declined.

On this occasion, before I could finish my laundry list of peccadilloes, he interrupted to ask: "Have you had problems with sexual sins?" He went on to say that I shouldn't feel guilt about masturbation because not to masturbate was abnormal. The American Kinsey Report on sexual behavior, he said, stated that 99.9 percent of all males masturbated. Then he asked if he could see my penis so that he could manipulate it to discover whether I had any of the "well-known deformities that lead to excessive erections." Nothing wrong with masturbation, he conveyed, it was just not good for the health to do it too much.

I stood up and left the room. I said nothing about the incident to anyone in authority in the seminary because I felt that it would be my word against his. In any case, even penitents in those days believed that the seal of Confession applied to them as well as to the confessor.

Thereafter, whenever we passed, he would smile and greet me as if nothing had happened. The following year he was removed from the seminary; perhaps his superiors got wind of his behavior. I later heard that he was appointed chaplain to a boy's preparatory boarding school, to care for the souls of an even younger age group than ours.

In years to come there would be a clear distinction in my mind between gay people and sexually predatory men; but I do not mean to suggest that even back in the late 1950s we seminarians associated being gay with sexual abuse. In our cloistered situation and narrow upbringing, being "gay" or homosexual, or identifying fellow seminarians or our teachers as such, was not part of any conversation I was aware of at the time. I thought I understood the meaning of the word "homosexual," yet I was unsure what it meant in terms of sexual expression. We were all of us aware that Father McCallum was a different kind of character from the rest of our community of priests.

Since the majority of our seminary priests, like the students, had themselves been recruited before puberty, it is not surprising that most of us, including the teaching staff, were heterosexual. The increase in the recruitment of gay men, more than the proportion in the population as a whole, arose after the Second Vatican Council when junior seminaries were abolished in most countries.

Prominent among the many allegations in Archbishop Viganò's letter was a searing denunciation of homosexual rings within the clergy, rising to the highest levels of the hierarchy. Homosexuality, he asserted, was associated with the phenomenon of clerical sexual abuse as well as a general culture of corruption. "These homosexual networks," he wrote, "which are now widespread in many dioceses, seminaries, religious orders, etc., act under the concealment of secrecy and lies with the power of octopus tentacles, and strangle innocent victims and priestly vocations, and are strangling the entire Church."

Pope Francis, he was alleging, encouraged gay lobbies, and brought forward gay prelates in the Curia. Knowing that McCarrick was homosexual, he nevertheless failed to ostracize him from the Vatican and enforce the restrictions on him ordered by Benedict.

Yet the link between homosexuality and abuse was challenged not only by liberals but by advocates of victims of abuse. Head of the Survivors Network of Those Abused by Priests (SNAP), and a survivor himself, Peter Isely declared: "This is infighting between curia factions that are exploiting the abuse crisis and victims of clergy sexual abuse as leverage in the struggle for Church power. The sexual abuse crisis is not about whether a bishop is a liberal or a conservative. It is about protecting children."

The sexual abuse crisis had been "weaponized," as some put it, in the right-left battle, and in the process had been weaponized against Francis. In the meantime, it was apparent that the survivors' interests were obscured in a blame-game conflict; moreover, a deeper understanding of the true nature and origins of the abuse was being neglected. Francis found himself in the middle of this internecine quarrel as he prepared to explore the origins of the priestly sexual abuse and decide what to do about it.

———————

Links between homosexuality and clerical abuse have been mooted for decades and proved inconclusive if not a red herring or plain wrong. Historian of religion Philip Jenkins has remarked on the interplay between clergy abuse and the opportunities it affords various interest groups to promote their own hobbyhorses. In his groundbreaking study, *Pedophiles and Priests* (1996), Jenkins noted how the moral panic generated by the phenomenon becomes a useful basis for other, partisan claims.

As the Vatican was pressured to resolve the abuse crisis, it encountered many-layered complexities, including the problem of terminology. While it is obvious that not all homosexuals are pedophiles, it is also obvious that the term "pedophile" splits into a variety of characteristics—ranging across sexual interest in infants, pre-pubescents, pubescents, and post-pubescents, and from males to females.

Making connections between clerical abuse, the "sexual revolution" of the fifties and sixties, the generally lax culture of the post-Vatican II period, and the emergence of homosexuality in seminaries and religious houses, has been irresistible. Jenkins remarked that even trained sociologists, like the priest-sociologist Andrew Greeley, fell for the association between homosexuality and sexual abuse. Writing in the *National Catholic Reporter* back in 1989, Greeley denounced the "blatantly active homosexual priests" appointed and promoted within dioceses. "Lavender rectories and seminaries are tolerated," he declared, thirty years ahead of the shock "revelations" of Frédéric Martel's *In the Closet of the Vatican*. "National networks of active homosexual priests (many of them church administrators) are tolerated," wrote Greeley. Homosexual priests are allowed to hold assignations for sex parties, and "perhaps a quarter of the priests under 35 are gay, and perhaps half of that group are sexually active." According to Jenkins, Greeley's analysis suggests that, at the very least, laxity toward homosexuality opens up tolerance toward clerical sexual abuse of minors.

Nor could Francis ignore the statistics of sexual tendencies within the priesthood in previous decades. Richard Sipe, former priest, practicing psychotherapist, and researcher on priestly sexuality, wrote prolifically throughout the 1990s on the clerical abuse phenomenon. He had worked with more than five hundred offenders over several decades and developed a range of categorizations and predispositions. While precluding a simplistic either/or explanation—clericalism/or homosexuality—he could assert several generalizations: For example, "seventy to eighty percent of priests who sexually abuse have themselves been abused as children, some by priests." Furthermore, he noted that a high percentage of those who later abused young-sters "were in effect given permission for such activity by a priest or religious superior who himself crossed the sexual boundary with the priest abuser during the time he was studying for ordination."

Sipe also insisted that celibacy, while being "an issue in under-standing abuse and the power structure of the church," did not "by itself solve the sexual problems of the Catholic Church." By the same token, thirty years on, given the global extent of the offenses, it was unrealistic to expect Francis to resolve the crisis by himself. He would need the Church behind him. Albeit six years already into his papacy, he called a summit to thrash out the state of things and a plan of action.

———————

The four-day "summit on clerical sexual abuse" was held in the hall of Paul VI in the third week of February 2019. It was hardly the beginning of a process to deal with the crisis as there had been scores of meetings and discussion groups on the issue since the beginning of the papacy. Yet neither of his predecessors organized such a high-profile meeting. Some two hundred bishops, together with survivors, child protection experts, lawyers, and church leaders, including heads of women's con-gregations and cardinals, were gathered under the chairmanship of Francis, who started by calling for a "conversion of spirit."

He issued twenty-one points for "reflection" including basic reporting and responding rules, participation of lay experts in investi-gations, a requirement to report allegations to civil authorities, codes of conduct for priests, more rigorous screening of candidates for the priesthood. Cardinal Blasé Cupich set out a plan for the accountability of bishops, and regulations for handling the reporting of abuse.

Francis declared that "abuse is always the result of an abuse of power, an exploitation of the inferiority and vulnerability of the abused, which makes possible the manipulation of their conscience and of their psychological and physical weakness."

The meeting's schedule was structured around three broad themes: responsibility, accountability, and transparency. Archbishop Scicluna, the abuse investigator in chief, talked of a "road map" that included an increase in the numbers of canon lawyers handling cases, the speeding up of processes, and the prompt removal of convicted abusers from public ministry. Scicluna now joined the Congregation of the Doctrine of the Faith (CDF), the body responsible for prosecuting cases. The CDF had defrocked Cardinal McCarrick in the previous week, demonstrating the level to which clerical guilt had risen and Francis's readiness to act.

The delegates heard victims' harrowing testimonies. They listened to a woman who had been impregnated three times by a priest. He began raping her when she was fifteen and forced her into three abortions. Another woman said that she had been abused by a priest for five years from the age of eleven. At one point, the hall fell silent after a horrendous account of an abuse survivor had been read out by Fr. Hans Zollner, a child protection specialist.

Throughout the four days of the summit, survivors' groups had been demonstrating outside. Even before the summit ended there were complaints that nothing "concrete" had been decided, eliciting the unfortunate response from Archbishop Scicluna that Francis had been "very, very concrete." Many of the "concrete" measures announced at the summit were already in force, or in the pipeline; much of the meeting had been spent listening to the survivors and hearing words of sorrow, commiseration, and regret, on behalf of the clergy.

Addressing the meeting, Francis took a spiritual view of the scourge. Child abuse, he said was like "sacrificing human beings, frequently children, in pagan rites." He went on: "Consecrated persons, chosen by God to guide souls to salvation, let themselves be dominated by their human frailty or sickness and thus become tools of Satan. . . . In abuse we see the hand of the evil that does not spare even the innocence of children. No explanations suffice for these abuses involving children." Above all the measures announced and to be announced, Francis repeated his call for a "change of heart," an alteration of spiritual attitude. It did nothing to assuage the survivor groups in Rome.

After the summit ended there were bitter complaints from advocates' groups that a "zero tolerance" policy had not been met. Archbishop Scicluna reiterated that zero tolerance, meaning "removal from ministry," had been met; but that it did not involve automatic laicization—a process requiring a "canonical trial." Here Francis found himself in conflict with the survivors: Laicization at the first moment of an allegation, in his view, raised questions of justice, particularly where evidence was lacking.

Francis was criticized both in Rome and beyond for commenting that sexual abuse of children included not only clerical but other abusers including members of families. Was this an attempt, some advocacy leaders asked, to water down the culpability of clergy? Yet it could be argued that by including other forms of child abuse he had demonstrated by contrast how much more heinous is sexual abuse in a religious context; that clerical abuse is in a sphere of abuse all by itself.

———————————

Coinciding with the summit, Cardinals Raymond Burke and Walter Brandmüller released a letter aimed at the participating bishops and heads of religious orders stating that in their view the sex abuse scandal was a consequence of a "homosexual agenda." The view, widespread across conservative clergy and laity, was reinforced several weeks after the end of the meeting by a 6,000-word letter by Emeritus Pope Benedict.

Initially he blamed clerical sexual abuse on the sexual revolution of the 1960s, including the odd idea that the availability of sexually explicit in-flight movies on airplanes had been a factor. Added to which, he cited secularization, the absence of God in society, the liberalizing of theology, including moral theology, following the Second Vatican

Council. "It could be said," he wrote, "that in the twenty years from 1960 to 1980, the previously normative standards regarding sexuality collapsed entirely, and a new normalcy arose that has by now been the subject of laborious attempts at disruption." At the same time he identified homosexuality in seminaries as a factor in the clerical abuse crisis. Despite some improvement, he went on, there were "homosexual cliques in seminaries which acted more or less openly and significantly changed the climate in the seminaries."

Benedict had no inclination, it seemed, to issue an apology for any part he might have played in the cover-ups; yet his key role as head of the Vatican department that dealt with abuse gave him the right, he believed, to have a say: "Since I myself had served in a position of responsibility as shepherd of the church at the time of the public outbreak of the crisis, and during the run-up to it, I had to ask myself—even though, as emeritus, I am no longer directly responsible—what I could contribute to a new beginning."

The intervention of Benedict revealed that the retired pope was far from resigned to a life of obscurity and silence. He was still playing a part and his followers saw a useful role for him despite his age, and perhaps because of it.

———————————

Against the background of long-running disputes over alleged links between homosexuality and sexual abuse, a Jesuit priest, Father James Martin, was working pastorally within the LGBT communities while combating homophobia among clergy and bishops. Matters came to a head for him on June 12, 2016, when Omar Mateen murdered forty-nine people and wounded fifty others at Pulse, a gay nightclub in Orlando, Florida. It was the most ferocious attack on LGBT people in the United States as well as the deadliest terrorist attack in America since 9/11. Mateen was shot dead at the scene. Acquaintances said that Mateen disparaged gay men and lesbians, and he had a history of conflicted attitudes about his sexuality. His father told journalists that his son became enraged when he saw men kissing in public.

Father Martin says that he was shocked by the absence of any recognition by the US Catholic bishops that the atrocity had been committed against gay people. In consequence he was moved to write a short book, *Building a Bridge: How the Catholic Church and the LGBT Community Can Enter into a Relationship of Respect, Compassion, and Sensitivity*. Citing the Catholic Catechism, Martin pleaded that the bishops should accord "respect, compassion, and sensitivity" for gays, lesbians, and transgender men and women. By the same token, LGBT people, he went on, should accord a corresponding respect to the clergy, remembering that clergy are often unfamiliar with LGBT people; moreover, that priests may have pursued a priestly calling as a solution to their own attraction to the same sex.

Father Martin's initiative was not appreciated by all his fellow Catholics. Some who affected to agree with his main point criticized him for failing to emphasize the Church's requirement of chastity for homosexuals, even though he said many times that he was not challenging any Church teaching on the matter.

His advocacy for the Catholic LGBT community became a focus of interest during the abuse summit talks, and his views were sought in particular on the charge that priestly abusers were in the main homosexuals. In one interview he said, "The vast majority of gay priests are faithful, are hardworking and celibate, and have never abused anyone, [and] are still afraid to come out. Why? One reason is the current poisonous environment. As a result, the only public model of the gay priest is the abuser." For this reason, he argued, the stereotype of the gay priest abuser has become fixed in people's minds. He went on to accuse the "far right" of conducting a "witch hunt for gay priests, and attacking LGBT plus people in general."

He was nevertheless convinced that Francis's oft-quoted "Who am I to judge?" had disrupted Catholic perceptions decisively: "He has gay friends," said Martin, "and he's written about LGBT people compassionately." Hinting that Francis might have been responsible for the initiative, he said: "The Vatican pointedly used that term [LGBT] when it invited me to give a talk at the World Meeting of Families in Dublin. . . . The talk was called Showing Respect and Welcome in our Parishes for LGBT People and Their Families."

Francis made no substantive statements about the circumstance of gays and lesbians within the Church, yet from time to time he demonstrated in individual encounters his acceptance of members of the Catholic LGBT community (on January 11, 2020, he would embrace a transgender person he had invited into the Vatican). At the same time, he had been clear in his rejection of gender fluidity, or gender spectrum theory.

Francis was to show publicly his regard for the pastoral work of James Martin by granting him an audience of thirty minutes on September 30, 2019; the two were photographed sitting close together in amicable conversation. It was the third meeting Martin had enjoyed with Francis since the beginning of the papacy. The friendly, easy postures of the two men, Jesuit and Jesuit pope, were eloquent, and the photo and caption went viral.

Writing from Rome in *America* magazine, Vatican correspondent Gerard O'Connell confirmed that the meeting was seen in Rome "as a highly significant statement of support and encouragement for this US Jesuit . . . well known as a public speaker, author and for his pastoral ministry to LGBT people." By meeting Martin in the library of the Apostolic Palace, where Francis normally greeted high-ranking guests, Francis indeed seemed to have shown more than casual approval of the priest. A source told O'Connell that Francis had read Martin's book *Building a Bridge* and wished to offer him encouragement.

———————

While Francis dealt daily with the repercussions of the worldwide priestly abuse scandal, he was all too conscious of the effect the crimes of a minority was having on the majority of good and faithful priests.

Their lives and work had been made all the more difficult; many felt a sense of guilt for the crimes of that minority.

In August 2019, on the feast of St. Jean Vianney, patron of Catholic parish priests, Francis wrote a letter to the priests of the world, the pastors who, as he put it, serve "in the trenches, bearing the burden of the day and the heat, confronting an endless variety of situations in your effort to care for and accompany God's people."

It contained not only his encouragement of all those priests, innocent of abuse and yet suffering in consequence of the criminal priests, but his thoughts beyond the summit on the source and nature of clerical abuse and the priesthood.

He acknowledged that "in more than a few places, our priests feel themselves attacked and blamed for crimes they did not commit. . . ." But just as soon he turned to the victims. "In these years, we have become more attentive to the cry, often silent and suppressed, of our brothers and sisters who were victims of the abuse of power, the abuse of conscience, and sexual abuse on the part of ordained ministers. This has been a time of great suffering in the lives of those who experienced such abuse, but also in the lives of their families and of the entire People of God."

He was "firmly committed," he went on, to carrying out reforms "so that the culture of abuse would have no room to develop, much less continue, but he acknowledged the "task is neither quick nor easy." He admitted that in the past "omission may itself have been a kind of response," but "today we desire conversion, transparency, sincerity, and solidarity with victims to become our concrete way of moving forward."

He wrote now in shocking and unprecedented terms of the cleansing of the priesthood and the Church, which had inferences for the origins of spiritual abuse. "The Lord is purifying his Bride and converting all of us to himself. . . . He is rescuing us from hypocrisy, from the spirituality of appearances. He is breathing forth his Spirit in order to restore the beauty of his Bride, caught in adultery."

Abandoning the usual image of the Church as the spotless Bride of Christ, he was citing the sixteenth chapter of Ezekiel, in which Jerusalem is likened to a bride turned prostitute. But stunningly, Francis was invoking the chapter as a metaphor for the Catholic Church of today. "It is the history of the Church, and each of us can say it is our history too." All priests, he went on, should accept the shame: "In the end, through your sense of shame, you will continue to act as a shepherd. Our humble repentance, expressed in silent tears before these atrocious sins and the unfathomable grandeur of God's forgiveness, is the beginning of a renewal of our holiness." Contained within the Ezekiel chapter is the account of the whore bride descending to the human sacrifice of children, an image that Francis employed for priestly sexual abuse, as we saw earlier.

He had further words of encouragement for the priestly vocation, and the counsel that pastors should avoid thinking of their limitations, "brooding over our troubles." Again and again, he expressed his gratitude for their commitments, working through the diverse activities and service of the pastoral life: care of the sick, the elderly, the dying; preaching the Gospel; celebrating the Eucharist, until he arrived at a perspective on the priesthood that might be taken as a description of his own message to the entire Church.

> *Thank you for the times when, with great emotion, you embraced sinners, healed wounds, warmed hearts, and showed the tenderness and compassion of the Good Samaritan. Nothing is more necessary than this: accessibility, closeness, readiness to draw near to the flesh of our suffering brothers and sisters. How powerful is the example of a priest who makes himself present and does not flee the wounds of his brothers and sisters!*

During the years in which news of sexual abuse cases came almost daily with sickening regularity, I was conscious of the sorrow and depression among many of my priest friends. At the same time, I learned of those daily insults and attacks on priests in Ireland and throughout the United Kingdom. Although the movie *Spotlight*, portraying abusing priests and cover-ups in the Boston diocese, was based on fact, the idea of the Catholic priest as pedophile or suspected pedophile had entered popular culture in scores of movies. In Martin Scorsese's 2006 film *The Departed*, two priests are taunted in a restaurant by the villain Frank Costello as if he assumes them to be guilty merely *because* they are priests. It took the 2014 film *Calvary*, by John Michael McDonagh, to depict the suffering of innocent priests on behalf of the guilty. A parish priest in rural Ireland, played by Brendan Gleeson, is murdered sacrificially by an abuse victim precisely *because* he is a good priest. The victim-murderer says: "I'm going to kill you, Father, *because* you are innocent . . . . no point in killing a bad priest but to kill a good one . . . that would be a shock." A great many priests had been paying for the crimes of fellow priests in less brutal and final ways, and Francis's letter, a powerful and uplifting expression of gratitude and encouragement, revealed his companionship with them while expressing his sorrow for the victims.

———

PART FIVE

CHURCH IN THE WORLD

World in the Church

CHAPTER FIFTEEN

GOD OF MANY RELIGIONS

Reaching Out to Judaism and Other Faiths

I n Buenos Aires, Jorge Bergoglio as archbishop made friends with Rabbi Abraham Skorka, then rector of the Latin American Rabbinical Seminary. Starting in 1997, they met regularly, their discussions ranging over theology and scripture as well as sports and Latin American poetry. Later they held public discussions on moral questions, including abortion, euthanasia, and gay marriage. In time they began to record their conversations and published some of them in their book, *On Heaven and Earth* (2010). Skorka wrote: "During our chats, the main topic and focus of concern was, and continues to be, individual people and their problems." They called each other "brother" and met frequently after Bergoglio became pope.

Francis's friendship with Rabbi Skorka was both a manifestation and catalyst for his love and understanding of Judaism and the Jewish people. In December 2015 Francis made a solemn, historic gesture of reconciliation by officially renouncing the ancient official duty, indeed "right," of Christians to convert Jews. The document read: "The Catholic Church neither conducts nor supports any specific institutional mission work directed towards Jews." Underpinning that "right" to convert all Jews was the ancient view that Judaism was an abomination. As James Carroll, historian of religion and Catholic commentator, viewed the matter: "Across the centuries, the mad Christian impulse to convert Jews has erected not only pillars of anti-Semitism but also underlying structures of biological racism, white supremacy, and Western contempt for, among others, Arabs and Muslims."

Proselytizing zeal in all religions brought much misery to the world and continues to be a source of religious violence. But Francis was invoking the proposition of religious pluralism: not just the principle of freedom of religion, but acknowledgment of the members of other faiths as sisters and brothers; recognition that their faiths were parallel spiritual journeys with their own worth and truth.

————————

The wider significance of the solemn renunciation of the ancient imperative to convert the Jewish people was its application to other faiths. How would it in time affect Catholic attitudes toward Islam? And how would it affect Catholicism itself?

"Christendom no longer exists," proclaimed Pope Francis, to the evident shock of the cardinals and bishops sitting before him in a resplendent marble hall of the Vatican. "Today we are not the only ones who produce culture, nor are we the first or the most listened to." Delivering his Christmas address to the Curia in 2019, he was bent on disrupting the notion of the Catholic Church as the one and only religion worthy of respect, influence, and status, even in the West. Nor had it the right to dominate: Christen*dom*. It was a year in which Francis was actively adjusting the relationship between Catholicism and other faiths, while seeking to rebalance the Vatican center with Catholicism's local Churches. Resistance to these adjustments, he said, was "an attitude of rigidity born of the fear of change, which ends up erecting fences and obstacles on the terrain of the common good, turning it into a minefield of incomprehension and of hatred."

He was defending his reform of the Church's central government, raising the department for evangelization above that of the department for doctrine. By "evangelism" he did not mean the imperative to convert, to proselytize, but to encourage in Christians themselves a change of heart, a renewal. This was not good news for Catholics who were convinced that a crucial obligation of Christians is to impose the good news on non-Catholics, to bring nonbelievers into the fold. Francis was instructing the faithful *not* to proselytize, *not* to convert those of other faiths, but to make friends with them.

In the first week of February of that year, Francis did something no pope, even the inveterate globe-trotter John Paul II, had done: He celebrated Mass in Abu Dhabi, United Arab Emirates, on the Arabian Peninsula, a region where the Eucharist is viewed as an act of sorcery—hence anathema to Islam. The scene was Zayed Sports City Stadium, where 120,000 worshipers gathered, including 4,000 Muslims, led by the crown prince of Abu Dhabi, Sheikh Mohammed bin Zayed Al Nahyan.

The principal symbolic moment came when Francis embraced Dr. Ahmed el-Tayeb, Grand Imam of Egypt's Al-Azhar University (known by some as the Vatican of the Sunni world). El-Tayeb, with a reputation for tolerance, although not toward Jews and Israel, was notable for his attempts to reconcile Sunni and Shia Muslims. The imam and Francis signed a declaration titled "Human Fraternity for World Peace and Living Together," condemning religious violence and pledging to promote peace and dialogue between Islam and Christianity. The document declared that Muslims of the East and West, together with the Catholic Church and the Catholics of the East and West, accept "the adoption of a culture of dialogue as the path; cooperation as the code of conduct; reciprocal understanding as the method and standard."

The document spoke of an ideal of religious pluralism, of respect for religions different from one's own; then it went further:

> *The pluralism and diversity of religions, color, sex, race, and language are willed by God in His wisdom, through which He created human beings. . . . His divine wisdom is the source from which the right to freedom of belief and the freedom to be different derives.*

Therefore, the fact that people are forced to adhere to a certain religion or culture must be rejected.

This historic act of friendship and reconciliation with another faith was yet another disruptive shock for conservatives. It contrasted with the uproar caused in the Muslim world by Pope Benedict in September 2006, when he delivered a speech at Regensburg University in Germany, citing a derogatory view of Islam. Benedict quoted from a book in which the Byzantine emperor Manuel Palaeologos said: "Show me just what Muhammad brought that was new, and there you will find things only evil and inhuman, such as his command to spread by the sword the faith he preached."

Benedict was denounced by Muslims throughout the world as a result of that quotation. But now it was the turn of Catholic conservatives to denounce Francis. The most hostile was a twenty-page letter signed by a group of senior theologians, including the noted Oxford scholar and Dominican priest, Father Aiden Nichols, whom I admired when he taught at my own university, Cambridge, and someone I counted as a friend. I was shocked by his evident role as leader of the signatories, and the vehemence of his accusations. Addressed to all the bishops of the Roman Catholic Church, the letter accused Francis "of the canonical delict [from the Latin for a violation of law or right] of heresy," demanding that the hierarchies of the world take "the steps necessary to deal with the grave situation of a heretical pope."

The letter took the opportunity to cast a wide net of papal heresy, including Francis's teachings on marriage and the family and his indulgence toward gays and lesbians. But high among the pope's alleged heresies was "his work in interfaith dialogue," a clear denunciation of the joint declaration with the Sunni faith leader. The letter concluded that "the evil of a heretical pope is so great that it should not be tolerated for the sake of some allegedly greater good."

The charge that Francis crossed the boundaries of respect for other faiths and Christian denominations was by now familiar; it was noted that he even received blessings from Lutheran and Anglican priests and bishops, a symbolic gesture of his acceptance of their authentic priestly status. George Neumayr declared that "like his fellow liberal Jesuits, Pope Francis often seems to exude enthusiasm for every religion except his own. In his extreme ecumenism, he is conforming to the lowest-common-denominator culture of a post-Christian age."

The disruptive significance of Francis's acceptance of other religions "as willed by God" has to be understood against the history of Catholicism's traditional claim to exclusivity. Moreover, the upheaval he was creating has to be understood in the light of the struggles of modern philosophers of religion to find a basis on which one set of fundamental dogmas can coexist, validly and authentically, with quite a different set of fundamental dogmas of another religion. The social and political context of conflicting faiths and denominations had been resolved, up to a point, in the great American experiment: religious freedom under the auspices of a secular government. The kind of theorizing expounded in John Rawls's *Theory of Justice* is compelling. What makes for a good society? Is it to impose, top-down, sets of values and beliefs? Or is it to allow individuals and groups of individuals to choose their own sets of values and beliefs? The former, clearly, is a fundamentalist society with all its drawbacks. The latter, with all its diversity, will only work under a set of laws that protects diversity but regulates by law the limits of individual values and beliefs: for example, the prevention of the practice of female genital mutilation; or the prevention of a religion's assumed right to torture and kill infidels! Yet the protection of toleration through the separation of church and state, faith and government, has never resolved the underlying problem, how one religion not merely tolerates a rival religion but respects and even honors it.

———————————

Down the centuries the Catholic Church had turned its face resolutely against granting other faiths, or even other Christian denominations, a measure of recognition and validity. In the nineteenth century popes regarded even the Anglican Archbishop of Canterbury as a layman of dubious baptism, let alone dubious priesthood.

Anti-religious-pluralism tendencies continued in the Catholic Church until the Second Vatican Council, when they were challenged by the promulgation of the document *Nostra Aetate*, which stated that "the Catholic Church rejects nothing which is true and holy in these [other] religions."

"She has a sincere respect," the document continued, "for those ways of acting and living, those moral and doctrinal teachings which may differ in many respects from what she holds and teaches, but which none the less often reflect the brightness of that Truth, which is the light of all men." Pope John XXIII originally wanted the declaration to apply to the Jewish faith alone, but it was extended "to the work of God in all the major faith traditions." Moreover, the final declaration of the Council, titled *Dignitatis humanae* (*The Dignity of the Human Person*) was a historic declaration of religious freedom, spelling out the Church's support for the protection of religious liberty. The measure, drafted by the American Jesuit theologian John Courtney Murray, was hotly disputed, but eventually passed by a vote of the Council Fathers, 2,308 to 70. Nevertheless it was to become a matter of dispute between official Catholic teaching and traditionalists like Archbishop Marcel Lefebvre, who was convinced that the Council had fallen into heresy on the matter.

While the Vatican's Pontifical Council for Interreligious Dialogue attempted to reach out to other faiths, John Paul II took some notable ceremonial steps: In 1986 he was the first pope to enter Rome's synagogue to pray with the Chief Rabbi. Later he invited leaders of other religions to pray with him at Assisi, a gesture that attracted denunciations from the Catholic ultraconservatives. Yet beyond the rhetoric and ceremonial gestures, the Catholic recommendation of respect for other religions lacked a firm theological underpinning.

There were philosophers on the margins of Church influence who had thought creatively about a basis for religious pluralism during the interwar period. One was the prominent German Catholic philosopher, Max Scheler, product of a Lutheran father and Catholic mother. He was to influence the philosophical work of both Karol Wojtyla and Edith Stein. Scheler argued that religious pluralism was like different groups on a journey toward a mountain range that was truth. The truth was seen from different vantage points and different stages of the groups' journeys without altering the range itself, or invalidating the pilgrims' vision of the truth.

One of the leading post–World War II theologians, the German Jesuit Karl Rahner, had another proposal that he called the "anonymous Christian." He argued that a person whose free response to his world included an act of loving surrender to the "world's Absolute Horizon" makes an act of faith worthy of salvation. On this basis, it was possible to accord respect to followers of other religions because they were somehow "subconsciously" Christian, a reflection that smacked of religious cultural imperialism to those of other faiths, and to Catholic conservatives as vague waffle.

Next came the modest proposal of a French Jesuit, Jacques Dupuis, a professor at the Gregorian University in Rome who slaved for some years over a book titled *Toward a Christian Theology of Religious Pluralism*. He proposed that the fullness of truth is not revealed until the Second Coming. So while not denying the uniqueness of Christian revelation, he suggested that the Catholic Church, like other great world religions, is traveling toward that fullness; that all religions, including Catholicism, are united in the humility of their lack of full truth. The solution had echoes of Scheler. But this proved unsatisfactory to Cardinal Ratzinger and Pope John Paul II, who could not accept that the Catholic faith lacked anything but the fullness of truth. It led to the temporary suspension of Father Dupuis's right to teach and a series of hostile cross-examinations of the hapless professor in

Ratzinger's Vatican offices. At one point Dupuis was accused of asking erroneous questions of his interrogators. It ended with Dupuis being taken to the hospital with an ulcer.

Finally, on January 28, 2000, Pope John Paul read out a statement on an occasion celebrating the work of the Congregation for the Doctrine of the Faith. The Revelation of Jesus Christ, he said, is "definitive and complete." He went on to insist that all other faiths are deficient compared to "those who have the fullness of the salvic means in the Church."

Next came the resounding declaration titled *Dominus Iesus,* signed by Ratzinger in August 2000, in which the errors of religious pluralism were spelled out, as "relativism" and "subjectivism," to which he added an extraordinary claim from which it could be inferred that the Anglican and Episcopalian churches are not proper churches. The statement enraged both Catholics and non-Catholics. Against that background, Francis's open-arms gestures toward other Christian denominations and other faiths was a welcome interruption.

The Church's attitude toward Islam, however, remained a crucial test of its intention to welcome religious pluralism—its determination not merely to tolerate other religions but to grant them respect, and even honor them and make common spiritual cause with them.

———————

At the end of March 2019, Francis visited Morocco, where he met and prayed with Muslim leaders. At his first weekly general audience in Rome after the trip, Francis started with a question: "People might ask themselves, 'Why is it the pope visits Muslims and not just Catholics?'" Christians and Muslims are "descendants of the same father, Abraham," he said, and the visit was an opportunity for "dialogue and encounter with our Muslim brothers and sisters." He went on to another question: "People wonder: 'Why does God allow so many different religions in the world?'" The reason, he continued, is that there are theologians who believe that it is "God's permissive will . . . this reality of many religions. Some emerge from the culture, but they always look toward heaven and God. . . . What God wants is fraternity among us, which is why we must not be frightened by difference. God has allowed this."

Francis was not to produce a fully worked-out theory of religious pluralism. He was not to square the circle of how the Catholic Church was in possession of the deposit of truth, and yet rival truths were to be respected, honored even, their devotees regarded as sisters and brothers. Yet his practice of holding polarities, seeming contradictions in tension, once again became the guiding principle. He was evidently correcting the impression he might have given that God somehow deliberately created many different religions, rather than that God *allowed* the creation of different religions within the freedom of the human condition.

But then, a Church that relates in an open fraternal way with other religions, and the "separated brethren" of non-Catholic Christians, is one thing. How should Francis deal with the calls for differences of belief and practice within the Catholic Church itself? Francis appeared to be sanctioning freedom for bold yet prudent change within the Catholic Church, encouraging degrees of independence among national groups of bishops. How should local Churches pursue the creative changes he advocated while remaining within the doctrinal fold of the Church as a whole? Of all the national communities of Catholics across the world, the Church in Germany seemed bound for trouble in its enthusiasm for reform.

CHAPTER SIXTEEN

EUROPE AND THE FAITH

A Post-Christian Continent

A s 2019 came to an end, there was somber news from countries across Europe with historic ties to the Roman Catholic Church. In France, the "Daughter of the Church," Cardinal Philip Barbarin, Archbishop of Lyon, had been given a suspended jail sentence (later rescinded) for allegedly covering up knowledge of clerical sexual abuse. Churches were being vandalized throughout the country—set on fire, statues and stained glass smashed. In just one month, tabernacles (the locked receptacles in which sacred consecrated wafers, or hosts, are stored) had been broken into in four different churches, the hosts scattered and desecrated.

In Spain new figures, published in May 2019, showed that while two thirds of Spanish citizens identify as Catholics, only half of them attend Mass. The majority of "Catholic" young do not agree with Church's teachings on premarital sex, sexual orientation, marriage, and contraception. The numbers of priests are down 10,000 since 1975, and their average age is sixty-five.

In Germany, where about a third of the population identifies as Catholic, the Church appeared to be heading for conflict with Rome. In 2018, the year of a shattering report on child abuse in the country, Church revenues rose by 3.3 percent to 6.64 billion euros, and yet 216,078 German Catholics were recorded as officially lapsing that year.

The reason for the enhanced income was higher wage levels through the previous year. Germans registered as church attenders are charged a compulsory church tax, between 8 and 9 percent (depending on the state) deducted at source by tax authorities. Those who officially leave or "sign out" of their church no longer pay the tax; but it means they no longer should receive the sacraments or a Catholic funeral. Those revenues not only sustain Catholic education and charities in Germany but make substantial contributions to the Vatican and missionary activities throughout the world. Germany's bishops, impatient for change, announced that they were going to organize a series of synods without waiting for Rome.

Seeing where things were heading, Francis wrote an open letter to the German faithful in June 2019, advising that their discussions should eventually take in the whole of the Church rather than the national Church in isolation. They must, he wrote, "walk together" with the larger Church, lest it end up "increasing and perpetuating the evils it sought to solve."

He said that while the Church engages with the changing world, it is "anchored principally on fidelity to the deposit of faith and tradition." Reform, he went on, "has never had the presumption of acting as if nothing existed before; on the contrary, it focused on valuing what good was done" and conserving its fruitful "roots." Then he delivered his oft-quoted saying from Gustav Mahler: "Tradition is not the worship of ashes, but the preservation of fire."

Again, he was emphasizing the need to hold apparent opposites in tension, not least the need to honor tradition while being ready to reform and grow; the importance of the papal office in balance with the bishops and the people; the center in tension with the peripheries. In his own person, moreover, he was daily demonstrating his capacity to behave as a local pastor while assuming the extraordinary role of the Bishop of Rome.

The German impatience prompted rebukes from other senior cardinals. Introducing an interview with Cardinal Raymond Burke that was highly critical of the German Church, *First Things* editorialized: "Half a millennium after the Reformation, Germans are making trouble again for the Roman Church. This time, Germany's Catholic bishops have set out to remake the Church in their own liberal image." Conservative Cardinal Rainer Maria Woelki of Cologne said that he and his brother cardinals detected "a kind of Protestant Church Parliament" in the making, while Cardinal Gerhard Müller invoked Nazi history.

Müller declared that the German bishops had perpetrated a "suicidal act" similar to the Catholic members of parliament, the Zentrumspartei, whose votes awarded Hitler with dictatorial powers in 1933. Müller had intended to shock, and there was nothing like playing the Hitler card to get people's attention.

Nevertheless, in January 2020 some 230 German Catholics, bishops, and laypeople, including a formidable constituency of women, met in Frankfurt to thrash out rules for conducting a German "synodal path" to reform. Led by the redoubtable Cardinal Reinhard Marx, head of the German Bishops Conference, the group started a process toward change irrespective of the pope and Rome. Among the topics for debate were whether there should be a married priesthood; should women be ordained deacons; should there be joint Communion for Catholics and Lutherans. The delegates expected their synodal path to continue for at least two years, and they warned that their concluding "opinions" might be more than "nonbinding."

The problems with the German Church had hardly begun.

While Francis routinely surveyed the crises of the Church in Europe, he had not neglected his own diocese, Rome, and the faithful of Italy at large. Taught by his grandmother, he spoke Italian fluently, infused with the slightly guttural accents of the Piemonte and the Spanish of his native Argentina. The family's Italian roots were in the far northwest of the country, the region around Turin, a distinctive part of Italy that was once the kingdom of Savoy. Southerners sometimes refer to these northerners as *Tedeschi*, Germans; and there is a saying, *Piemontesi falsi ma cortesi*—"The Piedmontese, false but courteous," for their allegedly two-faced charm. There would be frequent visits to basilicas and parishes in his diocese of Rome; trips to the shrines of the Holy House at Loreto and the tomb of Padre Pio, the stigmatic Franciscan saint of Pietrelcina, as well as to prisons, hospitals, and charitable institutions around Italy, with flying visits to earthquake zones, slum districts, and refugee encampments out on the beltways of towns and cities up and down the peninsula.

Meanwhile the antagonism between Francis and Matteo Salvini, the voluble, bearded leader of Italy's populist Lega Party, made headlines year after year. Tensions began shortly after Francis's election when he visited the island of Lampedusa, attended by the full panoply of media coverage. Francis was filmed on a launch out at sea observing the arrival of rescued migrants; he met and spoke with families, many of them Muslim, on land. Francis wanted to welcome refugees with Christian charity. Salvini believed that charity begins at home and wanted all illegal immigrants banned from disembarking.

Salvini had forged an alliance with Steve Bannon, the architect of Donald Trump's presidential victory in 2016. Seeking to establish a worldwide populist movement with Italy as its center, Bannon was planning an "academy" at an abandoned hilltop monastery near the village of Colleperdo, forty miles east of Rome. Bannon described the institution as an academy of the Judeo-Christian West, a "modern gladiator school" that teaches the basic culture and truths of Western people. Bannon attempted to call a conference on his ideals under Vatican auspices but was turned down. He responded by declaring Pope Francis "the enemy" and "dead wrong." Bannon's religiosity was matched by that of Salvini, who had a habit of clutching a rosary at political rallies and invoking Our Lady of Medjugorje, venerated at a shrine in Bosnia where the Virgin is said to be delivering daily messages with a right-wing political bias. Salvini calls for the return of Christian Europe, for crucifixes to be displayed in school classrooms, and for Holy Days to be restored. After Francis slapped the woman who grabbed him in St. Peter's Square on New Year's Eve, 2019, Salvini posted a video to his two million followers on Instagram. It featured his girlfriend grabbing his arm; instead of slapping her, he caresses her cheek. To demonstrate his attachment to traditionist Catholicism, he affected allegiance to Emeritus Pope Benedict, wearing a T-shirt proclaiming "Benedict is my Pope."

Francis declined to engage with Salvini or Bannon, although he attacked Trump for building "walls instead of bridges," and sent half a million dollars to aid migrants on the US-Mexican border. After a visit to a refugee camp on the island of Lesbos in Greece, he brought back to Rome twelve Syrian migrants, and housed them in Vatican accommodations.

Francis frequently addressed the people of Italy with characteristically disruptive, unscheduled tactics. There were his phone calls with complete strangers; the unrehearsed back-of-the-plane press conferences, always in Italian; and those lengthy interviews with favored journalists at Santa Marta. From the beginning of the papacy, no favored journalist caused more consternation than Italy's best-known columnist—Eugenio Scalfari, cofounder and formerly editor in chief of *La Repubblica.*

The effect of the Scalfari-Francis special relationship was to exasperate the Roman press corps. Vatican correspondent Hilary White complained on the website OnePeterFive that the Francis-Scalfari liaison made journalists "behave like a flock of partridges . . . a great deal of panicked fluttering and confusion and running about in circles, pecking each other." She saw it as a typical example of Francis's "applied chaos." Some Vatican correspondents were inclined to dismiss Scalfari as a "joke" or a "silly old fool," albeit through gritted teeth.

I had known Scalfari and Carlo Caracciolo, the cofounder of his newspaper *La Repubblica* and its sister, *L'Espresso*, since the mid-1980s, when the periodicals set up a syndication alliance with my newspaper,

The Observer. Scalfari was then, and remained into his nineties, a strikingly upright, slender man with hungry eyes, an angry beard, and a relentless, argumentative intelligence. His newspaper is nationwide rather than local, and idiosyncratically to the left. No editorial opinion column in Italy was more independent of region, religion, and political party than Scalfari's.

Francis befriended him as what was tantamount to an occasional, alternative, unscheduled freelance press representative. While the tendency was to blame or ridicule Scalfari for his unreliable papal interviews, Francis, by continuing the association, made clear his satisfaction with its outreach, tone, tendency to upset, and capacity to embrace a wide variety of Italian opinion.

A militant atheist and staunch anti-clerical, Scalfari deplored the relationship between the Italian state and the Catholic Church, underpinned by Mussolini's original treaties with the Vatican in 1929. He argued for the rescinding of the treaties, which would have meant the end of the Vatican's sovereign status, making the pontiff a mere migrant in a foreign state, and the loss of many privileges including tax benefits and diplomatic immunity.

Scalfari had campaigned for abortion, divorce, sexual freedoms, IVF treatment, euthanasia, and the decriminalization of recreational drugs. He was for de-Christianizing Italy and Europe. He was warm toward Gramsci-style Italian Communism (a "historic compromise" third way) and yet an enthusiast for free enterprise and free trade. He was every pope's nightmare until Francis arrived.

To the surprise of regular readers of *La Repubblica* and the horror of thinking Catholics who knew Scalfari's reputation, Francis embarked on one of the strangest "odd couple" relationships ever forged in the history of the modern papacy. Francis awarded Scalfari unsupervised, lengthy private interviews. He would phone the aged journalist, or write letters to him (the first was nine pages long), in certain knowledge that Scalfari would report what had passed between them in his popular column, which in turn would be reported across the Italian media—broadcast, print, and internet.

Scalfari would scribble an account of their meetings from memory after the meeting. There was no strict record, shorthand or audio, of the occasionally shocking views, tantamount to heresy, attributed to Francis over the years. And yet Francis himself was not inclined to disown such statements, nor was he dissuaded from continuing the colloquiums. The question of reliability arose in Scalfari's first interview. According to Scalfari, Francis complained that the trappings of the Vatican court are "leprosy," and that too many of his bureaucrats were "Vaticancentric." Official denials of the leprosy comment were quickly proclaimed by the Vatican, but by Christmas Francis was repeating such aspersions on his Curia to their faces. He had evidently used Scalfari as a kite-flying exercise.

Among the juicy items in subsequent interviews, Scalfari could report that Francis did not believe in immortality of the soul for people dying in a state of mortal sin: They would not be punished in eternal fires but simply "annihilated." According to Scalfari, Francis said that "after death, the souls of individuals who apologize are exculpated by God and participate in his consideration . . . yet the individuals who don't atone, and along these lines can't be absolved, vanish. . . . Damnation does not exist—what exists is the vanishing of corrupt souls." This was of course technically heretical, albeit welcome news to the sinful; as a basic tenet right up front in the official catechism, Catholics believe that the soul *cannot* die.

In another interview, Scalfari reported that Francis had denied the divinity of Jesus Christ during his earthly existence. "Anyone who has had the good fortune to meet with him and speak with him in utmost confidence—as I have done several times," wrote Scalfari, "knows that Pope Francis conceives of Christ as Jesus of Nazareth: a man, not an incarnate god. Once incarnate, Jesus ceases to be a god and becomes a man, until his death on the cross."

What was Francis up to—exposing himself so enthusiastically to the untender mercies of Italy's most notorious religious skeptic, to the extent of being characterized, with supporting quotes, as a careless purveyor of theological nonsense, at least as far as Catholic teaching is concerned?

Whatever the authenticity of Scalfari's reported papal indiscretions, Francis surely must have realized their power to draw in a wide sector of Italian Catholics on the margins. For example, Scalfari likely probed the question of God's infinite love versus hell's eternal torment, and got an answer that retained the doctrine tempered by God's infinite mercy.

By the same token, I can only imagine that Scalfari was probing Francis on the question of Christ's humanity and his divinity, when the tricky question of the theological problem known as the hypostatic union (two natures in one person) came up. Was Christ *really* a human being like you and me? Francis had preached on this theme at a general audience on December 21, 2016. He was talking about hope being a journey, and how God fulfilled his promise made in the words of the prophet Isaiah: "Behold, a young woman shall conceive and bear a son, and shall call his name Immanuel." Francis went on: "God fulfills his promise by becoming human; not abandoning his people, he draws *near to the point of stripping himself of his divinity*. In this way God shows his fidelity and inaugurates a new kingdom which gives a new hope to mankind." It is easy to imagine that Scalfari lost something in theological translation, and that Francis was not too concerned at the garbling of the finer if crucial point of one of the great mysteries of Christian revelation. His aim was not to take Scalfari and his readers through a theological disquisition on theories of hypostasis, but to stress that Jesus is the "one in whom the hope of God and the hope of humanity meet."

In the tradition of Jesuit missionaries down the centuries, Francis was not afraid of disrupting the strict boundaries of doctrine to draw his listeners into a wider understanding. In that same sermon he asked: ". . . is my interior life static, closed? Is my heart a locked drawer or a drawer open to hope . . . ?"

This breaking of strict boundaries, to reach out by adapting doctrine to local culture, was a familiar tactic of Jesuit missionaries in the seventeenth century. Among many instances, the Jesuits on the Huron mission in what is now Ontario requested the mother house back in Rouen, France, to alter the doctrine of transubstantiation, the change of bread and wine into the body and blood of Christ. The Hurons saw the Eucharist as cannibalism; they were not against cannibalism when it came to their enemies, but they never ate their friends!

The adaptation of doctrine to Italy's skeptical, secularist constituencies via Scalfari is reminiscent of the Jesuit accommodations to Confucianism during their long attempt to evangelize China from the seventeenth century onward. The life of the Catholic Church in China indeed posed significant challenges for Francis, as it did to his predecessors John Paul II and Benedict XVI. In the *Annus Horribilis* of 2018, he took an initiative to resolve the circumstance of two rival Catholic Churches and sets of bishops, the government-sponsored Church and the underground Church that had suffered much persecution. Francis took a risk-laden step to interrupt the impasse over the divided Catholic communities in the country. It was another instance of his determination to shift the balance from the center to the local.

CHAPTER SEVENTEEN

THE TWO CHURCHES IN CHINA

Francis Takes Risks for Unity

I n 1955 a pale, haunted-looking priest visited our junior seminary to talk about his experiences as a missionary in China under Mao Zedong. The priest recounted how he was arrested and thrown in jail, where he suffered mental and physical torture for two years. He was subjected to solitary confinement, beatings, starvation, sleep deprivation, and nonstop propaganda. He explained that his tormentors were attempting to induce terror, humiliation, feelings of guilt. It was the first time I heard the term "brainwashing."

The priest said that he was taken eventually to the border with Hong Kong and released. He was free, but his health was permanently broken. He spoke of the courageous priests and faithful still serving the needs of the Church underground. Yet he said little, as I remember, about China's history and culture. He said even less about the history of the Christian missions to China, starting in the eighth century, resuming in the Middle Ages and then again with the Jesuits and Franciscans in the seventeenth century. He confined himself to the evils of atheistic Communism and the stories of current persecutions.

Today there are two forms of Catholic Church in China. The Church that has retained direct links with Rome, its bishops nominated by the pope, its priests ordained by those bishops, is widely referred to as the underground or unofficial Church. It has suffered oppression and harassment and has many martyrs. The other Church, often referred to as the "official" Church, has valid bishops and priests and its sacraments are valid too, but its allegiance is to the regime, which approves its bishops and regulates its activities. This official Church is less persecuted and more prosperous, and it operates openly. It is closer to the pre-Vatican II Church in the West in its liturgies and devotions.

Catholics in China, from both Churches, number about ten million and appear to be in decline, while Protestant Evangelicals are on the rise at sixty or seventy million. The success of the Evangelicals is arguably owed to the movement's strongly indigenous nature, free of foreign control; the capacity of their pastors to work independently in isolation; and their willingness to acquiesce, working with the local authorities and the regime where necessary. Catholics, with their strong links to Rome and the pope, whether official or unofficial, are regarded as a foreign influence.

Richard Madsen, a sociologist specializing in China and a former Maryknoll missionary in the country, describes in his book *China's Catholics* how the two groups, official and unofficial, work together and yet apart. He describes an "official" Church Mass on the Feast of the Assumption at St. Joseph's Cathedral in the northern coastal city of Tianjin. The Assumption is an important feast day for Chinese Catholics. It was a Saturday: The church was packed; the bishop celebrated in Latin in the old rite with his back to the congregation, attended by many acolytes and clouds of incense. About a hundred children made their First Communion, the girls dressed in white dresses and veils.

Meanwhile, outside the cathedral, a group of "underground Catholics" were kneeling, saying the rosary in competition with loudspeakers relaying the service inside. Later, after the official congregation departed, the rival unofficial congregation entered the church for their own Mass in Chinese: These were the inheritors of the Church in communion with Rome who saw themselves as authentic Chinese Catholics. This was just one manifestation of the variety of ways the two Churches operate in China.

Since the Communists came to power in China in 1949, after the protracted civil war, all faiths and their practices have been spasmodically attacked or barely tolerated at best. During the Cultural Revolution (1966 to 1976), hundreds of thousands of places of worship, including temples, mosques, and churches, were confiscated or demolished. Buddhism, Taoism, Islam and Christianity—Catholic and Protestant—only survived through courage and readiness to face persecution. The deaths of thirty-three Trappist monks of the Abbey of Notre Dame de Consolation, slaughtered after a grueling march in 1947, are remembered by Catholics in China to this day, each monk individually by name.

The antagonisms between China's estimated ten million Catholics have been a vexing issue for the papacy ever since Deng Xiaoping's 1978 policy of "reform and opening" following the end of the Cultural Revolution and the death of Mao in 1976. The regime-approved Catholic Church is known as the Chinese Catholic Patriotic Association (CCPA). It was established in 1957 by the regime's Religious Affairs Bureau to supervise and keep a close check on Catholics. The following year Pope Pius XII condemned the CCPA when its bishops consecrated new, Communist-approved bishops. He ordered their excommunication. The unofficial or underground Church, which has maintained communion with the pope, sees itself in continuity with the earlier persecuted Church, uncooperative with the regime; many of their priests suffered, like our seminary visitor back in the 1950s. Today the underground Church is largely supported by foreign charities, especially in the United States, and by Catholics in Hong Kong.

After the death of Mao, Deng Xiaoping allowed the return of religion under a policy promulgated in 1982. The regime apologized for past persecutions, realizing that religion cannot be suppressed easily and that it is best to work with it rather than against it.

As Catholics began to practice with greater confidence and open-ness, the split between the official and the unofficial churches revived. John Paul II hoped for a papal visit. He wrote to Deng pleading for the forging of links between the Vatican and the government. Answer came there none. Benedict XVI wrote to the unofficial Church, referring to the CCPA as "incompatible with Catholic doctrine." Meanwhile a number of the illegitimate bishops were being quietly reconciled to the Holy See via back channels, a fact acknowledged in Benedict's letter.

On his election, Francis was determined to revive contacts and bring to a head the long-running anomalous situation between the two Churches. Amid the tribulations and travails of the *annus horribilis*, 2018, he was involved in secret negotiations with the regime. While dealing with the upheavals of the Viganò affair he reached a discreet "provisional" accord in an attempt to end the seventy-year dispute over the two Churches.

Signed on September 22, 2018, the provisions have not been pub-lished, but reports from various correspondents indicate that the pope would have the final say over the choice of bishops, while the Chinese government would have a role in vetting the short lists. Moreover, the long-term strategy appears to be that the unofficial, underground Church, should acquiesce alongside the official Church, meaning that it subjects itself to the regime's control.

For several groups, within China and outside, the initiative was a betrayal of the underground Church and its many martyrs. Francis was accused by Cardinal Joseph Zen, resident in Hong Kong, of selling out to Xi Jinping. Ever since his consecration as Bishop of Hong Kong, he had been a strong supporter and fundraiser for the underground Church in China, a constant thorn in the side of the Beijing govern-ment. In 2014, a year into Francis's papacy, Zen said that Hong Kong tycoon Jimmy Lai had given him HK$20 million to assist the under-ground Church. The links between wealthy and influential Catholics in Hong Kong and the underground Church have added to the complexity of the situation against the background of Hong Kong pro-democracy riots. Zen has harshly criticized Pope Francis, accusing him of being naïve about the bishops of the CCPA, whom he describes as "slaves."

Funding for the underground Church also comes from the United States, where conservative voices have sternly rejected Francis's China policy. Writing in *National Review*, George Weigel declared: "An immense moral capital is being built up in China by those religious communities that refuse to bend to Communist repression. By contrast, religious communities identified with the regime will bear the stigma of that regime when it collapses, as Communist regimes inevitably do." American Catholic commentators who supported the unofficial Church through their years of persecution were understandably baffled and angry.

Did Francis hope to change the China-Catholic story in the interests of long-term survival? It is tempting to compare the 2018 Rome-China agreement with the treaty negotiated between Hitler and the Holy See in the summer of 1933, known as the Reichskonkordat.

That accord provided that Hitler would guarantee German Catholics the right to practice and educate children in exchange for withdrawal of Catholics from social and political action. In association with the deal, the Catholic Center Party, the last democratic party in Germany, agreed to vote in the Enabling Act that awarded Hitler his dictatorship, and straightaway disbanded itself voluntarily. The treaty demoralized the Catholic opposition, scandalized a younger generation, and made Hitler look acceptable in the eyes of the world. The historian Owen Chadwick called it "one of the most controversial acts in German history."

Under Paul VI three decades later, the Vatican attempted to pursue a concordat between Poland and the Soviet Union. Archbishop Karol Wojtyla, the future John Paul II, blocked the scheme, perhaps influenced by the disaster of the Reichskonkordat. Had he not done so, the events of 1989 and onward might have turned out differently.

There are significant differences, however, between the German accord, and indeed Catholicism in Poland, the Soviet Union in the

1970s, and the situation in China today. The German Church was not divided, nor was it a minority group. Poland's population was predominantly Catholic, and far from divided; the Soviet Union was failing. Ten million Catholics in China's population of 1.4 billion is minuscule. There is little hope that the Catholic population is ever likely to offer any kind of meaningful opposition to Beijing. Francis, who has said little or nothing about his aims in China, may well be seeking to end a situation in which the regime has been dividing and ruling the Chinese Church: a tactic Xi could pursue to the destruction of both groups.

The principal objection to the current secret accord focuses on the nomination of bishops rather than any doctrinal or liturgical issue. The Reichskonkordat was also about nomination of bishops. The Vatican sought to impose the new Code of Canon Law's (1917) insistence that the pope and only the pope should nominate bishops. Yet Eugenio Pacelli, who negotiated the deal, never succeeded in securing that provision in the final treaty. Down the centuries the process of nominating bishops has involved many different practices, depending on local circumstances, even including the laity. Taking the long view, involving the regime to the extent of allowing them a veto on episcopal nominations, might well be entertained by Rome in order to unify the Church in China.

It is possible that Francis is dealing with the regime much as Jesuit missionaries adapted to Chinese imperial officialdom five hundred years earlier. His agreement with the government over nomination of bishops is another example of his capacity to hold opposites in tension and move forward by interruption. Cardinal Parolin, secretary of state in the Vatican and principal negotiator of the accord, said that Francis's secret China deal is the Vatican's vision to "help advance religious freedom, to find normalization for the Catholic community there, and then for all other religions to have space and a role to play in society."

The comment lends encouragement to a view expressed by Richard Madsen, who argues that normalization of relations between the two

Churches, and between the Vatican and Beijing, would create opportunities for Catholics, alongside other Christian denominations and non-Christian religions in China, to encourage the "principles and virtues of civil society." Madsen saw parallels between the two Churches in China and divisions within Catholicism at large:

> ... besides nourishing the flower of faith, martyrdom also produces the thorn of division. It raises the heat in discussions about who is a worthy member of the community. It tempts the community to self-righteousness and even to revenge.

It is undeniable that Francis's China policy is risky, a complex "game" reminiscent of the Chinese board game Go, which involves competing influence and rival territories, where each move can have far-reaching consequences. Ownership of churches and shrines, competing diocesan boundaries and rival bishops, have long created confusion and antagonism, a taste of what schism might mean in the Catholic Church at large.

Other difficulties lie ahead: A papal visit, for example, could require that the Vatican sever relations with Taiwan. Richard Madsen wrote back in 1998 with a degree of prophetic realism when he declared that normalization of the Catholic Church within China could not occur until more liberal-minded successors to John Paul II and Deng Xiaoping are in place. Francis fits the bill, but Xi, the most autocratic leader since Mao, clearly falls well short of it.

Francis has been widely criticized for his silence on the situation of the Uighur Muslims in Xinjiang, drawing comparisons with Pius XII's silence on the Holocaust. It appears out of character for a pope who sought accord with Islam and visited, at personal risk, the oppressed Myanmar Muslims in 2017. In the absence of an explanation it could prove a blot on his papacy.

PART SIX

BELOVED AMAZON

In the Heart of the Church

CHAPTER EIGHTEEN

PACHAMAMAS IN THE SANCTUARY

Francis Brings the Amazon to Rome

On Monday, October 18, 2019, a group of devout young Catholics broke into the church of Santa Maria Transpontina on the grand Via della Conciliazione near the Vatican. They made off with five identical wooden, brightly painted images of a naked pregnant woman, Amerindian in features and decorated with tribal facial marks. The images were placed within a side altar as if forming a shrine. Later the raiders filmed themselves as they cast the objects ceremoniously into the River Tiber. They believed the idols represented Pachamama, the pagan goddess of fertility worshiped in the Amazon region. As they saw it, the presence of the images in a Catholic church was a desecration. The video went viral, as did reactions.

Amid the Twitter storm, a religious sister, styling herself DigitalNun, blogged her view of the peculiar ambiguities of the case: "I am uneasy about the actions of those who threw the statues into the Tiber, just as I was uneasy about their being set up in the first place." She disapproved of the theft and attempted destruction, yet she worried that idolatry had crept into Christian worship at the very heart of Christendom.

There were reports that another Pachamama image took pride of place in the Vatican auditorium where two hundred prelates were gathered under the chairmanship of Francis for a synod on the future of the Amazon. Drawn from the nine countries within the vast Amazon basin that stretches from the Andes in the west to the Atlantic Ocean in the east, participants were to discuss the challenges and the future of the Church in those regions.

Meanwhile, a thirty-second YouTube clip showed Pope Francis blessing a Pachamama in the Vatican gardens before the synod began. The internet was buzzing with indignant expostulations against the desecration of Christian rites; or was it the Christianizing of pagan rites in the heart of the Eternal City by the pope himself? Pachamamas were springing up all over Rome, it seemed.

What was Pope Francis playing at? Was he advocating idolatry? Or was he teaching a lesson in enculturation, the adaptation of Catholic doctrine to local cultural beliefs? Yet who, or what, was being enculturated, the Amazon or the Vatican?

According to several synod prelates the objects were Amazonian images of the Virgin Mary. But Fr. Giacomo Costa, spokesperson for the synod, disagreed: "It is not the Virgin Mary. . . . It is an indigenous woman who represents life." Then a bishop declared: "Probably, those who used this symbol wished to refer to fertility, to women, to life. . . . Amazonia is meant to be full of life."

A Pachamama image also took pride of place when a band of barefoot indigenous people from the Amazon came before the tomb of St. Peter, joined by Francis. They sang the ancient hymn to the Holy Spirit, "Veni Creator Spiritus," then processed out of the basilica bearing a canoe and holding aloft their Pachamama.

Among the many tweets, blogs, and Instagrams, several hundred signatories lent their names to the declaration that "the undersigned Catholic clergy and lay scholars protest against and condemn the sacrilegious and superstitious acts committed by Pope Francis, the Successor of Peter."

Reacting to these accusations of idolatry, an indigenous leader, Delio Siconatz Camaitieri, said: "You are a bit restless, I see . . . perhaps you don't understand what the Amazon needs. Do not harden your hearts, we believe in one God! Do we have our rituals? Yes, but we must integrate them with the heart that is Christ."

Speaking to the crowds in St. Peter's Square, Francis said: "The church is not a fortress, but a tent capable of expanding and offering access to everyone. The Church is 'going out' or it is not the Church, either it is walking, always widening its room so that all may enter or else it is not the Church." It seemed yet another gloss on his oft-repeated phrase about time being superior to space.

At the weekend Pope Francis, evidently seeing the drowning of the images as an act of vandalism, issued an apology not for the presence of the objects but for the deliberate act of iconoclasm that took place: "As bishop of this diocese, I ask forgiveness from those who have been offended by this act." He added that the images had been rescued; that they were undamaged and were in the safekeeping of Italy's police chief.

He also had words for prelates who scoffed at the feathered head-dresses worn by participants at the synod's opening ceremony, including an odd feathered crown he wore on his own head. They should take a good look, he said, at the weird three-cornered hats they like to wear in their own sanctuaries.

The controversial Amazon synod, held in Rome during October 2019, was an event Francis had planned from the beginning of his papacy. He recognized the importance of Latin America, home of some 43 percent of all Catholics, and the Church's current center of gravity. The faithful of the Amazon region suffer widespread poverty, endangered indigenous communities, unemployment, racism, homelessness, lack of schooling and health care; the indigenous peoples are oppressed moreover by devastation of the rain forests due to slash-and-burn agriculture, extraction, and pollution. The synod was the first meeting of its kind to focus on a specific territory, bringing together all its bishops. It has been estimated that it was preceded by consultations spread over two years involving some 50,000 people. It would come to be known as the synod that openly discussed the possibility of a married priesthood, but the delegates were principally preoccupied with the sufferings and privations of indigenous peoples, and the environmental catastrophe exploding in the rain forests.

As a prelude to the synod, Francis brought the Amazon right into the Vatican sanctuary. Yet he had also taken himself out to the peripheries, visiting that one year alone no less than eleven countries on the Church's margins. Crisscrossing the planet, he signaled his concern for migrants, poverty, indigenous people, and the environment, reaching out to non-Catholic Christianity and to other religions, especially Islam and Judaism. His destinations that year included Panama, Romania, Morocco, the United Arab Emirates, and Japan. In Tokyo the students and faculty of Sophia University presented him with a sculpture of Kannon, a Buddhist goddess of mercy, who resembles images of the Virgin Mary; during the persecutions of Christianity in Japan, the faithful would pray to Kannon's image, seeing in her the presence the Mother of God. Kannon was, in turn, an adaptation of Hindu deity Guanyin. The incident echoed the papal reverence paid to the Pachamama of the Amazon.

Among the many synod declarations and recommendations on the circumstances of poverty, the synod bishops, all from Latin America, voted 128 to 41 to allow married men of proven maturity and goodness of life to be ordained as priests where there was an absence of clergy. They also voted that a commission should study the possibility of ordaining women as deacons.

The Church now awaited the response from Francis in the form of the document known as an "apostolic exhortation." For many, the seven years of his papacy led up to that point. Some speculated that it was the "defining" moment of his pontificate. As it happened, he would remain silent on the prospects for married priests or for deaconesses. The response to the synod would disappoint all those liberals who were hoping for the immediate opening up of priesthood to married men.

Against the background of the synod and the controversies over a married priesthood, the "Two Pope" situation and the Francis-Scalfari "odd couple" relationship were about to assume an extraordinary new significance, demonstrating Francis's talent for resilience and irony.

In the first half of January 2020, Benedict became involved in a row over a book titled *From the Depths of Our Hearts: Priesthood, Celibacy, and the Crisis in the Catholic Church*. The book was promoted as a coauthored work by "Benedict XVI/ Robert Cardinal Sarah" (Sarah was the seventy-four-year-old prefect of the Congregation of Divine Worship, originally from Guinea, who was publicly reproved by Francis for his extreme traditionalist views.) The preface and conclusion were signed by both, and their names appeared prominently and coequally on the cover: To the amazement of many, the resigned pope was presented as Benedict XVI without the "Emeritus" above a photograph of the former pontiff in his prime. Benedict was also credited solely with the authorship of one of the chapters. In an excerpt that ran in *Le Figaro*, Benedict appeared to have written: "I believe that celibacy has great significance as an abandonment of an earthly realm," and that for priests staying on the path to God, "celibacy becomes really essential." The coauthors also stated in the allegedly joint introduction that following St. Augustine of Hippo they cannot remain silent: "*Silere non possum.*" And that allowing married men to become priests would put the Church in grave danger.

The publication of a book extolling the merits of priestly celibacy, written by two elderly senior prelates, one of them an ex-pope and world-class theologian, might have appeared unremarkable in any other circumstance. Unfortunately, the publication seemed timed to the release of Francis's apostolic exhortation, the summation of his deliberations on the Amazon synod, and his response to calls for ordination of married deacons in the Amazon region.

The media reaction was effervescent. Was Benedict interfering with the teaching role of his successor? Or was he being manipulated? A headline in the *New York Times* expressed the nub of the matter: "Two Popes and One Big Furor After Benedict Weighs in on Priestly Celibacy." In reaction to the gathering storm, *Vatican News* published a note asserting that the book was written in "filial obedience to Pope Francis" and "in a spirit of love for the unity of the Church."

Benedict's minder, Archbishop Gänswein, lost no time attempting to defuse the situation by issuing a denial of the coauthorship via the Italian news service, ANSA. Benedict's name and photograph on the cover were to be withdrawn. But whose idea was it to present the coauthorship in the first place? If it wasn't Benedict, then it was surely Cardinal Sarah. And what role had Benedict's secretary and constant companion played? And how was the coauthorship to be rescinded? The French translation, published by Editions Fayard, was already in the bookshops. The English-language version was not due out for several weeks; but the publisher, Ignatius Press of San Francisco, refused to alter the coauthorship citations or remove Benedict's photograph from the cover.

Meanwhile, Cardinal Sarah jumped to his own defense on social media: "The polemic that has sought to smear me . . . by insinuating that Benedict XVI was not informed of the publication of the book *From the Depths of Our Hearts* is deeply abject. . . . I sincerely forgive all those who slander me or who want to oppose me to Pope Francis. My attachment to Benedict XVI remains intact and my filial obeisance to Pope Francis remains absolute." But no sooner had he expressed his ever-so-holy attachment to Benedict than he put the aged ex-pope in the wrong by implication. On January 14, Sarah published correspondence showing that Benedict had indeed seen and approved the text of the book, including the introduction, the conclusion, and the cover. So what now? Next Sarah reported that he had met with Benedict in person, and there was "not one misunderstanding" between them.

Apart from the immediate dispute over editorial understandings and misunderstandings, the affair, instantly dubbed Bookgate, illustrated yet again the inherent dangers of two living popes, or rather a living pope and an active "undead" one, living side by side. Should a resigning pope be allowed to stay on within the Vatican, still dressed in white, still retaining his papal title, still publicly involved with doctrinal matters, with scope to call the current pope's doctrinal authority in question?

The harsh criticisms of Cardinal Sarah, a hero of the conservatives, provoked an enraged response from the pen of George Weigel. He took to the pages of *First Things* to claim that the retired pope and his coauthor, Cardinal Sarah, were being "bullied" by the liberal media. He wrote of the "calumnies," the eruption of "online hysteria," "the cacophony," "the extraordinary venom spewed at the pope emeritus and the cardinal." The attack on Benedict was "exceptionally nasty—and deeply ill-informed," the attack on Cardinal Sarah "was equally vicious—and just as ill-informed." The piece gives a vivid sense of the deplorable state of conflict within the Catholic media. Yet what enraged Weigel most about the attacks was the claim that Benedict was ailing mentally, whereas the aged pope's mind, Weigel could confirm, was "clear as a bell." Above all, however, the "calumnies were amplified" by the vindictive and untruthful charge that the coauthors were interfering with the "discernment" of Pope Francis, "that the theological and pastoral defense of clerical celibacy is an act of disloyalty to Pope Francis; and that they should just shut up."

According to his usual practice, Francis made no official comment on the row. Instead he opted to engage in a characteristic display of disruption. Bypassing his own press aides, he took into his confidence his favorite outsider columnist, the nonagenarian atheist Scalfari. The consequent piece appeared in *La Repubblica*, Scalfari admitting that he had not actually written a shorthand note of what Francis said, but had made a "loose reconstruction."

Scalfari started by characterizing the coauthored book in question as part of an opposition campaign led by Cardinal Sarah against Francis. "The Emeritus Pope," he wrote, "had received a request from Cardinal Sarah for a text on priestly celibacy." Scalfari then launched into his account of the controversy:

Sarah was against Francis on celibacy and expected Benedict to make common cause with him. Benedict produced a text which formed a contribution to the polemical book Sarah submitted to the publisher. Most major Italian periodicals headlined the story which, had it been true, would have sparked a major row, assembling under the banners of a cardinal and emeritus pope, resigned but active, a constituency of truculent bishops unhappy with the pope, so putting Pope Francis in difficulty. . . . So Ratzinger declared that he had not sided with Sarah, nor had he authorized a coauthored book with him. Hence Benedict offered Francis his entire support.

Scalfari concluded: "Our Pope didn't take the Sarah faction seriously, and he accepted Ratzinger's brotherly support on the day we met." The support was of course that Benedict repudiated his joint authorship of the book, thus scuppering any claims that he, the emeritus, was attempting to outflank the reigning pope. Scalfari went on to ask Francis "what his inner reaction was to the existence of a group in opposition to his pontificate." The pope allegedly responded that: "there is always someone opposed in an organization that embraces hundreds of millions of people around the world." Scalfari concluded that the issue with Ratzinger was therefore closed—"*caso e chiuso*"—"... and the small or great opposition that still remains standing ought to be considered a fairly normal phenomenon in such structures."

All the same, the "unofficial" nature of the information, and the source, could always be modified, emphasized, or denied at a later date if it were deemed necessary. The circumstance reminded me of an early lesson I was given by a Curial source on the difference between Vatican information that is *officioso* as opposed to *unofficioso*. Unofficial information had its uses and considerable power; yet it could always be finessed, as circumstances required. Or it could be withdrawn invoking the scholastic principle: *quod gratis asseritur, gratis negatur*, "what is freely asserted is freely denied."

CHAPTER NINETEEN

AMAZON SYNOD

Priestly Celibacy and the Rain Forests

I n February 2005, a seventy-three-year-old American nun, Sister Dorothy Stang, was gunned down on a dirt road in the state of Para, a region of the Amazon basin in northern Brazil. She was on her way to a community meeting when she was accosted by two armed men—Clodoaldo Carlos Batista and Raifran das Neves Sales, employees of a livestock company. Sales shot her in the stomach. As she fell face down on the ground he fired another round into her back before shooting her in the head four times. She had been defending small farmers in the area by attempting to thwart plans to extend big cattle ranching.

Brought up in Ohio, one of nine children, Sister Dorothy lived and worked for forty years alongside four other religious sisters, educating the poor of the region and working with the Pastoral Land Commission, which defends the rights of rural workers. She set up twenty-one communities working with local people on agriculture and sustainable development projects, housing, and school construction. She raised funds to finance the building of a dam to generate electricity and campaigned against the sequestration of land, forest, and water by big business. As a teacher she trained faith leaders. Her death revealed the breadth of a missionary vocation in the Amazon region and its perils.

In honor of Sister Dorothy, Francis issued his Amazon letter (apostolic exhortation) to the world on the fifteenth anniversary of her death—February 12, 2020. Entitled *Querida Amazonia*, Beloved Amazon, the document expressed his considered thoughts on the three-week Amazon synod held the previous October. Both sides of the Catholic media divide had awaited the publication with heightened anticipation.

A week before its appearance, LifeSiteNews ran a comment headlined: "Pope Francis's post-Amazon Synod Exhortation Could Be Worse Than Everyone Thinks." Robert Royal, the American Catholic writer and social scientist, warned readers to brace themselves for Francis's support for a married priesthood. It would be a disaster leading to schism, he averred. By the end of the piece, however, he wondered whether Francis might retreat and leave the celibacy rule unaltered. Yet this would not be due, he wrote, to the pope's own discernment on the matter so much as the timely influence of the Benedict/Sarah book. Either way, he insisted, Francis was about to be reckless, or a coward. He concluded that "virtually everything in the Church is up for grabs, not only celibacy and deaconesses, but marriage, sexuality, Hell, the Devil, Communion, teaching authority." If nothing else, this kind of commentary demonstrated that Francis could not win, could not be allowed to win, whatever he did or said, or did not do or say.

In the event, *Beloved Amazon*, when it appeared, failed to fulfill Royal's expectations. The document was a passionately written plea for the defense of a region and its peoples under threat from commercial and social exploitation. While focusing on the particular issues of unemployment, poverty, migration, and oppression, the exhortation transcended the political and economic perspectives by invoking the spiritual dimension of their forest environment as creation. Francis did not mention the married priest proposal, nor women deacons; and, according to reliable reports, the document had been completed for the press on December 27, well ahead of the Benedict/Sarah book.

———————

At 15,000 words, the exhortation *Beloved Amazon* is written in Spanish with wide-ranging citations of Latin American writers: Mario Vargas

Llosa, Pablo Neruda, Vinicius de Moraes, Ana Varela, Tafur Jorge Vega Marques.

With climactic disasters unfolding around the world from Brazil to Australia, the gentleness of Francis's tone does not obscure his anger and sorrow for the natural environment and everyday injustices and perils suffered by the people of the *selva*; nor the courage of the Christian pastors, missionaries like Sister Dorothy Stang, and the many volunteers, indigenous and foreign, men and women, working in the Amazon region. The poetic note of the writing is striking as he pleads for the world to understand the Amazon in terms of a personal love relationship involving the creator rather than an exploitable commodity.

He dreams, he writes, of a region that struggles for the rights of the poor, especially among the indigenous, who are suffering from the greed of foreign and local businesses plundering their natural habitats. He deplores the circumstance in which peoples are "considered more an obstacle needing to be eliminated than as human beings with the same dignity as others and possessed of their own acquired rights." Concern for the environment, he declares, is inseparable from concern for people.

Next he dreams of a world that recognizes the cultural value of the Amazon. The globalized economy is threatening "human, social and cultural wealth . . . each distinct group in a vital synthesis with its surroundings, developing its own form of wisdom."

He repeats themes from *Laudato Si'* and its meditation on the environment as God's creation in which everything is connected. The care of people and the care of ecosystems, he declares, are inseparable. He writes of enculturation whereby the Church "reshapes her identity through listening and dialogue with the people, the realities and the history of the land in which she finds herself." There are reminders here of the Pachamama upset. He is pleading for "new faces with Amazonian features," moving beyond an imported Church of European culture.

Then he talks about how the Church's teaching should manifest itself in time and place in a manner transformed by its locale and peculiar culture. Finally, he addresses the problem of bringing the Eucharist to remote places where there are no priests. He does not ask for a change to the celibacy rule. He pleads for more vocations, especially for missionary priests, and greater participation of the laity, women in particular. No mention of ordaining women as deacons. So he has sidestepped the two issues that had created so much consternation, for and against.

The reception of the exhortation revealed, once again, the crosscurrents and whirlpools of media coverage outside the Church and within it. The *Washington Post* announced that Francis "backs away from a potentially major reform." The *New York Times* headlined that Francis "rejects proposal to allow married priests in remote areas." Damian Thompson, a fervid traditionalist, writing in Britain's conservative weekly *Spectator*, wrote that "The only thing we can say for certain about *Querida Amazonia* is that the Pope has thrown his professional sycophants under the bus." He meant—all liberals. He went on to predict that the disappointment will be "unendurable" for the liberals who had been pinning their hopes on the beginning of the end to the celibacy rule for clergy as the beginning of the end of clericalism and a harbinger of a female priesthood.

If the liberals found the exhortation unendurable they were managing to control their hysteria reasonably well, but the disappointment was palpable. Heidi Schlumpf of the liberal, usually Francis-friendly *National Catholic Reporter*, reported reactions among clergy and laity in the liberal wing of the Church, confirming that Francis had "disappointed those hoping for an opening of clerical roles to married men and women, with many noting that the pope failed to extend his prophetic voice about environmental injustice to injustices in his own house, the church." She added that "many women were especially outraged over the document's language of complementarity."

Two crucial suggestions of the final report needed the go-ahead from Francis: One was the formation of a group of bishops special to the Amazon basin; the other was a liturgical rite, a form of religious ceremony and regular prayer life, special to its peoples. This would necessarily involve, again, enculturation: the languages and culture of the peoples, and recognition that so many of the Catholic communities are led by laypeople, more than half of whom were women. A Church with Amazonian features, Francis wrote, requires the stable presence of mature and lay leaders endowed with authority. Referring to the Pachamama figures that prompted accusations of idolatry, he said: "It is possible to take up an indigenous symbol in some way, without necessarily considering it idolatry . . . a myth charged with spiritual meaning can be used to advantage and not always considered a pagan error."

For the papal biographer Austen Ivereigh, however, there were no disappointments. Francis, he argued, had other, more important goals in his sights. The document, Ivereigh went on, was "less about avoiding conflict than about seeing another path where the Holy Spirit is calling the Church." Instead of resolving the opposing views, left versus right, or choosing one over the other, Francis was keeping the polarities in tension in order to transcend them:

> [T]he mistake is to try to resolve it by allowing one side to defeat the other. Rather, by patiently and attentively holding together the polarity— positions that pull in a different direction— the leader allows for the possibility of a "third way" that the Holy Spirit offers.

Francis was not entirely explicit about the "third way"; and perhaps that was deliberate. It was something to be discovered by the local Church without rules and regulations from the center, under the guidance of the synod final report, or as Francis would say—the Holy Spirit.

———————

The role of women in the Amazon's future, and in parallel with the Church in the world, was central. It was bound to be contentious.

Francis wrote that women should play a central role; that their "services entail stability, public recognition, and a commission from the bishop . . . while continuing to do so in a way that reflects their womanhood." He wrote of the "tender strength of Mary" and suggested that clericalization of women would hamper their role. Just as he was trying to reform harmful clericalism, he appeared to be saying, why should women be encouraged to become clerics? There was a progressive view, after all, that sought the desacralization of the priesthood, as the only way of rooting out the worst aspects of clericalism. By this view women were no more in need of a sacralized vocation than men.

But the theologian Massimo Faggioli found Francis's language on women "typically and woefully inadequate" while the effusive praise of the "feminine" was "counterproductive." Feminist theologians went further, arguing that Francis was exemplifying men with creation and women with the created, that men represented Christ while women represented the Virgin Mary. In a stinging essay in *The Tablet*, Professor Tina Beattie, a theologian at Roehampton University in London, charged that Francis was woefully ignorant of ecofeminist studies that identified nature with womanhood and womanhood with nature, not as the vulnerable sweet Virgin in need of protection by the male archetype, but as the Mother Earth figure of "awesome maternal potency." She charged that Francis's concept of woman was "mired in a sentimental fantasy." In the "real world, gender roles and identities are agile and malleable," but Francis, she wrote, imagines woman as an archetype "frozen in time, its function being to 'soften' male culture with feminine tenderness and receptivity."

Undoubtedly Francis's attitude toward women was colored by his generation and background; nor would one expect the aging Argentine Jesuit to be abreast of studies in gender fluidity and ecofeminism. Yet her criticisms along with many others from left and right were perhaps equally frozen in the view that a pope should be an all-knowing, all-wise, and a virtually infallible source of magisterial ratiocinations.

One of the more surprising reactions to *Beloved Amazonia* was that of Cardinal Müller, who had clashed with Francis over Communion for the divorced. The cardinal, as if with a deep sigh of relief, saw the exhortation as a bid "to ensure a harmonious, creative, and fruitful reception of the whole synodal process." Noting that the letter is written in a "personal and attractive tone," the cardinal wrote that he was convinced that the "Pope does not want to fuel existing political, ethnic, and inner-Church conflicts and conflicts of interest, but rather to overcome them." The pope, he wrote, "wants to win all Catholics and Christians of other denominations, but also all people of good will for a positive development of this region."

Commenting on the first three chapters, he wrote that the text had "the liberating power of the gospel of Christ and not an academic study . . . [and a] reconciling effect of reducing internal Church factions, ideological fixations, and the danger of inner emigration or open resistance." He hoped that the interpreters would refrain from unnecessary harshness and take up the concerns of the Holy Father like true sons and daughters of the Church "in a spirit of agreement and collaboration." He ended with a homiletic trope, declaring that divine providence would resolve the absence of priests. "Let us simply leave the last word to the Lord in this overwrought discussion. . . . 'The harvest is abundant but the laborers are few; so ask the master of the harvest to send out laborers for his harvest.'"

Francis had disrupted notions of what was widely expected of the papacy, and the inference to be drawn by his admission that he was not all-knowing, all-powerful, was yet to sink in. It began with his assertion that his exhortation was not meant to replace the final document of the Amazon synod, but was more a set of marginal glosses. He asserted: "I have preferred not to cite the Final Document in this Exhortation, because I would encourage everyone to read it in full." He was saying that it was up to individual souls and local communities to apply their own rediscovery of Christian evangelization.

Even in the case of married priests, Francis had not given the go-ahead; but neither had he definitively ruled it out. The discussion had been initiated at the synod, and there was every possibility that the Church would come to it little by little. As Cardinal Martini warned in his interview with me in 1993, change within the Church needs a sense of gathering momentum to discover the way through a dilemma, while avoiding splits much greater than the Lefebvre split following the Second Vatican Council.

The entire process of the synod, the Final Document, and the exhortation, choreographed by Francis, indicated what the Catholic writer and Jesuit Tom Reese described as a change to "business as usual in the church." The synod's final document, Reese wrote, "profited from the participation of many people who know better than the pope or the Roman Curia the problems and issues of the Amazon region, since they live there, they experience its suffering, and they love it passionately." Don't just read it, Francis was saying: Apply it.

The point of a synod was the collective journey of those for whom the issues were crucial, those who were living through the concerns that were raised. A synod could only work if the participants took responsibility and came to the solutions "little by little." It was not going to work if people always looked to the pope for every answer. Francis had clearly demonstrated a historic shift by altering the relationship between the final document of the synod and his papal exhortation.

CHAPTER TWENTY

WORLD, INTERRUPTED

Francis in the Time of Coronavirus

O ne evening in the week before Easter 2020, as coronavirus deaths mounted throughout Italy and the world, Francis stood looking out over the empty square of St. Peter's. It was dark, raining; he was a lone white figure shimmering in a spotlight, the city silent save for the distinctive Italian clarion sound of ambulances taking patients to hospitals. An icon of Mary the Protectress of the Romans was on display. Francis prayed before the image, then kissed a crucifix that had reputedly saved the city from plague in the sixteenth century. His text was from Mark, where Jesus and his disciples are caught in a storm. Jesus is fast asleep and the frantic disciples wake him whereupon he counsels faith and hope.

Even as commentators were still worrying over the institutional and doctrinal status of the Amazon synod and the exhortation, the coronavirus had been spreading in Wuhan, China. It was soon to reach Rome and the Vatican. The first cases were reported in Italy on January 31, 2020, when two Chinese visitors tested positive. By late February clusters of new cases were reported in Lombardy, in northern Italy. In late February it was reported that Francis was suffering from "an indisposition"; it turned out to be a common cold. But several Vatican bureaucrats came down with the virus and were isolated.

By early March the disease was spreading apace throughout the country and across the world.

Francis had isolated himself as best he could and used the available technology to livestream services, homilies, and addresses, amid messages of hope, prayers for the sick and dying, and encouragement and praise for medical and essential workers. All the evidence is that he carried on his usual varied workload.

On March 11, Italy's prime minister, Giuseppe Conte, announced the shutdown of all nonessential businesses save for food shops and pharmacies, ordering people to stay at home unless employed in essential services. On March 12, the papal vicar of the diocese of Rome, Cardinal Angelo De Donatis, ordered that all churches be closed. The next day, after talking with Francis, he announced that while public Masses would be cancelled, the churches should remain open for lone visits keeping social distance from other worshipers. By the third week of March some fifty priests had died of the virus in Italy. Many were elderly; most had been working pastorally among the sick.

Laudato Si' and the Amazon document were written against the background of the looming, irreversible environmental disaster of global warming. The pandemic also revealed, if any needed reminding, the potentially fragile interrelationship between human beings and the natural environment. Governments and health systems were struggling with immediate problems of testing and providing intensive care beds, respirators, and protective clothing. Meanwhile the economic and social fallout added parallel dimensions of future calamity. The world appeared headed for a historic recession; whole industries, businesses large and small, faced bankruptcy, with mass unemployment and a sweep of new poverty in its wake.

Even as governments struggled with present emergencies, there were voices urging new thinking on the environment, globalization, labor, and the complex relationships between societies and the earth's ecology. Francis's message in *Laudato Si'* and *Beloved Amazon*, as well as frequent, impassioned addresses throughout the world over the previous seven years, now appeared prophetic as the pandemic unfolded.

On September 20, 2018, he spoke to a disabled workers' group on the theme of value and work: "Our world needs a burst of humanity, which leads [us] to open our eyes and see that he who is before him is not a commodity, but a person and a brother in humanity." He spoke heatedly of the exploitation and enslavement rooted in a utilitarian conception of the human person and the need for society to go beyond the false and damaging equivalence between work and productivity.

The "burst of humanity" responding to the pandemic prompted echoes of his views, voiced by economists, political theorists, world leaders, and public opinion around the world. In light of the risks and caring self-sacrifice of frontline health workers, there was widespread talk of ensuring "redistribution of respect" beyond the crisis. As the coronavirus epidemic and fatalities increased, the global warming crisis was not entirely marginalized by commentators. Parallels with climate change were made with the damaging consequences of slower or reversed economies as well as environmental benefits in conservation and pollution reduction. *Laudato Si'* argued for the interconnectedness of the entire planet, human-ecological-economic-political-spiritual. This compelling view of the world, increasingly referred to as the Anthropocene, stood to offer a vision of hope beyond the COVID-19 global interruption.

According to an Oxford University research team, 71 percent of Europeans were now in favor of a universal basic income, a policy long urged by Francis. Emmanuel Macron and Angela Merkel proved receptive to his calls for debt relief and economic stimulus in parts of Africa, Latin America, and Asia.

On March 28 Francis sent a handwritten letter to a social rights judge in Argentina. He wrote of the universal anxiety at the "geometric progression of the pandemic"; that health and life were the priority to avoid "a viral genocide (*genocidio virosico*)"; that the world must avoid the potential future consequences of the pandemic: the spread of hunger, unemployment, violence, loan sharking—"the true plague of dehumanized delinquents" (already experienced in Italy as the Mafia took advantage of the situation).

He ended by recommending the vision of the London-based Italo-American economist Mariana Mazzucato, with her condemnation of a kind of global economy that chooses extraction of value rather than its creation. He was referring to her 2018 book, *The Value of Everything: Making and Taking in the Global Economy*, which calls for a stronger role for the public sector in the economy. "I believe [her vision] can help to think about the future," he wrote. He informed the judge that the department he had established for integral development was inspired by Mazzucato's ideas.

Her book argues that when "value extraction" substitutes for "value creation," the result may well be a rise in GDP, yet wealth is concentrated increasingly in the hands of the few and inequality becomes rampant. Francis, in accord with economists like Thomas Piketty and Joseph Stiglitz, consistently criticized reliance on the "trickle-down" effect to eradicate poverty, pointing to inequalities caused by globalization. Francis's notions of "value," however, extended beyond standard accounts of the "common good" to a Franciscan vision of a spirituality that sees the relationship between human beings and nature as graced by creation.

After Easter 2020, in the midst of the pandemic, he published "a plan for the rising up again," *Un plan para resucitar,* in the Spanish weekly *Vida Nueva.* Reflecting on worldwide suffering and the hope of the Resurrection, he wrote that "we live surrounded by an atmosphere of pain and uncertainty . . . we ask who will roll away the stone?" The stone, like the pandemic, "threatens to bury all hope," especially for the isolated elderly, the poor, the exhausted and overwhelmed carers on the frontlines. They ask, he wrote, "Who will roll away the stone? . . . But the Lord goes before us on our journey and removes the stones that paralyze us."

Signaling the sufferings caused by racism and xenophobia, he went on to say that the pandemic was an opportunity in which the Holy

Spirit could inspire a new imagination "to make new things . . . frontiers fall, walls crumble, and all the discourse of the fundamentalists dissolves in the face of an imperceptible presence which shows the fragility of which we are made." At this moment in history, Francis declared, we have also understood that for better or worse all our actions affect others because everything is connected in our common home. He went on to speak of other epidemics: poverty, unemployment, hunger, racism, pollution, the coming consequences of global warming. He concluded that we should look to "the necessary antibodies of justice, charity, and solidarity," leading to "a civilization of hope" as opposed to a civilization of "anguish and fear."

During the course of the pandemic Francis offered daily prayers and homilies to encourage the faithful and inspire hope in the world at large. Catholics across the world experienced many spiritual privations: the suspension of the sacrament of healing; the ban on gatherings for weddings, baptisms, and funerals; above all, the deprivation of Holy Communion at Mass. The storm of tweets and blogs on the enforced withdrawal of the Eucharist revealed how much it was missed, valued, needed. There was an irony indeed in the reflection that the call for ordaining married men in the Amazon was an attempt to satisfy a hunger for the Eucharist in response to the dearth of priests there; that there were places where Catholics were permanently deprived of the Eucharist for many months and even years. Now that hunger was being felt among Catholics around the world. Among the many recommendations Francis made about prayer and worship during the pandemic was his call for another kind of Communion.

Like many cradle Catholics of my generation, I was taught in childhood about "Spiritual Communion." In the run-up to making our First Communion we were supposed to feel deprived of the Eucharist. So to comfort ourselves we were told we should come close to Jesus in an act of imagination. We were encouraged to think about Jesus as a close friend who was with us whenever we chose to think about him. The nuns who taught us were careful to avoid the impression that this companionship could ever be a substitute for actual Eucharist. In later years, even in the seminary, it was never discussed or recommended again.

During the pandemic Francis started to talk of that same "Spiritual Communion" during his livestreamed early morning Mass. He varied the words from day to day, but he also provided a formal prayer based on a tradition known as Communion "by desire"—practiced by mystics and pastors down the centuries, including during epidemics of the past, like the Black Death, when many priests died and people were cut off from the Eucharist in church. This was his prayer, first broadcast on March 21, 2020: "I embrace You as if You were already there and unite myself wholly to You."

Francis was also advising priests to use that pastoral "economy" practiced in the Eastern Orthodox Churches to provide spiritual care in exceptional circumstances. He spoke of an Italian bishop who had called him on the phone, worried about giving absolution for sins outside of formal individual Confession. Francis said that the priest had consulted canon lawyers who said that it should not be done. Francis told him: "Bishop, fulfill your priestly duty." The bishop took it as a green light. Francis said: "I found out later that he was giving absolution all around the place."

As the pandemic progressed across the world, clergy wondered whether there would ever be a bounce back once the emergency was over. Writing in *The Tablet* on May 16, 2020, sociologist Stephen Bullivant predicted that with fewer priests, many of them aged and vulnerable to the disease, and fewer laypeople, the shrinking of Mass attendance would likely be accelerated.

Francis appeared to be well aware of this. At his Easter Sunday Mass in 2020 in an empty basilica, attended by a handful of assistants who had self-isolated with him in Santa Marta, he gave an address to the city and the world, *Urbi et Orbi*, in which he talked of Easter as the contagion of hope in the midst of the contagion of the virus. "Like a new flame this Good News springs up in the night: the night of a world already faced with epochal challenges and now oppressed by a pandemic severely testing our whole human frailty," he said. "The Church's voice rings out: 'Christ, my hope, has arisen!'" A very different contagion was in prospect: "It is the contagion of hope."

On October 3, 2020, Francis issued a lengthy letter, an encyclical, to the entire human race, Catholic and non-Catholic, titled *Fratelli Tutti*, by which he meant "to all brothers and sisters" (although he would be castigated for not explicitly articulating "sisters"). It is an extended sermon pleading for radical change in a post-coronavirus world: for societies more caring of those in need, less governed by naked market capitalism. Once again, he criticizes the assumption that trickle-down economics solves the crises of poverty; once again, he insists that wealth creation must be accompanied by fairer wealth distribution.

He calls for the banning of capital punishment, rejection of war, and repudiation of populism and populist leaders who pander to the "basest and most selfish inclinations."

The encyclical appeals to our universal sibling bonds, our brotherhood and sisterhood in the spirit of St. Francis, as a basis for social democracy. Francis expresses his sadness for all those who have suffered and died throughout the pandemic, especially those who lacked treatment because of unequal distribution of medical resources. "Once this health crisis passes," he writes, "our worst response would be to plunge even more deeply into feverish consumerism and new forms of egotistic self-preservation."

PART SEVEN

CONTAGION OF HOPE

The Legacy of Francis

CHAPTER TWENTY-ONE

THE FRANCIS EFFECT

Opposing Verdicts on Francis

By the seventh year of Francis's papacy, the harsh verdicts of many conservatives on the papacy were settled and unremitting—ranging from more-in-sorrow-than-in-anger to acerbic to enraged. The more severe attacks added to the pressures on him, including the barrage from Viganò; yet he showed remarkable resilience. On the plane back from Madagascar in 2019, he said: "Of criticisms, I always see the advantages. Sometimes you get angry, but the advantages are there. . . . I do not like it when critics are under the table. They smile, they let you see their teeth and then they stab you in the back. This is not loyal, not human."

People of my generation grew up in a militant, defensive Church that viewed criticism of a living or recently dead pope as disloyalty to the Church. After the Second Vatican Council it became routine to criticize popes, and the liberals led the way, starting with criticism of Paul VI over his position on contraception, and especially of John Paul II and Benedict for their conservatism. Yet the criticisms of these popes were reasonably polite. At the same time, and paradoxically, the Vatican embarked on the serial beatification of recently deceased popes, creating a kind of dead saintly popes society. Even popes whose reigns had been controversial, such as Pius IX, got promoted (a gang tried to throw his coffin into the Tiber as the cortege made its way to his resting place). In the view of liberals, it was a purely political move to counterbalance the beatification of John XXIII.

The busy papal sainting project has been boosted by the abolition of the role of devil's advocate under John Paul II (one wonders how his own canonization process might have prospered under a tough devil's advocate). John Paul II allowed that "outsiders" should nevertheless be heard; hence he countenanced a sharp critique against Mother Teresa by Christopher Hitchens in the run-up to her beatification in 2003.

Yet adjudicators within the saint-making department are hardly equal opportunity hosts to criticism. I've yet to hear that a critic of Pius XII has been given a hearing by the Vatican. At the same time such critics are instantly labeled as "smearers" by the conservative media. When Professor Hubert Wolf of Münster University produced evidence from the recently opened Pius XII archive that the wartime pope was anti-Semitic, he was instantly dubbed a "detractor" in the *National Catholic Register*.

———————

The relentless opposition to Francis came in two forms. There were the prelates around the world, and members of the Curia within the Vatican, engaged in passive resistance, sitting out the papacy and waiting for it to end while giving the impression that they endorsed his agenda. There were members of the Curia and other senior cardinals, like Sarah and Burke, who showed positive resistance by giving interviews and addresses, or collaborating in books—disagreeing with Francis publicly, albeit with cold politesse. Mostly these critics would disparage Francis by inference, when talking in general terms about the state of the Church. "Every day," declared Cardinal Sarah, "I receive calls for help from everywhere from those who no longer know what they are to believe. Every day in Rome, I receive discouraged and suffering priests. The Church is going through the dark night."

Then there were the open enemies: the well-funded media platforms without paywalls attacking the pope 24/7; and, in parallel, the book-length condemnations in which authors spread themselves to build a case for the prosecution.

The rage, and contempt, of the conservative extremes clearly stemmed from a belief that everything they believed and held dear was under existential threat as a result of this papacy. There was, and ever had been since the end of the Second Vatican Council, a genuine anxiety about excesses of "reforms" that went haywire. Henri de Lubac, one of the great *Nouvelle Théologie* advisory figures at the council, eventually came to warn of the "resentment against the abuses of yesterday producing blindness to the benefits of the past." His sorrow and anger were registered at length in his *Motherhood of the Church,* published in English translation in 1982. A selection of his charges gives an impression of legitimate conservative grievances: disdain of tradition, the overweening arrogance of theologians, pressure groups appropriating the media, rejection of dogmatics, "a full flowering of pseudo-prophetic pretensions," and a "moral laxity presented as the mature person's irreversible progress."

Conservatives in those early days after the Council were also reacting to the understandable loss of traditional liturgies, poor translations of Scriptures, and such "abominations" as guitar playing and tambourines in church; Mass around the coffee table celebrated with Coca-Cola and bagels. The aberrations began to extend further across the boundaries of orthodoxy and into the realms of hippiedom and the New Age. Father Matthew Fox, along with his associate Starhawk, billed as a white witch, dabbled in ecological spirituality. Father Stephen Dunn, a Passionist priest and professor of Christian Ethics in the Toronto School of Theology, developed a spirituality known as the Cosmic Mass and devotion to the Mother Earth. Fox published an open letter in the form of a full-page display advertisement denouncing Ratzinger; he invited the cardinal to do circle dances with women and men, old and young, in search of "authentic spirituality."

Critics made an all too easy shift from such antics to Francis's inclusion of the environment as matter of theological and moral concern.

There was also a crude attempt to charge him with Satanism and official support of the LGBT movement. The letter to bishops, signed by certain theologians and clergy in April 2019, including Father Aidan Nichols OP, contained this item: "At the opening mass of the Synod on Youth in 2018, Pope Francis carried a staff in the form of a 'stang,' an object used in satanic rituals. During the Synod on Youth in 2018, Pope Francis wore a distorted rainbow-colored cross, the rainbow being a popularly promoted symbol of the homosexual movement." As it happened, the so-called "stang" was a rustic shepherd's staff given him by a youth group at the last moment before Mass as a substitute crozier. The "rainbow" cross was based on the logo for the Aparecida meetings of Latin American bishops, signifying the colors of the principal participating countries.

Much of the criticism, however, tended toward a mix of the doctrinal and the political. The British writer Henry Sire, who sometimes used the pseudonym Marcantonio Colunna, declared in his *The Dictator Pope* that Francis was "a papal tyrant the like of whom has not been seen for many centuries." George Neumayr, in *The Political Pope*, asked: "How did the papacy go from safeguarding doctrinal unity to shattering it? How did it go from fighting a sinful world to joining it? . . . The crisis created by this pontificate's toxic combination of political liberalism and doctrinal relativism is a historically singular one. . . . " Neumayr's pessimism assumed the loss of a papal golden age that many would dispute; more strangely, he failed to admit the toxicity of the clerical sexual abuse in former eras.

Then came the Catholic intellectuals, celebrated at seminars and conferences. George Weigel, biographer of John Paul II, a thinker described as an intellectual giant by Rupert Murdoch's Fox News, described the Francis Effect in terms of the trajectory of the Church as a whole: "At stake is the relationship of the universal Church to the local Churches: Is Catholicism a federation of national or regional Churches, or is Catholicism a universal Church with distinctive local expressions?" Weigel, as usual, was making a palpable either-or argument; yet he might have conceded that Francis was keeping the alternatives in tension.

R. R. Reno, editor of *First Things*, focused on Francis's papal style. Referring to the papacy as "the current regime," he declared that Francis "combines laxity and ruthlessness. His style is casual and approachable; his Church politics are cold and cunning. There are leading themes in this pontificate—mercy, accompaniment, peripheries, and so forth—but no theological framework." Reno summed up with a violent peroration: "He is an automatic weapon, squeezing off rounds of barbed remarks, spiritual aperçus, and earthy asides (coprophagia!). This has created a confusing, even dysfunctional atmosphere that will become intolerable, if it hasn't already." How the church politics of Francis could be cold and cunning, while his "leading themes" are "mercy, accompaniment, peripheries" is difficult to grasp; but there can be no mistaking Reno's fury.

It is noticeable that some of Francis's harshest critics were recent converts to Catholicism, suggesting that their ideals of the papacy were set higher than those of cradle Catholics. An example was American journalist Jonathan B. Coe, who wrote a fiercely personal piece of character assassination in the pages of *Crisis* magazine. Having charged that Francis had surrounded himself with "men of weak character with skeletons in their closets," he asserts that the Francis Effect consists of the manipulation of courtiers: "Character doesn't seem to matter; what matters is acquiring, consolidating, and wielding power while accomplishing a progressive agenda and pursuing vainglory." He concluded: "You can have honor without power and power without honor, but, when the two come together in the fallen human heart, they make for a deadly ecclesial cocktail."

A curious feature of the conservative attacks was an insistence that his extension of moral concerns to embrace neglected issues meant a repudiation of others, even though there were deep parallel connections. A case in point was his condemnation of nuclear weapons on the one hand and his condemnation of capital punishment on the other.

Both were linked to his defense of the sanctity of life and were consistent with Catholic ethics. But a circle of conservative Catholic opinion insists that his focus on these two issues meant that he was deliberately soft on abortion.

It is reminiscent of the joke about the fond mother who buys her son two ties for his birthday; when he comes to visit her, he is wearing one of them. Greeting him, she says: "So you didn't like the other one?"

Ross Douthat, op-ed columnist for the *New York Times*, wrote in his *To Change the Church* that the Francis Effect appeared to be "largely a media phenomenon, a shift in how the papacy is perceived by outsiders rather than an actual revival of enthusiasm within the church." Douthat believed that Francis's "field station" image of the Church, as a merciful community that welcomes back the fallen, the doubting, the lukewarm, has not worked. "There is no evidence beyond the anecdotal that a liberalizing pontificate is actually bringing the lapsed back to faith," he writes. Nor that it is "increasing Mass going, inspiring new vocations, or otherwise ushering in the great progressive renewal that John Paul allegedly choked off." Yet these are short-term trends, as he concedes, that cannot be "plausibly" blamed on the pope. "It will be decades before we can look at any 'Francis effect' in full and assess its consequences for Catholic practice and belief."

The observation is well made in a book that offers a measured critique of the papacy without rancor; and Douthat is right to draw attention to the fact that lapsed Catholics do not seem to be flocking back to the pews. Yet in his "field station" message, Francis had not promised a widespread return to practice, nor was he addressing the disaffiliated alone. The change of heart, the evangelization he hoped for, clearly was to begin with those who were already attending Mass, the people already in the pews. The Church might well get smaller before it began to heal and be a Church of healing.

Many parishes are closing in Western countries, their congregations dwindling and graying. A 2020 survey published by sociologist of religion Stephen Bullivant reveals that the most enthusiastic Catholics are under the age of thirty. Douthat suggests that the young tend to be more traditionalist, which, he points out, could be bad news for the liberals. And yet, according to Bullivant's research, Catholic youth gave a high rating to Francis on a span of issues, including his support of traditional Catholic teaching tempered by mercy and care of the poor. Bullivant says that Francis is popular among all age groups that attend Mass regularly, but especially the young. He concludes, "I think this indicates that the disengaged Catholicism more prevalent in older generations isn't common with young people. If you're going to Mass as a young person, it's because you really want to be there."

———————

Those mainly on the liberal wings tend to approve of Francis, claiming that his "effect" is progressive. Liberals make less noise because their critiques tend to be less newsworthy, less sensational. Characteristic of liberals, perhaps, many of them hover between praise and criticism, endorsement and reservation. A Catholic medical practitioner, writing to me, exemplifies this ambivalent viewpoint, generally warm but with qualifications:

> Compared to his predecessors, he does seem to have the "common touch"—more parish priest than distant Pontiff. His warmth, sympathy, and modesty personify for many, I imagine, the Christian virtues, mitigating to some extent at least the terrible damage to the Church's moral standing from the fallout from the abuse scandals. Most reasonable people, Catholic and non-Catholic, would acknowledge this.
>
> My reservations would be that he has "left undone things that he ought to have done" in not resolving the two substantial issues that threaten the Church's future as an institution—the ever ageing and shrinking priesthood and the theologically unsound (and unacceptable to the vast majority of the faithful) imprimatur against contraception.

I have the impression the narrative here is that Francis favors the necessary steps of lifting the celibacy requirement and revisiting (or revoking) Humanae Vitae *but has been thwarted in his endeavors by his conservative critics (Cardinal Sarah, etc.). Perhaps, but popes need to be strong-willed as much as saintly and any favorable verdict on his papacy must be tempered by this ineffectiveness in not facing down his opponents. The pieties of* Laudato Si' *and virtue signaling of washing the feet of Muslims are not enough!*

Yet how different on the matter of the Francis Effect and the washing of feet is the perspective of papal biographer Austen Ivereigh, a leader of liberal opinion on Francis: "The Francis Effect is as impossible to measure empirically, as it is real," he writes. Echoing the predictive comments of Gary Wills at the outset of the papacy, Ivereigh writes that the "Francis Effect is a new way of being Catholic in our time. It is no longer enough to adhere to a narrow range of doctrines and a few pious practices . . . but who you are and whether people can see that primary encounter—in prayer, in life—with Jesus Christ." If there is an "iconic image" of the papacy, he declares, it is the "foot-washing in prison, the act that so offended the traditionalists and the nativists." He concludes: "The Francis Effect is to liberate religion from its attachment to power and self-sufficiency, from its tribal superiority, and turn it outward, *ad gentes*, so that the Church lives no longer for itself but to serve humanity."

That view of the Francis Effect as a pastoral impact shared and given major impetus by lay Catholics is a point strongly made by John Gehring, author of *The Francis Effect*. "Pope Francis teaches us," he writes, "that Christianity is not a collection of abstract principles that can be reduced to parsing and defending faceless propositions. The shattering mystery of the Incarnation is that God stands with us in our pain, anxiety, joy, and longings. This gritty theology requires us to take risks and act." Gehring, who has worked with migrants at the Mexican-US border, adds, "I have been graced to work with and learn from young, undocumented immigrants who leave me in awe of their courage."

Among many positive clerical reactions is a pastoral comment, anecdotal but consistent, that contrasts with the pessimism of Cardinal Sarah above. Cardinal Timothy Dolan of New York said at the seven-year mark: "People will approach me to say, 'I've been away from the Church for years, but Pope Francis is drawing me back,' or 'I'm not a Catholic, but I sure love this pope.' . . . He is helping people take a fresh look at the Catholic Church, and thereby come to know Jesus, and experience His love and mercy."

A personal survey of opinion yields many similar stories. Whether the respondents and interviewees are practicing Catholics or not, clergy or lay, there are three consistent views of the Francis Effect: that he raised global consciousness of rampant inequality; that he made us aware of the destruction of the environment (the biggest existential risk to all our futures) as a moral failing; that he repeatedly appealed for empathy, forgiveness, and charity—which he calls mercy and hope.

Janet Soskice, a philosopher of religion at the University of Cambridge, writes to me: "With Francis I feel a certain lightness of heart, in the midst of concerns. I am proud as a Catholic that his first encyclical was *Laudato Si'*, on the environment, which is so needed and has been an encyclical for the whole of the Catholic Church and beyond, not only to other Christians but to anyone who cares about our planet and social justice today. His election, whatever he is able (or not) to achieve as Pope, and Benedict's resignation, signify that the Church can change."

Experiencing the Francis Effect in living, concrete, terms, a parish priest of some thirty years tells me: "Francis said find the suffering Christ in your parish . . . after years of neglect of that suffering, I looked for it and found homeless, lonely, hungry people. . . . I got the parish together and we started to help . . . an obvious thing for any parish, but we'd never done it . . . and the parish has come alive. There is a sense of dynamism and hope in the parish that had been absent; I'm convinced it is down to Francis, but it was there among the people just waiting to be galvanized."

A convert Catholic tells me: "I get the feeling that the ministry is for everybody, not just the priesthood, which was why I became a Catholic at the Second Vatican Council. I came into the Catholic Church because of the Council, it was such a time of new hope. But the previous two popes, John Paul II and Benedict, were rowing back on that . . . they saw the ministry to be all about the clergy, they were clamping down . . . but for Francis we are all invited into the ministry."

An elderly woman, who has spent years working as an art therapist with schoolchildren and in hospitals, goes to church only two or three times a year. She tells me: "I've been struck by one thing, which has changed my whole attitude to gay people. . . . I saw a BBC documentary where he seemed to know by instinct these two pilgrims in a group of eight who were most in need of comfort. And especially a black gay man . . . who was an atheist . . . Francis came up and hugged him . . . Francis pressed his cheek hard against the man's cheek, and this big strong cynical black man wept . . . and it seemed to change his whole life, and it has changed my life too."

The short story writer Tobias Wolff, who for years has run the creative writing project at Stanford University, emails me: "It seems to me that in their anxiety to 'defend the faith,' as they understand the faith, some Catholics hunker into a combative crouch, wielding narrowly curated orthodoxies as a cudgel, radiating judgment and condemnation, to the point that their faith is hardly recognizable as Christian. Pope Francis is a Christian. Everything he says and does proceeds from a truly humble, open-hearted care for others. If I have to choose between Francis and the versions of Catholicism that seem determined to find him in error, I will go with the Christian."

Eamon Duffy, the church historian and historian of the papacy, writes to me tersely, at tweet length, but tellingly: "His decentralization, validation of lay experience, etc., are very close to the Church of John Henry Newman. I have been waiting for a pope like this for fifty years."

Another respondent, an office worker in his mid-forties, left the Church in his late teens, finding the "whole thing" irrelevant, a "waste of time." Married, divorced, and married again, now with two children, he says: "I got interested because he seemed very human. . . . I was in Rome and went to the big general audience one morning out of curiosity":

> I liked the way he talked very simply about Jesus in the gospel. He was a long way off, but he seemed close, and very human. After that I started to read the Gospel of St. John and it struck me that if you latched on to just one of Jesus' sayings and thought about living it, it would change your life. I decided that I wanted to be a Christian again. I think that I'm Catholic again, but without all the paraphernalia. . . . That's how I see Francis.

This span of approval from the conservative and liberal camps gives an impression of reactions to Francis as well as the diverse nature of Catholics and their expectations. I have spoken with many men and women whose spiritual lives have been reawakened and disturbed by Francis; who have seen themselves and the Church, and other Christians and faiths, in a new light. Through all the disruptions, upheavals, and antagonisms, I have detected a sense of renewed spiritual energy among Catholics whatever their standpoint within the Church, an energy that burns brightly beyond the politics and the divisions.

Francis talked of the strength of this energy in terms of the Holy Spirit on Pentecost Sunday 2020, when he joined with the Anglican Archbishop of Canterbury in a message to the ecumenical prayer movement known as Thy Kingdom Come. It was in the form of a video message broadcast globally. The movement, started in 2016 and expanded globally to 172 countries, embraces all Christian denominations. Participants meet in mass gatherings, and in smaller ones. The lockdowns due to the coronavirus gave rise to new opportunities for digital gatherings, including a 24/7 "upper room" of prayer.

At Pentecost, Christians remember the descent of the Holy Spirit in the shape of tongues of fire over the heads of the apostles, praying together in an upper room. The Pentecostal gift of tongues, said Francis, should enable us to speak to each other across barriers. He spoke of the way the Holy Spirit "infects" the entire world with Pentecostal energy, while the "deadly virus" ravaging the world in the pandemic had parallels with the viruses of war, poverty, racism, and greed.

He hoped that Christians would become more united as "witnesses of mercy" for the human family in a world experiencing a "famine of hope." The Catholic Church has its many Pentecostal, charismatic, movements. By his companionship in prayer with the Archbishop of Canterbury, Francis was demonstrating that if he could unite with the head of the Anglican Church, then the Pentecostal energy could find ways of uniting the divisions and overcoming the antagonisms within his own Church.

CHAPTER TWENTY-TWO

A YOUNG CHURCH

Our Hope for Years to Come

Close to my home in central London, the River Thames is spanned by the Waterloo Bridge. A few hundred yards from the bridge on the south side is the modest church of St. Patrick. It is a simple unadorned upper room, painted white, served by a community of Franciscan friars. The congregations are dwindling, mostly the elderly Irish, a few recent migrants and asylum seekers; the daily eight o'clock Mass is attended by twenty or so women and men, most of them on their way to work. The Mass is brief, pared down to its ultimate simplicity, the Word and the Eucharist at dawn. In the background is the roar of London as the commuters pour out of Waterloo train station heading for the City.

Yet every Monday night this same unadorned church fills to capacity with young people, mostly in their twenties. Many are obliged to stand or sit on the floor. They belong to a charismatic Catholic group known as the Cenacle; they come into this central travel hub from all over London for their special weekly service. The group is run by laymen and women, but they have their priest who comes from the East End of the city each week to celebrate the Mass. Our Franciscan parish priest hears Confessions at the back. For two and a half hours they sing and pray and testify. After Mass the church is lit by candles; the priest raises the Blessed Sacrament in a monstrance and members in need of healing come up front and kneel while the people sing and pray. The devotion is palpable: One senses a vibrancy and dynamism in the spirituality and friendship. They are a Christian community from scattered locations, in touch on their iPhones.

On the north side of the Thames, a short walk from Waterloo Bridge in the district known as Covent Garden, there is another Catholic church, Corpus Christi. Unlike St. Patrick's, this church is richly decorated with ornate tiles, marble, gilt filigree, and stained glass; an old-fashioned Confessional box stands at the back; there are statues of the saints with votive lamps. Five red glass oil lamps burn over the sanctuary before the gorgeous tabernacle. At the same time, every Monday evening, worshipers come from every corner of London to attend a Latin Mass performed with decorum and Gregorian chant. Most members of the Monday congregation are members of the Latin Mass Society, which has international links and affiliations with various "sodalities" of traditionalist prayer groups. Members will meet at other Latin Mass venues, travel on pilgrimage together, and benefit from training sessions in liturgy and Latin. Membership and communication benefit from online facilities and livestreaming of Masses. Traditionalist visitors love this little church. Cardinals Burke and Sarah have celebrated Mass here. It is no secret that Francis is not keen on Latin Masses with priests turning their backs on the congregation, but neither has he sought to thwart or ban them.

While both churches, north and south, are home to local parishes and occasional visitors, it is the presence and energy of the groups, also known as movements, divergent in expression and yet Catholic to the core, that reveal a future path for the Church. These two regular assemblies of Catholics represent perhaps the polar opposites of similar groups in the United Kingdom and across the world. Some lean toward various forms of charismatic practice, others are more traditionalist; just as some express themselves in prayer and liturgy, others seek action in practical social work. Some are inspired by devotions to the Virgin Mary, others to particular saints—Padre Pio, Therese of Lisieux, Vincent de Paul; there are specific works of mercy—migrants, refugees, the sick, the dying, the homeless; some focus on children, or particular regions—Asia, Africa, Latin America. The rich variety of Catholic groups, stimulated by the varied manifestations of Catholic imagination, is often obscured by the media clash of liberals and conservatives. And while there has been talk of schism during the papacy of Francis, the vibrant associations of Catholics show that what Catholic groups hold in common is stronger than their differences, even when those differences grow strident. Francis has urged the faithful to understand that being Catholic essentially means keeping contradictions and oppositions in tension, rather than shearing apart or reaching unsatisfactory reconciliations.

And here the "Two Popes" come together. Pope Benedict, as a younger man looking ahead during the post-Vatican II traumas, saw the potential of these groups and movements to renew the Church. In a broadcast in German in 1969, Benedict, then Joseph Ratzinger, said: "[The Church] will be seen much more as a voluntary society, entered only by free decision . . . it will make much bigger demands on the initiative of her individual members. . . . In many smaller congregations or in self-contained social groups, pastoral care will normally be provided in this fashion. . . . The Church will be a more spiritual Church, not presuming upon a political mandate, flirting as little with the Left as with the Right. . . ."

While many parishes are closing in Western countries, their congregations dwindling and graying, the groups and movements are youthful, expanding. Their vibrancy and energy show that young Catholic Christians are less inspired and affiliated by ideas and by doctrinal definitions than they are by prayer, the Mass, and engagement with the world, its joys and sorrows, as it is.

The growth of the movements has owed much to each of the popes since John XXIII, but Francis has revived their spirit and energies when they seemed in danger of flagging and declining. Yet what permanent changes has he wrought that will continue his vision for the future Church?

By the beginning of the eighth year of his papacy, Francis revealed that his legacy had been shaped toward a profound influence in social and environmental spheres rather than in dogma, and with a powerful spiritual message of compassion and clemency. For a continuation of this trend we must look to the cardinals he has created, who share his pastoral concerns and spirituality.

He has promoted men not from major metropolitan dioceses but from distant regions and especially developing countries. By his seventh anniversary he had passed over bishops in dioceses such as Milan, Venice, and Philadelphia. Not only would the new breed of cardinals determine the choice of the next pope in conclave, but also the fate and future of the Church in years to come. By October 2019, he had chosen 53 percent of the College of Cardinals. By 2020 there were already fewer cardinal bureaucrats working within the Curia, down from 35 percent at his election to 26 percent. There were fewer Italians, from 24 percent down to 18 percent. The Americans were down from 10 percent to 7 percent. Latin Americans, Africans, and Asians were up; white cardinals down. Cardinals from the global South now accounted for 44 percent of the college.

A sample of the new cardinals tells its own story. Michael Czerny, seventy-three, a Jesuit dedicated to immigration issues and policies with expertise in Africa, was working in the Department for Promoting Integral Human Development. He was thought to have drafted *Laudato Si'*. Bishop Alvaro Ramazzini Imeri of Huehuetenango, seventy-two, a Guatemalan, was working with indigenous people in Latin America, battling exploitative extraction corporations and attracting death threats. Archbishop Matteo Zuppi, sixty-four, from Bologna, had earned the nickname *vescovo dei poveri*—"bishop for the poor." He had been a long-serving member of the international Community of Sant'Egidio, which works for the destitute and homeless internationally. Archbishop Miguel Ayuso Guixot, sixty-seven, had been involved in religious pluralism for many years, in particular Christian-Muslim relations. Likewise, Francis promoted Ignatius Suharyo Hardjoatmodjo of Jakarta, Indonesia, and Cristóbal López Romero, sixty-seven, of Rabat in Morocco—both in Muslim-majority countries. From Africa he chose a peace and reconciliation leader, Archbishop Fridolin Ambongo, fifty-nine, of Kinshasa, Democratic Republic of the Congo; from the Caribbean he promoted Archbishop Juan de la Caridad García Rodríguez, seventy-one, of Havana, Cuba, a campaigner for Catholic education who led efforts to help the afflicted after the 2008 hurricane that laid waste to the country. Archbishop Jean-Claude Hollerich, sixty-one, a Jesuit and formerly a missionary in Japan, was president of the Commission of the Bishops' Conferences of the European Community. Making him a cardinal ensured that he would take an evangelizing approach to the European countries.

All of these cardinals embodied in one way or another Francis's vision for the Church. They will continue with his priorities. And while it is inadvisable to predict how the conclave will vote, it seems probable that they will choose somebody who will not undo his legacy. Meanwhile their presence and work will be an encouragement to broad constituencies of faithful around the world.

From the beginning Francis repeatedly appealed to the "synod" as a means of governance and reform for the long-term future. The word, from the Greek *sinodus*, meaning a meeting or council, at its root combines *syn* (with) and *odos* (path). Reinstituted by Paul VI in 1967, the synod, Francis remarked, was "new as an institution but ancient in its inspiration." Some believe that the story of the two disciples on their way to Emmaus, meeting the risen Jesus, was the very first synod. For Francis the synod is not just a meeting together but "walking together"; hence the early Christians were often known as "followers of the Way." An example of an early synod was the meeting called by "apostles and presbyters" in Jerusalem to decide whether pagan converts needed to be circumcised before baptism. The synod became a means of settling disputes or matters of special urgency for particular regions.

As we have seen, Paul VI, impressed by the power of the Second Vatican Council to deepen the understanding and practice of the faith, declared that regular synods should be a way of continuing the benefits and influence of the Council. In particular, the synods were meant to create an emphasis on the combined discernment of pope and bishops. Under Francis's two successors, John Paul II and Benedict XVI, synods proved disappointing to many. John Paul II had a tendency to ignore the recommendations of the bishops and go his own way.

Francis publicly expressed his vision for synods of the future in the fall of 2015: "The journey of synodality is the journey that God wants from his Church in the third millennium. . . . A synodal Church is a listening Church, aware that listening is more than hearing. It is a reciprocal listening in which each one has something to learn." The entire Church, he declared, is synodal, both generally and specially, a community that recognizes unity in a diversity of cultures and geography; an institution that allows for local discretion in harmony with universal authority. Yet he admitted that while "walking together—laity, pastors, the bishop of Rome—is an easy concept to express in words" it is "not so easy to put into practice."

He went on: "We must continue on this path. . . . The world in which we live and which we are called to love and serve, even with its contradictions, requires from the church the strengthening of synergies in all areas of its mission."

Francis boosted the power and authority of future synods in 2018 when he decreed that the final document of a synod, when approved with "moral unanimity" and approved by the Pope, becomes part of the official teaching of the Church. The decree also gave greater scope for the input of the laity and real debate: all sides being heard.

Francis's vision of the synodal future has sparked a lively, at times angry debate among clergy and laity. The theologian Massimo Faggioli saw synods as the answer to crises within the Church that had political parallels within democracies: a decline in participation and representation, combined with media distortions—fake news and bias. Faggioli writes that it must be "the alternative to the lecture circuit where competing agendas vie for media attention and ideology-driven donors . . . [it] takes place in a real, lived ecclesial community and not in the realm of Church fiction or virtual religion." He went on: "It is about being pastoral rather than trading in sarcasm and sound bites especially through social media. . . . The synodal process puts the assembly of real people who participate in and represent the Church at the center, and not a media audience whose market value is in its divisiveness."

Faggioli might well have reckoned his point justified by George Weigel's riposte: Synodality, he wrote, "provides cover for effecting serious changes in Catholic self-understanding and practice for which there is little or no doctrinal, theological, or pastoral warrant." The final report of the Amazon Synod, he charged, was a "masquerade," in "language sodden with clichés." Focusing on the notion in the final report of the *sensus fidelium*, the idea of the faithful expressing an opinion, was "gobbledygook."

Unfazed by such criticisms, Francis decided to establish a synod on the topic of synods, scheduled for 2022. His response to the doubters was to keep talking, keep consulting, leading the Church inexorably toward a more inclusive, participating future.

CHAPTER TWENTY-THREE

FRANCIS THE MODERNIST

Myths of Tradition and Liberalism

A s a junior seminarian in the late 1950s I was intrigued by a passage I came across in a battered old novel I found in the limited selection of pious works of fiction in our student library. Titled *My New Curate*, by Canon Patrick Sheehan, and published at the turn of the twentieth century, it portrayed the priestly life in a country parish in rural Ireland. There was a chapter in which the priests of the diocese came to the bishop's house to discuss questions about liturgy and theology. A dispute arose between two of the clergy over the truth of the Bible as a divinely inspired text. A clever young cleric, who had been influenced by German critical scholarship, raised the question: Did the Virgin Mary speak the actual words of the great prayer known as the Magnificat in response to the Angel Gabriel, or was it a product of the imagination of the author of the Gospel of Luke? The clever priest cannot be convinced that the famous prayer was uttered by a young Hebrew country girl. The traditionalist priest responds that such an opinion is "blasphemous." Moreover, "it is the complete elimination of the supernatural, the absolute denial of inspiration." He thunders: "If the Magnificat is not an inspired utterance, I should like to know what is."

In other words, the Virgin Mary had been directly inspired by God to utter the famous prayer, and Luke the evangelist surely wrote down her utterance word for word.

That novel was my first inkling of the so-called modernist crisis that shook the Church in the final years of the nineteenth century and created even greater storms in the first decade of the twentieth, reverberating through to my junior seminary in the 1950s, where the next generation of priests were in formation for the future. Under the influence of the clerical culture of that time, I found myself siding with the traditionalist priest against the specious German scholarship of the smart young upstart just as Canon Sheehan intended me to do.

Understanding Pope Francis, the changes he has wrought, the disruptions he prompted, the individuals and groups he somersaulted during his papacy, has, and will be, told in many different ways. But how do we locate him within longer-term trends and conflicts that have created dissension within the Church since the late nineteenth century?

Of the many verdicts on Francis's papacy, there is one that goes to the heart of his disruptive cognitive dissonance. He has been accused of being a "modernist," an incendiary term within the Catholic Church that a hundred years ago was equivalent to being called a heretic.

The heresy of modernism, and its parallel error liberalism, was first dramatically condemned by Pope Pius IX in his *Syllabus of Errors*, published in 1864. Among the eighty false tenets excoriated in that sulfurous syllabus is this: that it is heresy to claim that "the Roman Pontiff can, and ought to reconcile himself, and come to terms with, progress, liberalism, and modern civilization."

Pius X, who succeeded Leo XIII to reign through the first decade of the twentieth century until the outbreak of the First World War, was even more castigating of the "modern" than was Pius IX. He described attempts to reconcile Catholicism with modern civilization as a "synthesis of all heresies." If Pius IX and Pius X were right, then we face the shocking proposition that Francis has indeed been guilty of heresy.

Pius X would become a model for priests until the mid-to-late-1960s, when his charisma faded save for a small, ever loyal group. He was one of ten children, the son of a village postman in rural Treviso, northern Italy. He walked four miles to and from school every day. He was a devout man who after ordination rose to be the spiritual director of a seminary. He was slow-moving, a little overweight, and tended to wear his papal tiara askew; he refused to eat alone, as was the custom of popes, nor would he allow himself to be carried in the traditional papal litter fanned by ostrich feathers like an emperor.

He was gravely anxious about the future. He feared that the Church was in steep decline, headed for breakup. He saw in democracy, religious freedom, and religious pluralism a great danger to the Church—relativism, the conviction that any religion is as good or as bad as any other, or as no religion at all. He feared the influence of secularism, especially in education, the rule of the mob implied in the popular vote. He feared above all the notion that doctrines might be subject to change. Hence he was alarmed by what he deemed the Church's nightmare within: a small, mainly unrelated, circle of Catholic scholars, ordained and lay, across Europe and especially in Germany, who were seeking to apply contemporary intellectual and scientific disciplines to Catholic teaching.

They were interested in exploring Christian claims from the perspectives of history, anthropology, psychology, the natural sciences, contemporary textual criticism. Already there were Protestant theologians working in these fields. These Catholic scholars, now called "modernists" as a term of abuse by Rome, considered it essential to keep up with their Protestant peer group. Was the Genesis story of creation literally true? Or was it purely poetic? How many authors wrote the books of Isaiah: surely not just one? Might one endorse Darwin's theory of evolution? What did it mean for doctrine to develop? Change? Already Cardinal Newman, who had spent decades studying original texts of the Early Fathers, had written on this theme. He had been suspect for a time, but under Leo XIII his reputation as an authentic Catholic theologian had been restored. To understand Christianity, the Church, and its doctrines, it was essential to study its history.

But Pius X conceived a particular detestation of church historians and their tendency to poke their noses into dark corners. His spymaster in chief, a Monsignor Umberto Benigni, who was hired to hunt down modernists, proclaimed that "history is nothing but a continuous, desperate attempt to vomit. For this sort of human being there is only one remedy: the Inquisition!" Pius X believed that the modernists were set to undermine the Church in the new century. He wrote two devastating encyclicals against them. The first added sixty-five more errors to those listed by Pius IX: Highest on the list was of course "modernism" itself, which constituted "the compendium and poison of all the heresies." The second defined the power relations between the papacy and the entire Church. It declared that intellectual questions within the Catholic Church are not a matter for scholarly peer group discussion, as the modernists argued, but a moral matter to be resolved by papal authority. As the saying went at the time, "The Pope's will: God's will."

Pius X ordered those identified with the least taint of modernism to be summarily sacked from their teaching posts, their writings banned. It was enough to be seen with a newspaper with liberal tendencies. When his advisers counseled compassion, he said: ". . . They should be beaten with fists. In a duel you don't count or measure the blows, you strike as you can." Benigni's spy network spread in parishes and seminaries across the world. Tale bearing, tittle-tattle, rumors were the order of the day. Much injustice was done.

The foremost English-speaking so-called modernist was George Tyrrell, a brilliant young Jesuit priest of Irish descent. He wrote of a God revealed through religious imagination and symbolism, a God open to all peoples and cultures. He argued that religious experience, and salvation, is attainable by all human beings, including non-Catholics and non-Christians. He cast doubt on the idea of eternal hellfire. He raised conscience above dogma, challenged the pretensions of clericalism, the creeping infallibility of the pope, the superstition of many popular miracles. He preached a form of democracy in the Church, claiming that ministry should be shared between the ordained and the laity. His insistence that God is both present, and to be found, "in the collective mind and conscience of the community" especially infuriated Pius.

There are significant parallels between the teaching of Francis and the condemned ideas of George Tyrrell and other "modernists." The parallels would grow closer and multiply with the next generation of courageously rigorous scholar-theologians who followed in the 1930s: the group known as *Nouvelle Theologie.*

In *Laudato Si'* Francis attributes authentic spiritual expressions to indigenous "pagan" peoples; he preaches the "economy" of mercy, and the importance of the spirit over the letter. Francis and Tyrrell would have agreed on the role of conscience. Tyrrell saw Christ as the voice of individual conscience "subtly intertwined with our own soul." At the very beginning of the *The Joy of Love,* Francis echoes the role of conscience and responsibility of all the members of the faithful. He wrote that he wanted to be clear that "not all doctrinal, moral, or pastoral issues need to be settled by interventions of dogma." While teaching and practice are necessary, "this does not preclude various ways of interpreting some aspects of that teaching or drawing certain consequences from it." Conscience does not necessarily restrict one to the letter of the law, he argued, but "recognizes with sincerity and honesty what for now is the most generous response that can be given to God."

Poor Tyrrell was isolated. He lacked peer-group restraints and became reckless, outlandish, a troublesome member of the Jesuit order. He was finally excommunicated. When he died, aged forty-seven, his health wrecked by the treatment meted out to him by the anti-modernist thought police, he was denied burial in consecrated ground. The priest who read a service over his coffin was disciplined by his diocese.

The terror-stricken reaction to the perceived dangers of Tyrrell and his circle was equally outlandish in Rome, with far-reaching consequences for the Church in subsequent generations. To ensure the rejection of the modernist heresy for all time, in 1910 Pius X published a directive obliging ordinands to swear an anti-modernist oath, which they did until the late 1960s, and continue to do to this day in modified form. It requires acceptance of papal teaching, and acquiescence at all times in the meaning and sense of such teaching as dictated by the pope. The effect of the oath was to destroy peer group exchange, and to put the Church into theological deep freeze for generations.

It is a supreme irony of the past century of Catholic history that the Church of Pius X, and the Piuses that followed him—Pius XI and Pius XII—congratulated themselves on their defense of unchanging "tradition," *semper eadem.* Yet they were presiding over a Church that was itself a historic innovation, a novel, reactionary Church based on the anxieties of Pius X.

The spirit of diversity and dynamism, the quest for authentic Christianity, nevertheless survived. The *Nouvelle Théologie* group defied the stagnant seminary studies in theology and philosophy approved by the Piuses. Important figures included the Jesuit Henri de Lubac; the Dominican friars Marie-Dominique Chenu and Yves Congar; the American John Courtney Murray. Like Newman they studied the Early Fathers; they read the original texts of Thomas Aquinas, Bonaventure, and Duns Scotus; they called their work *resourcement,* to explain that they were not making innovations but rediscovering lost significance. In his book *Surnaturel (The Supernatural)*, de Lubac claimed that the spiritual life was a dimension of what it meant to be human, rather than an "added" grace mediated by the Catholic Church. Francis was influenced by them and was squarely within their tradition.

These "new" theologians were at first disciplined for their writings, sacked from university and seminary posts, and barred from publishing. In the late 1950s, however, the movement began to meet and publish again despite oppression. A longing to end the citadel, "unchanging" Church of the Piuses finally erupted at the Second Vatican Council, called by the elderly John XXIII, elected in 1958 after the death of Pius XII. John XXIII himself, as a young seminary professor, had been reported for modernist tendencies for merely quoting a few lines from one of those authors banned by Pius X. He had escaped censure only by abjectly humiliating himself, pleading his case in person in Rome and in a letter described by his biographer Peter Hebblethwaite as "groveling." His abject apologia indicates the extent to which even the best are undermined by the oppression of an overbearing "religious superior."

Under John XXIII and the Second Vatican Council the "new" theologians became advisers to the attending bishops. By its end in 1965 the Church no longer saw itself as a citadel but as a pilgrim people of God on the move. There was a call for authority by collegiality rather than rule from the papal apex. Many of the ideas once labeled modernist heresy were allowed scope, tested by scholarship and peer group discussion. Yet anti-modernist traditionalism has lingered on; the problem with "change," "development," and "engagement" has continued on through the late twentieth century and into this one. The Church of Pius X exerts a residual influence over the minds, consciences, and nostalgia of a constituency of Catholics, most of whom, nowadays, had no experience of living under his auspices. In its extreme form, this brand of "traditionalism" is promoted by the group known as the Society, or Fraternity, of Pius X. The group quarrels with many of the reforms of the Second Vatican Council. An extreme form of Pius X adulation claims that the last valid pope was Pius XII.

It has been hard for Catholic writers to see Pius X as he really was since he was canonized by Pius XII in 1954, describing him as a "glowing flame of charity and shining splendor of sanctity." But Cardinal Pietro Gasparri, secretary of state under Pius X and one of the most eminent Curial cardinals in the modern period, had another view. In his as yet unpublished deposition for the canonization process, he roundly condemned him. "Pope Pius X," Gasparri told the tribunal, "approved, blessed, and encouraged a secret espionage association outside and above the hierarchy, the Cardinals; in short he approved, blessed, and encouraged a sort of Freemasonry in the Church, something unheard of in ecclesiastical history." His case against Pius X's canonization went unheeded.

Typical of Francis's capacity to confound expectations, he was seen occasionally praying in the early morning at the tomb of Pius X in St. Peter's Basilica. It is tempting to wonder what this encounter between Francis, the pope of mercy, and the shade of St. Pius X, the scourge of modernism, signifies.

———————

We are accustomed to seeing the Catholic experience in prosperous Western countries through the twentieth century and into this one in terms of the irresolvable conflict between so-called conservatives and liberals. In broad terms it plays out as a struggle between permanence and change, tradition and progress, authority and conscience, definitiveness and openness. Yet there is another perspective, characterized by the philosopher of religion Charles Taylor as the conflict between the quest for religion's highest spiritual aspirations and the appeal to prudence—the scaled-down, humanistic acceptance of our limitations and frailties. Taylor states his warning against the all-or-nothing pursuit of religion bluntly: The highest spiritual ideals also "threaten to lay the most crushing burdens on humankind." The great spiritual visions of human history "have also been poisoned chalices, the causes of untold misery and even savagery."

The practice of prudence through mercy, the scaling down of high aspirations, nevertheless involves a loss, which Taylor characterizes as spiritual lobotomy. "We deceive ourselves," writes Taylor, "if we pretend nothing is denied thereby of our humanity." But is this the last word? Are none of us spared the choice between either spiritually impoverished prudence, or wounding and self-wounding zeal?

Francis does not accept this as the last word. He calls for a third way, a *prudenza audace*, an audacious prudence, which keeps the apparent opposites, with their accompanying rewards and dangers, in tension. When historians come to scrutinize in depth the prodigious flow of Francis's teachings, they are unlikely to find the least evidence of divergence from the magisterium of the Church. And yet, they will find a consistent Christian counsel of prudence and clemency that recognizes human frailty: the way we are.

CHAPTER TWENTY-FOUR

WHO IS HE LIKE?

Francis and Gregory the Great

W here does Francis stand within the history of the popes? Which other pope in the long history of the Church is he most like? He is not alone among popes of the past two centuries in launching disruptive initiatives. Pius IX, author of the *Syllabus of Errors,* had himself declared infallible in faith and morals, under certain conditions, at the First Vatican Council in 1870. The dogma sent shock waves through Europe, contributing to the persecution of Catholics in Germany. It would oblige future popes to defend their predecessors' decrees, even when they knew them to be wrong.

In the early 1960s the elderly John XXIII called the reforming Second Vatican Council, or Vatican II, the greatest renewal of the Church since the Council of Trent half a millennium earlier. He released a surge of spiritual energy. Yet among its many consequences, an estimated 100,000 priests abandoned their calling in the years following Vatican II, and heated disputes over the Council's letter and spirit rage to this day. The extremes of some progressive Catholics led to what even liberals would call "the runaway Church."

Pope Paul VI, despite the collective urging of many bishops and moral theologians to the contrary, published in 1968 his encyclical *Humanae Vitae,* confirming the sinfulness of contraception in every circumstance. Many millions of the faithful who had been practicing contraception fell away from the Church. Those Catholics who remained yet ignored the ruling established a gulf between the Church's teaching and actual practice that continues to this day.

On June 12, 1987, John Paul II addressed more than a million faithful near Gdansk, scene of the shipyard strike that launched the Solidarity movement in Poland in 1980. He spoke of workers' rights and explained the meaning of the common good, and solidarity "as one another . . . never one against another." He left the Polish leader Wojciech Jaruzelski presiding over a collapsing regime. From this point the Soviet system began to unravel.

Then there was Benedict, the first pope in history to voluntarily resign—heralding a stunning disruption that will now be open to popes for all time, along with the tensions and difficulties that two living popes might bring.

Yet we need to return, I would argue, more than sixteen centuries to the papacy of St. Gregory the Great to find a pontiff as positively and widely disrupting as Francis. Pope Gregory 1 (590–604) shook up the office of the papacy with reverberations right down to the twenty-first century. He was the first pope to declare himself the "Servant of the Servants of God" (*Servus servorum Dei*) and to actually mean it and practice it. Many popes, including recent ones, have adopted the title, while hardly living it.

Francis, like Gregory, has lived the sobriquet "Servant of the Servant of God," not merely by declining showy vestments, papal pomp, and extravagance, as did Gregory, but by stressing his role as being "of service"; acknowledging his readiness to abase himself, confess his mistakes, his ignorance, his fallibility, and his sinfulness. In 2020 Francis dropped "Vicar of Christ" from the list of official titles published in the Vatican yearbook. The Second Vatican Council had declared that all bishops are vicars of Christ; Francis wished to be known simply as Bishop of Rome, in which role he was a successor of the disciple Peter.

Pope Gregory ordered that the Church should be governed through those meetings of bishops, the synods. The pope and his Curia, he declared, were "a fraternal service in communion and to communion"; and he wrote that "Peter, the first in authority among the apostles" was also first "in humility." Gregory matched the principle of "primacy of Peter" to the "principle of the synod," the local discretion of bishops, in the service of the priesthood and the laity.

Francis will be remembered for his care of migrants, the homeless, and the outsider, and for his deep friendship with the Jewish people and love of the Jewish faith. While constrained by Christian attitudes of the age, Gregory was famously and controversially a protector of the Jews. He wrote a letter condemning the compulsory baptism of Jews, and we find him insisting on their right to freedom in civil affairs and their right to worship in their synagogues.

Pope Gregory was preoccupied with the condition of the poor and the outsider. He relieved the plight of refugees fleeing the cruel incursions of the invading Lombards. These homeless, starving migrants threatened the very welfare of Rome, but Gregory pressed his pastors and parishes into service, in addition to drawing on his family's revenues, which he had personally renounced.

He preached using simple words and in brief. Reminiscent of Francis's "field hospital" church, in his book *Pastoral Care* he likened bishops to medical practitioners. He was severe on corruption and is credited with the phrase *corruptio optimi pessima*: The corruption of the best is the worst of all. Francis quoted the phrase in his document *The Holy Year of Mercy*, adding that corruption "is a sinful hardening of the heart."

Gregory is remembered for his initiatives during the Plague of 590, which was probably the return of an early pandemic that had claimed a great many victims in Europe. He became pope in consequence of the death of Pelagius II, who had died of the disease. Gregory organized a series of processions through the city, from St. Peter's to the basilica of St. Mary Major. Cardinals, bishops, and abbots joined the file along with the citizens of Rome. During the final procession, legend has it, St. Michael the Archangel appeared on the top of the castle that now bears his name, Castel San Angelo. He was seen to be sheathing his sword, a sign that the epidemic would cease.

On March 18, 2020, as Italy was ravaged by the coronavirus pandemic, with many hundreds of people dying every day, Francis walked alone along part of the route of the procession against the plague taken by Gregory the Great, as if to represent the world in pilgrimage, united with him through digital technology. He ended his walk in the church of St. Marcello, famous for its miraculous crucifix, attracting pilgrims during a sixteenth-century epidemic. He prayed there alone. Francis was making an act of popular piety at a time of crisis—to console and offer hope; he was walking in the footsteps of Pope Gregory.

———————

Looking back over the reigns of John Paul II and Benedict XVI, biographers remark on their academic credentials, their doctorates and university professorships. John Paul was a philosopher of religion, steeped in phenomenology—an abstruse philosophy with restricted interest for the wider faithful; Benedict was an eminent theologian in his own right, and like John Paul a former university professor. It has been customary, however, to think of Francis as a man of emotions rather than intellect. He himself has often stressed the importance of "realities over ideas."

While Francis has consistently addressed the faithful, and the world, in accessible concrete language and images, those who have explored his younger life attest to the depth and breadth of his reading and intellectual resources. At the same time, it is possible to trace the powerful influence of philosophers who enabled him to grasp the dynamic of opposites in tension. During the 1980s he began a thesis on the ideas of Romano Guardini, the Italo-German philosopher of religion, precisely on the power of unreconciled opposites. He never finished it, but he evidently developed and pursued his reading and thinking over the following ten years.

His love of literature spanned Shakespeare, Rilke, Hölderlin, Gerard Manley Hopkins, Manzoni, Neruda, and especially Jorge Luis Borges. When Bergoglio was teaching creative writing at Santa Fe, Argentina, he got to know Borges, who visited the school and talked to the pupils. Bergoglio had an intense liking for a short story by Borges titled "Aleph."

The central character enters a cellar where he comes upon a minuscule, iridescent sphere "of almost unbearable brilliance" that contains the entire universe, past, present, and future. He calls it the Aleph. Borges gives an astounding impression of the prodigality of nature and humankind, of history and emotions within the sphere. In the Aleph his character sees the entire earth from every point and angle, individuals, plants, trees, animals, cities, oceans: "I felt dizzy and wept, for my eyes had seen that secret and conjectured object whose name is common to all men but which no man has looked upon—the unimaginable universe. I felt infinite wonder, infinite pity."

Jorge Bergoglio's attachment to this literary expression of universal sympathy and pity, embraced by the virtue of mercy, is matched by a parallel story in the writings of Gregory the Great. In his dialogues, Gregory writes of the life of St. Benedict. One night the saint was praying by the window of the tower in which he lived. While deep in contemplation, he experienced a vision of the entire world—past, present, and future—as if in a flash of lightning. How, asked Gregory's interlocutor in the dialogue, could God make the entire world small enough to fit into a bolt of lightning? Gregory answered that God did not shrink the world, but he expanded Benedict's soul in the act of contemplation, enabling the world to enter his heart.

Francis, who spent several hours of every day in silent prayer, periodically spoke of the need for contemplation in the midst of a busy life. There could be busy prayer, of intercession, of supplication, of the liturgy and the rosary, but contemplative prayer, he often said, was the prayer that gave rise to hope. The Borges story and the Benedict story are reminiscent of a paragraph in *Laudato Si'* (p. 79) where he speaks of the universe "shaped by open and intercommunicating systems" and how we can "discern countless forms of relationship and participation." He goes on to think of "the whole" as open to "God's transcendence, within which it develops." Hence there is a mystical meaning, he writes, quoting a Sufi poet, "in a leaf, a mountain trail, a dewdrop, in a poor person's face."

His insights were so often a marriage of the literary and the spiritual imagination. Speaking to students at the Gregorian University in Rome, he told them that theology was only fruitful when it was done in a spirit of prayer: "doing theology on one's knees," he said.

If Francis is reminiscent of Gregory the Great, he also resembles the greatest Church disrupter of the Middle Ages, his papal namesake Francis of Assisi. While in prayer, the saint heard a voice saying: "Francis, repair my Church, which has fallen into disrepair and is in danger of collapse." On the day Cardinal Bergoglio was elected, taking the name of Francis, he was well aware of the many ways the Church had fallen into disrepair. He recognized, moreover, the drastic measures to be addressed. Like St. Francis, and unlike any other pope in history, Pope Francis has extended the idea of the Church to include the planet and its ecology, following the Franciscan vision of nature as a "sister" or even "mother." Pope Francis has elevated environmental morality to the highest order. Moreover, he has linked the suffering of the poor to environmental damage through overextraction and environmental destruction.

Francis combined the spirituality of St. Francis with the spirituality of Ignatius of Loyola. As church historian John W. O'Malley observes, Ignatius taught that "change is more consistent with one's scope than staying the course. It consists as well in the courage and self-possession required to make the actual decision to change and convince others of the validity and viability of the new direction."

A writer in *First Things* records that he taught for a number of years at a Jesuit university: "I'm familiar with a pastoral approach that treats disruption and rule-breaking as a spiritual tonic. . . . This Jesuit adoption of a number of multiple, even contradictory ecclesial masks helps us understand why Pope Francis can tack so quickly from 'liberal' to 'conservative' positions."

Jesuit pedagogy traditionally involves deliberate shock tactics to make way for new thinking. Jesuit missionary methods routinely involved the reversal and interruption of received norms to attain their objectives. "To produce a change, a disruption that breaks up the comfort of a situation is needed," writes an expert on Jesuit education. "This is the first step named *unfreezing* in which an old behavior will be shaken up before introducing a new behavior."

The most profound nudge of all his disruptions is summed up in his chosen motto, which connects with all the themes of this book, *miserando atque eligendo*—"by having mercy and choosing." He consistently, daily, reminded the faithful not to despair of God's mercy, and to extend mercy, forgiveness, clemency, and love to others. On December 8, 2015, he launched the Year of Mercy, which he had started by invoking the words spoken by Portia in *The Merchant of Venice*:

> *The quality of mercy is not strained;*
> *It droppeth as the gentle rain from heaven*
> *Upon the place beneath. It is twice blest;*
> *It blesseth him that gives and him that takes. . . .*

In his letter to the faithful at the culmination of that year, he wrote that mercy is "the very foundation of the church's life." He never saw mercy as an individual, occasional virtue, but as a core collective movement within Christian culture and spirituality—allied and in parallel with the same impulse in Judaism and Islam. "May the works of mercy also include care for our common home," breaking the logic of violence and selfishness that dominates political and economic life, "making mercy felt in every action that seeks to build a better world."

A PERSONAL
POSTCRIPT

Twenty years ago, I published a book titled *Breaking Faith: The Fate and Future of the Catholic Church*. John Paul II had been pope for a quarter of a century; he was ailing with Parkinson's disease. Catholics were wondering what kind of pope might follow him. For all that he had been a great pope, the Church was in an unhappy state even before the full extent of the sexual abuse scandals emerged.

As I completed that book, which attempted a survey of the Church in the world, I came to think in the final pages of the predicament closer to home. I looked at my own family and friends, and especially those demoralized within the faith. There was my mother, deprived of the Eucharist; my brother, deprived of a blessing at his second marriage. And I had a niece, married in church at twenty-five, whose husband left her within two years for another woman. They divorced. If she were to marry again she would be characterized as an "adulterer," unable to go to Communion. She was urged to apply for an annulment, but John Paul had tightened the rules. She asked: "Uncle John, does God hate me that much?"

Among close friends: a priest bullied by his bishop for conducting a popular service of general absolution during Lent, a service of Reconciliation banned by John Paul; an academic colleague who declined to write a favorable review of a book on women priesthood because it would negatively affect her future career in Catholic education; an actively gay friend refused Communion at the funeral Mass of his mother; a priest friend who left the ministry without permission to marry (John Paul had tightened the rules that allow laicization); he and his wife languished in a state of excommunication, denied the sacraments.

These were everyday problems of ordinary Catholics close to me who found themselves discouraged, disillusioned, and marginalized, driven away from the sustenance of the sacraments, sometimes in despair of their religion, sometimes moving into communities of faith that had more compassion. The ecclesiastical culture under John Paul encouraged an oppression aimed at reinstating the sin-cycle of former years.

I wrote in *Breaking Faith*:

> *What if we had a pope who genuinely believed that those in trouble, with broken lives, broken relationships, and broken faith, are in greatest need of inclusion and love? A pastoral pope for our time would be a pope who focused his concern on the lost sheep; who ceased to speak of the sinfulness of the faithful, their "culture of death," their "secularism," "indifferentism," and "selfishness." He would recognize that each and every pastor is "father"—the original meaning of the word "pope," within his own faith community. A pope who would mend the breaking faith of our Church must love all the faithful without exception . . . and see in the very least of them—the sinners, the marginalized, the dissidents, the discouraged—the continued future of the Church we love.*

Benedict was, in so many ways, a fine pope; but he was not the pope my extended family and many friends had hoped for. Francis, so patently, has filled that role. Today we are in a very different kind of Church; and while there are constituencies who long to bring back the

Church of John Paul and Benedict, and even the Church of Pius XII, the disruptions of Francis cannot be undone.

Turning closer to home, as I finish this book, I dedicate it to my granddaughters. Having worked for three decades in a university, I have a sense of their generation, the children of the twenty-first century. They live in very different time zones and mentalities from the generations of their uncles, aunts, parents, and grandparents—some of whom are still living, as Cardinal Martini once said to me, in the 1990s, some in the 1960s, and some in the nineteenth century.

My granddaughters, and many I know of their generation, are committed to their religion by a free decision. They are more open to minorities and other faiths, people of difference; they are not motivated by a fear of God. Their values are genuinely Catholic: Here Comes Everybody. They follow the spirit as well as the letter; their moral concerns are wide, rejecting racism, inequality, and prejudice; relieving poverty and homelessness; combating climate change. They have little interest in theological quarrels or the niceties of liturgical rubrics, or in anathematizing fellow Catholics, let alone people of other denominations and faiths. They do not treat their religion as a secure haven from the real world. They know the Church's teaching on essentials but they are nonjudgmental. They are more capable of holding opposites in tension than my generation or that of my parents.

They face a future of rising world poverty, unemployment, migrant crises, the consequences of climate change amid mounting global debts. I have written this book, convinced that Francis interrupted our Church for the future shocks of the interrupted world of my grandchildren, their children, and their children's children. He has disrupted the walls of separation; taught the interrelatedness of societies and nature; urged service for the common good sustained by hope in the boundless love of God.

John Cornwell

Jesus College, Cambridge, 2020

ACKNOWLEDGMENTS

I am indebted to many journalists for their extensive coverage of this papacy published in a wide circuit of Catholic and secular media platforms, as well as the ever-growing bibliography, including the biographies published in the early months of the papacy. I have spoken with many members of the clergy, within and outside the Vatican, up to the rank of archbishop and cardinal, most of whom preferred to remain anonymous. I am grateful to John Wilkins, Michael McGhee, Rory Doyle, Stephen Heath, and Eamon Duffy for reading this book in manuscript. For conversation and correspondence I thank Veronique Mottier, Christopher Lamb, Marco Politi, Robert Mickens, Joshua McElwee, Heidi Schlumpf, Henrietta Harrison, Brendan Walsh, Tobias Wolff, James Lefanu, Mariana Mazzucato, and Duncan Kelly. For special guidance I am grateful to Ian Johnson and Richard Madsen, and especially to my editor Laura Mazer and to Eva Avery. As ever, I thank Zöe Pagnamenta and Clare Alexander, and my publisher, Mark Tauber, for his enthusiasm and encouragement.

SOURCES

Introduction

Page 2: Francis on mercy and the Jubilee of Mercy: James Keenan, "The Scandal of Mercy," *Thinking Faith*, December 4, 2015.

Page 2: "Wills concluded": Gary Wills, *The Future of the Catholic Church with Pope Francis* (New York: Viking, 2015).

Page 3: "By 2018 Richard Rex": Richard Rex, "A Church in Doubt," *First Things*, April 1, 2018.

Page 3: "Francis would declare": Francis, "Justice and Mercy," Morning Meditation, February 24, 2017.

Page 4: "Hope is this living in tension": Francis homily, Santa Marta, October 29, 2019.

Page 5: "bold prudence, he called it": Francis quoted by M. Michela Nicholais in "La Prudenza Audace del Sinodo Per Amazzonia," *La Voce*, October 7, 2019.

Chapter One

Page 11: "One day he dropped an armful of documents": John Cornwell, *A Thief in the Night: The Mysterious Death of Pope John Paul I* (New York: Simon & Schuster,1989), 185–6.

Page 12: "Paul attempted to describe": Peter Hebblethwaite, *Paul VI: The First Modern Pope* (Mahwah, NJ: Paulist Press, 1993), 339.

Page 13: "By 2018 it was estimated": Tom Gjelten, "The Clergy Abuse Crisis Has Cost the Catholic Church $3 Billion," NPR, August 18, 2018.

Page 14: "Christendom no longer exists": Francis, Christmas Discourse to Curia, December 21, 2019.

Page 15: "Research by sociologist": Stephen Bullivant, *Mass Exodus: Catholic Disaffiliation in Britain and America since Vatican II* (Oxford: Oxford University Press, 2019), 56ff.

Chapter Two

Page 19: "a scandal known as Vatileaks": Gerald Posner, *God's Bankers: A History of Money and Power at the Vatican* (New York: Simon & Schuster, 2015), 474ff.

Page 21: "a T-shirt proclaiming": "Rome Cannot Be Home to Two Popes," *The Tablet*, May 30, 2019.

Page 22: "In a broadcast on German radio": Tod Worner, "When Father Ratzinger Predicted the Future of the Church," *Aleteia*, June 13, 2016.

Page 23: "His experience of Argentina's disastrous Dirty War . . . allegations of betrayal": Multiple sources, in particular Paul Vallely, *Pope Francis: Untying the Knots* (London: Bloomsbury, 2013); Austen Ivereigh, *The Great Reformer: Francis and the Making of a Radical Pope* (London: Allen and Unwin, 2014); Jimmy Burns, *Francis Pope, of Good Promise* (London: Constable, 2015).

Chapter Three

Page 29: "Antonio Spadaro . . . describes": Antonio Spadaro, "Interview with Pope Francis," *L'Osservatore Romano*, September 21, 2013.

Page 32: "His first formal address:" Francis, "Address of the Holy Father Pope Francis," March 16, 2013.

Page 33: "The choice of director": Paul Elie, "The Spiritual Nearness of Wim Wenders's 'Pope Francis: A Man of His Word,'" *New Yorker*, May 21, 2018.

Chapter Four

Page 37: "He did not mince his words": Harriet Sherwood, "The Pope Compares Fake News Consumption to Eating Faeces," *The Guardian*, December 7, 2016.

Page 37: "microcosm of jealousies": Marco Politi, *Pope Francis among the Wolves: The Inside Story of a Revolution,* trans. William McCuaig (New York: Columbia University Press, 2015), 174.

Page 37: "palace of gossipy eunuchs": Cornwell, *Thief in the Night*, 62.

Page 38: "at least 80 percent of Vatican bureaucrats": Frédéric Martel, *In the Closet of the Vatican: Power, Homosexuality, Hypocrisy,* trans. Shaun Whiteside (London: Bloomsbury, 2019).

Page 38: "British diplomat once captured": Owen Chadwick, *Britain and the Vatican during the Second World War* (Cambridge, UK: Cambridge University Press, 1986), 122.

Page 40: "The Catholic commentator Andrew Sullivan": Andrew Sullivan, "The Pope Is Not Gay," *Atlantic*, August 15, 2010.

Page 40: "in the words of the Irish writer": Colm Toíbín, "Among the Flutterers," *London Review of Books*, August 19, 2010.

Page 40: "Martel cites Archbishop Paul Marcinkus": Martel, *In the Closet*, 252–253.

Page 42: "If you can't find charity": Cornwell, *Thief in the Night*, 108.

Chapter Five

Page 50: "According to the business magazine": Andrew A. King and Baljir Baatartogtokh, "How Useful Is the Theory of Disruptive Innovation?" *MIT Sloan Management Review*, September 15, 2015.

Page 50: "Writing in *Forbes*": Irwin Kula and Craig Hatkoff, "Pope Francis: CEO and Epic Innovator," *Forbes*, November 12, 2014.

Page 52: "Kevin Systrom, cofounder of Instagram": Paige Leskin, "Instagram's Former CEO Once Flew to the Vatican Personally to Help Pope Francis Create an Account," *Business Insider,* November 20, 2019.

Page 53: "Back in 1996": Thomas J. Reese, S.J., *Inside the Vatican: The Politics and Organization of the Catholic Church* (Cambridge, MA: Harvard University Press, 1996), 279.

Page 53: "Francis took steps to revolutionize": Gerard O'Connell, "Pope Francis Establishes a New Vatican Secretariat for Communications," *America*, June 27, 2015.

Page 54: "a central content hub": Duncan Wardle, "Disrupt or Die, Former Disney Innovation Head Says," *National Business Review*, October 29, 2018.

Page 55: "direct-to-consumer offerings": Justin Moser, "Disney Restructures Its Business as Digital Disruption Shakes Up the Media Industry," *Los Angeles Times*, March 14, 2018.

Page 55: "According to Heidi Schlumpf": Heidi Schlumpf, "Pro-Trump Group Targets Catholic Voters Using Cellphone Technology," *National Catholic Reporter*, January 2, 2020.

Page 57: "as church historian Eamon Duffy has written": John Cornwell, *Breaking Faith: The Pope, the People, and the Fate of Catholicism* (New York: Viking, 2001), 34.

Chapter Six

Page 59: "The Italian banker Roberto Calvi": Posner, *God's Bankers,* 257ff.

Page 60: "on the verge of bankruptcy": Josephine McKenna, "Franciscan Order on Verge of Bankruptcy After Financial Fraud Is Uncovered," Religion News Service, December 19, 2014.

Page 60: "Pius IX fled into exile": David I. Kertzer, *The Pope Who Would Be King: The Exile of Pius IX and the Emergence of Modern Europe* (Oxford: Oxford University Press, 2018).

Page 60: "Earlier still, the Franciscans": Martin Schlag, *The Business Francis Means: Understanding the Pope's Message on the Economy* (Washington, DC: Catholic University of America Press, 2017), 162ff.

Page 61: "The Jesuit community at Salamanca": Schlag, *The Business Francis Means,* 34.

Pages 62: "Then there is the so-called Vatican Bank. . . . The bank came under the spotlight again": Cornwell, *Thief in the Night.*

Page 63: "nicknamed Monsignor Cinquecento": "The Vatican's Woes: Exit Monsignor Cinquecento," *Economist,* June 29, 2013.

Page 63: "Ten years on, the Cardinal Archbishop of Naples": John L. Allen Jr., "Facing Financial Scandals, Pope Creates New Vatican Watchdog," *National Catholic Reporter,* December 30, 2010.

Page 64: "Benedict's personal butler": Posner, *God's Bankers*, 468ff.

Page 65: "He lambasted clerical love of luxury": "Pope to New Priests," Catholic News Agency, April 26, 2015.

Page 65: "the $500,000 spent on 'remodeling'": John L. Allen Jr. "Defendant in Vatican Trial Says Cardinal 'Clarified' Affair with the Pope," *Crux,* September 22, 2017.

Page 65: "Francis strove to initiate proper governance and good practice": Austen Ivereigh, *Wounded Shepherd: Pope Francis and His Struggle to Convert the Catholic Church* (New York: Henry Holt, 2019), 45ff.

Page 66: "Chelsea property deal in London": Miles Johnson and Donato Paulo Mancini, "Police Investigate Holy See's Bet on Chelsea Property Project," *Financial Times,* October 14, 2019.

Page 67: "'the lids have been taken off the pots'": Cindy Wooden, "Financial scandal shows Vatican reforms are working, pope tells media," Catholic News Service, November 26, 2019.

Page 68: "Christopher Lamb, *The Tablet*'s Rome correspondent": Christopher Lamb, "Power Games in the Roman Curia Pose Greatest Threat to Financial Reform," *The Tablet*, November 19, 2019.

Page 69: "human rights lawyer Geoffrey Robertson": Geoffrey Robertson QC, *The Case of the Pope: Vatican Accountability for Human Rights Abuses* (London: Penguin, 2010).

Chapter Seven

Page 71: "Jorge Bergoglio was born in 1936": Vallely, *Untying the Knots*, 15ff.

Page 73: "a rise in poverty in Buenos Aires": Samuel H. Gregg, "Understanding Pope Francis: Argentina, Economic Failure, and the *Teología del Pueblo*," *Independent Review* 21, no. 3 (winter 2016/2017).

Page 74: "representing some of the poorest regions of the world, at Aparecida": Ivereigh, *Great Reformer*, 153ff.

Page 74: "in a series of conversations with his friend Rabbi Abraham Skorka": Jorge Mario Bergoglio and Abraham Skorka, *On Heaven and Earth: Pope Francis on Faith, Family, and the Church in the Twenty-First Century* (New York: Image, 2013).

Page 76: "an essay by Catholic economist Philip Booth": "Has Francis misunderstood the market economy?" *The Tablet*, December 4, 2013.

Page 76: "R. R. Reno, editor of the Catholic periodical": R. R. Reno, "Francis and the Market," *First Things*, February 2014.

Chapter Eight

Page 82: "'The document is riddled'": George Neumayr, *The Political Pope: How Pope Francis Is Delighting the Liberal Left and Abandoning Conservatives* (New York: Center Street, 2017).

Page 82: "Poorest, of the poorest": Wim Wenders, *Pope Francis: A Man of His Word* (2018).

Page 83: "'Bergoglian word-bombs'": R. R. Reno, "Crisis of Our Time," *First Things*, December 1, 2015.

Page 83: "'The earth, our home, is beginning to look'": *Laudato Si'* (London: Catholic Truth Society, 2015), 21.

Page 84: "'We were not meant to be inundated by cement'": *Laudato Si'*, 44.

Page 86: "'We are not God'": *Laudato Si'*, 67.

Page 87: "Christian spirituality, he declares, proposes": *Laudato Si'*, 222–4.

Page 90: "Connection between God and all beings": *Laudato Si'*, 233–6.

Chapter Nine

Page 90: "Di Giovanni told the Vatican media": Gerard O'Connell, *America*, January 15, 2020.

Page 91: "Known officially as the Pontifical Commission for the Protection of Minors": John Cornwell, "Women Come to Power," *Newsweek*, May 4, 2014.

Page 93: "As Cardinal Martini remarked in my interview with him": John Cornwell, *Sunday Times Magazine*, April 25, 1993.

Page 94: "Pope John Paul II refused to shake her hand": Greg Daly, "Eyewitness Accounts Challenge McAleese Papal Handshake Story," *Irish Catholic*, January 17, 2019.

Page 95: "'the authority of their housekeepers'": David Gibson, "Lost in Translation? 7 Reasons Some Women Wince when Pope Francis Starts Talking," USCatholic.org, December 19, 2014.

Page 95: "something of the Argentine machismo attitude": V. S. Naipaul, "Argentina: The Brothels Behind the Graveyard," *New York Review of Books*, September 19, 1974.

Page 95: "'strawberries on the cake' of theology": Hannah Roberts, "Women Theologians Are 'the Strawberry on the Cake,' Says Pope," *The Tablet*, December 11, 2014.

Page 96: "'Women, in the Church, are more important'": Adelaide Mena, "Women in the Church remarks urge a deeper theology," Catholic News Service, July 31, 2013.

Page 96: "'Masculinity and femininity are not rigid categories'": *Amoris Laetitia* (2016), 286.

Page 96: "John Paul II in his 1994 letter on the priesthood": *The Tablet*, July 15, 1995.

Page 97: "during my interview with Cardinal Martini": Cornwell, *Sunday Times Magazine*.

Page 99: "'real discrimination of woman'": Gerhard Ludwig Müller, "Women Deacons? A Perspective on the Sacrament of Orders," Zenit, January 17, 2002.

Chapter Ten

Page 101: "In the fall of 2013, Jacquelina Lisbona": David Gibson, "Did Pope Francis Really Tell a Divorced Woman to Take Communion?" Religion News Service, April 23, 2014.

Page 102: "'In God, justice is mercy and mercy is justice'": Francis, "Justice and Mercy," February 24, 2017.

Page 102: "Returning from Brazil in 2013": "Press Conference of Pope Francis During the Return Flight," July 28, 2013.

Page 108: "The columnist and author Ross Douthat": Ross Douthat, *To Change the Church: Pope Francis and the Future of Catholicism* (New York: Simon & Schuster, 2018), 97.

Chapter Eleven

Page 111: "As the first synod": Philip F. Lawler, *Lost Shepherd: How Pope Francis Is Misleading His Flock* (Washington: Gateway, 2018), 77ff.

Page 112: "The Church has never judged homosexual persons": "African Cardinal Sees Effort to Manipulate Synod," Catholic World News, October 17, 2014.

Page 115: "prefer a more rigorous pastoral care": *Amoris Laetitia*, 308.

Page 116: "four ruffled cardinals": Edward Pentin, "Full text of dubia cardinals' letter asking Pope for an audience," Catholic News Agency, June 20, 2017.

See Pope Francis on hope, including homilies given at Santa Marta from the Feast of the Immaculate Conception, December 8, 2016, and Easter 2017: *On Hope* (Chicago: Loyola Press, 2017).

Chapter Twelve

Page 126: "'A Church with wounds can understand'": Cindy Wooden, "Five Wounds of Christ: Pope Urges Recovery of Traditional Devotion," *National Catholic Reporter*, January 22, 2018.

Page 127: "'The day they bring me proof'": Junno Arrocho Esteves, "Pope Apologizes for Word Choice on Sex Abuse Crisis," *The Tablet*, January 24, 2018.

Page 128: "'Words that convey the message'": Evan Allen, "Cardinal O'Malley speaks out against Pope's comment on sex abuse victims in Chile," *Boston Globe*, January 21, 2018.

Page 129: "The Barros case was examined and reexamined, but there is no evidence": www.vatican.va, speeches, January 21, 2018.

Page 130: "'I have made serious mistakes'": Thomas Reese, "'I have made serious mistakes,' says Pope. 'I ask forgiveness,'" *National Catholic Reporter*, April 17, 2018.

Page 132: "An Investigating Grand Jury": Scott Dodd, "Pennsylvania Grand Jury Says Church Had a 'Playbook for Concealing the Truth,'" *New York Times*, August 14, 2018.

Page 133: "At his morning Mass at Santa Marta's": Sermon on Hope: Santa Marta, June 7, 2018

Chapter Thirteen

Page 138: "'families come in many different'": Harriet Sherwood, "Irish PM: time to move Catholic church from centre of society," *Guardian*, August 25, 2018.

Page 138: Pope Francis speeches in Ireland, August 2018: www.dublindiocese .ie/pope-francis-speeches-in-ireland

Page 138: "In the evening Francis met with a group of abuse survivors headed by Marie Collins": Marie Collins, "The Pope was honest when I quizzed him about abuse, but I despair after answers I was given," *Irish Independent*, August 27, 2018. Collins did not, according to this interview, say that Francis had never heard of the Magdalene Laundries (as was widely reported), but that he heard "detail": "He wasn't familiar with the detail of the Magdalene Laundries, the mother and baby homes, and the institutional schools. The survivors were very forthright in telling him exactly what went on in all those places and making it clear what they wanted him to do and say. As he listened, he asked for details and for clarifications."

Page 139: "I later obtained a transcript of the recording": Francis's comments were made on August 28, 2018. Transcript courtesy of Christopher Lamb.

Page 140: "Half a million tickets had been disbursed": Ken Foxe, "OPW reveals final headcount for papal Mass in Phoenix Park," *Irish Times*, September 19, 2018. The official report of the Office of Public Works put it at "almost certainly just under 152,000."

Page 140: "a 7,000-word letter issued overnight": "The Viganò Statement," The Catholic Thing, August 27, 2018.

Page 143: "The Great Accuser has been unchained": Sister Bernadette Mary Reis, "Pope Francis at Mass: Jesus the icon of the meek and compassionate pastor," *Vatican News*, September 18, 2018.

Page 143: "'it's about limiting the days of this pope'": Elizabeth Dias and Laurie Goodstein, "Letter Accusing Pope Leaves U.S. Catholics in Conflict," *New York Times*, August 27, 2018.

Page 143: "According to Michael Sean Winters": Michael Sean Winters, "Viganò letter exposes the putsch against Francis," *National Catholic Reporter*, August 26, 2018.

Page 143: "his homily during Mass at Santa Marta": Sermon on Hope: Mass, Santa Marta, October 23, 2018.

Page 144: "an open letter in French": "Open Letter by Cardinal Marc Ouellet on Recent Accusations against the Holy See," *Vatican News*, October 7, 2018.

Chapter Fourteen

Page 147: "When Francis uttered that phrase": "Press Conference of Pope Francis During the Return Flight," July 28, 2013.

Page 148: "this priest, Father Leslie McCallum": John Cornwell, *Seminary Boy* (New York: Doubleday Religion, 2006), 272–4.

Page 150: "Peter Isely declared . . .": "Blaming homosexuality . . . " Catholic News Service, February 20, 2019.

Page 150: "Philip Jenkins has remarked": Philip Jenkins, *Pedophiles and Priests: Anatomy of a Contemporary Crisis* (Oxford: Oxford University Press, 1996).

Page 151: "Greeley denounced": Quoted by Jason Berry, "Secrets, Celibacy and the Church," *New York Times*, April 3, 2002.

Page 151: "'seventy to eighty percent of priests'": Richard Sipe, *Sex, Priests and Power: Anatomy of a Crisis* (New York: Brunner-Routledge, 1995), 12.

Page 152: "The four-day 'summit on clerical sexual abuse'": Gerard O'Connell, "Francis presents 21-point 'road map' guide to guide discussion at abuse summit," *America*, February 21, 2019.

Page 154: "a 6,000-word letter by Emeritus Pope Benedict": "Full text of Benedict XVI essay: 'The Church and the Scandal of Sexual Abuse," Catholic News Agency, April 10, 2019.

Page 157: "the pastoral work of James Martin": See Bishop John Wester's response to Catholic News Agency account of Francis-James Martin meeting: "Archbishop Wester responds to recounting of Pope's words about Jesuit Fr. James Martin," *National Catholic Reporter*, February 21, 2020.

Page 158: "'our priests feel themselves attacked'": "Letter of His Holiness Pope Francis to Priests on the 160th Anniversary of the Death of the Holy Curé of Ars, St. John Vianney," August 4, 2019.

Chapter Fifteen

Page 163: "historic gesture of reconciliation": James Carroll, "Pope Francis and the Renunciation of Jewish Conversion," *New Yorker,* December 16, 2015.

Page 165: "The imam and Francis signed a declaration": "Document on Human Fraternity for world peace and living together: full text," *Vatican News,* February 4, 2019.

Page 166: "a twenty-page letter signed by a group of senior theologians": "Prominent clergy, scholars accuse Pope Francis of heresy in open letter," LifeSiteNews, April 30, 2019.

Page 167: "every religion except his own": George Neumayr, "The Pope's Pickle in Burma," *American Spectator,* September 6, 2017.

Page 169: "anonymous Christian": Karl Rahner, *Theological Investigations, Vol. VI: Concerning Vatican Council II,* trans. Karl-H. and Boniface Kruger (New York: Herder and Herder, 1971), 390ff.

Page 169: "the fullness of truth is not revealed": Jacques Dupuis, *Toward a Christian Theology of Religious Pluralism* (Maryknoll, NY: Orbis Books, 1997).

Page 170: "the errors of religious pluralism were spelled out": *Dominus Iesus,* August 2000.

Chapter Sixteen

Page 173: "In Spain new figures": Fernando Forte, "Attendance at religious services among believers in Spain 2019," Statista, May 14, 2019.

Page 173: "In 2018, the year of a shattering report on child abuse in the country": "German churches lose 430,000 Catholic and Protestant members in 2018," dw.com, July 19, 2019.

Page 175: "playing the Hitler card": "Cardinal Müller criticized for his Nazi comparison of Germany's synodal way process," *America,* February 6, 2020.

Page 177: "a typical example of Francis's 'applied chaos'": Hilary White, "Pope's Scalfari Message Is for Italians (Not for You)," OnePeterFive, October 21, 2019.

Page 179: "The question of reliability arose in Scalfari's first interview": Eugenio Scalfari, *La Repubblica,* October 1, 2013.

Page 179: "Francis had denied the divinity of Jesus Christ": James Roberts, "Scalfari claims Pope does not believe Jesus 'the man' was divine," *The Tablet,* October 10, 2019.

Chapter Seventeen

Page 184: "the two groups, official and unofficial, work together and yet apart": Richard Madsen, *China's Catholics: Tragedy and Hope in an Emerging Civil Society* (Berkeley: University of California Press, 1998), 1ff. The background history of the two Catholic communities in China is extensively told in Ian John Johnson, *The Souls of China: The Return of Religion after Mao* (New York: Pantheon, 2017). For a microhistory of one Catholic community in China: Henrietta Harrison, *The Missionary's Curse and Other Tales from a Chinese Village* (Berkeley: University of California Press, 2013).

Page 186: "he reached a discreet 'provisional' accord": Paul P. Mariani, S.J., "The Extremely High Stakes of the China-Vatican Deal," *America*, December 7, 2018.

Page 186: "Francis was accused by Cardinal Joseph Zen": "Cardinal Zen says Pope Francis being 'manipulated' on China," *Crux*, March 2, 2020.

Page 187: "George Weigel declared": "Did Pope Francis Just Make China Protestant?" *National Review*, September 24, 2018.

Page 188: "Cardinal Parolin, secretary of state": Junno Arocho Esteves, "Cardinal defends Vatican-China Agreement amid criticism," *National Catholic Reporter*, April 3, 2019.

Page 189: "the thorn of division": Madsen, *China's Catholics*, 141.

Chapter Eighteen

Page 193: "young Catholics broke into the church": Church Militant, "Vortex-Pachamama drowned," YouTube, October 21, 2019. See also LifeSiteNews, "Priest burns Pachamama," YouTube, November 4, 2019.

Page 194: "YouTube clip showed Pope Francis blessing": LifeSiteNews, "Video shows Pope Francis blessing controversial 'Pachamama' statue," YouTube, October 24, 2019.

Page 194: "several hundred signatories": Maike Hickson, "100 Priests, Lay Scholars Call Francis to Repent for Pachamama Idolatry at Amazon Synod," Pan-Amazon Synod Watch, December 11, 2019.

Page 195: "issued an apology": "Pope Francis apologizes that Amazon synod 'Pachamama' was thrown into Tiber River," *Catholic World Report*, October 25, 2019.

Page 195: "words for prelates who scoffed": "Pope: Indigenous People's Feathered Headgear No Sillier Than Vatican Hats," *Guardian*, October 7, 2019.

Page 197: "A headline in the *New York Times* expressed": Jason Horowitz and Elisabetta Povoledo, "Two Popes, and One Big Furor after Benedict Weighs in on Priestly Celibacy," *New York Times*, January 14, 2019.

Page 199: "'bullied' by the liberal media": "The Bullies and That Book," by George Weigel, *First Things*, January 29, 2019.

Page 199: "part of an opposition campaign": Eugenio Scalfari, "Celibato dei preti, papa Francesco: con Ratzinger il caso è chiuso," *La Repubblica*, January 15, 2020.

Chapter Nineteen

Page 201: "Sister Dorothy Stang": Roseanne Murphy, *Martyr of the Amazon: The Life of Sister Dorothy Stang* (Maryknoll, NY: Orbis Books, 2007).

Page 204: "The reception of the exhortation revealed": Heidi Schlumpf, "Disappointment, Outrage over Papal Document on the Amazon," *National Catholic Reporter*, February 12, 2020; Thomas Reese, "Pope Francis Punts on Married Priests, *National Catholic Reporter*, February 14, 2020.

Page 205: "'not always considered a pagan error'": Francis, *Querida Amazonia*, February 2, 2020, 79.

Page 205: "'by patiently and attentively holding together'": Austen Ivereigh, "Pope Francis discerns 'third way' for the Amazon," *The Tablet*, February 12, 2020.

Page 206: "'typically and woefully inadequate'": Massimo Faggioli, "Francis Sidesteps the Synod's Recommendations," *Commonweal*, February 14, 2020.

Page 206: "'mired in a sentimental fantasy'": Tina Beattie, "A 'frozen' idea of the feminine," *The Tablet*, February 20, 2020.

Page 207: "'personal and attractive tone'": Cardinal Müller, "'Querida Amazonia' Is a Document of Reconciliation," *National Catholic Register*, February 12, 2020.

Chapter Twenty

Page 211: "on the theme of value and work": Pope Francis, "The Work Is Not a Commodity," Zenit, September 20, 2018.

Page 211: "a viral genocide": Courtney Mares, "Francis warns of a coronavirus 'genocide' if economy prioritized over people," Catholic News Agency, March 30, 2020.

Page 212: "he published 'a plan for the rising up again'": Gerard O'Connell, "Pope Francis Shares His Vision for COVID-19 Aftermath," *America*, April 17, 2020.

Page 212: Stephen Bullivant on post-COVID statistics: "Churches after the storm," *The Tablet*, May 14, 2020. See Austen Ivereigh interview with Francis: "Pope Francis says pandemic can be a 'place of conversion,'" *The Tablet*, April 8, 2020.

Chapter Twenty-One

Page 219: "'Of criticisms, I always see'": Hannah Brockhaus and Ed Pentin, "Pope Francis says he welcomes constructive criticism," Catholic News Agency, September 10, 2019.

Page 220: "'I receive calls for help'": Cardinal Robert Sarah in conversation with Nicolas Diat, *The Day Is Now Far Spent*, trans. Michael J. Miller (San Francisco: Ignatius Press, 2019), 1.

Page 221: "His sorrow and anger were registered": *The Motherhood of the Church* (San Francisco: Ignatius Press, 1982), 25.

Page 222: "'At stake is the relationship'": George Weigel, "There's a Pony in Here Somewhere," *First Things*, October 28, 2019.

Page 223: "'combines laxity and ruthlessness'": R. R. Reno, "A Failing Papacy," *First Things*, February 1, 2019.

Page 223: "piece of character assassination": Jonathan B. Coe, "Understanding and Combating the Francis Effect," *Crisis*, February 27, 2019.

Page 224: "Ross Douthat, op-ed columnist": Douthat, *To Change the Church*, 190ff.

Chapter Twenty-Two

Page 233: "a broadcast in German in 1969": Tod Worner, "When Father Ratzinger Predicted the Future of the Church," *Aleteia*, June 13, 2016.

Page 236: "Francis publicly expressed his vision for synods": "Pope calls for 'synodal' church where all listen, learn, share mission," Catholic News Service, October 17, 2015.

Page 236: "decreed that the final document of a synod": Francis, *Episcopalis Communio*, September 15, 2018.

Page 237: "'trading in sarcasm'": Massimo Faggioli, "Catholic synodality as a response to the crisis of democracy," *La Croix International*, November 12, 2019.

Page 237: "language sodden with clichés": George Weigel, "The 'Synodality' Masquerade," *First Things*, November 13, 2019.

Chapter Twenty-Three:

Pages 240–246: For a portrait of Pius X and the anti-modernist campaign, see Owen Chadwick, *A History of the Popes, 1830–1914* (Oxford: Oxford University Press, 1998), 334ff.; Nicholas Lash, "Modernism, *Aggiornamento* and the night battle," in *Bishops and Writers: Aspects of the Evolution of Modern English Catholicism*, ed. Garrett Sweeney (Wheathampstead, Hertfordshire: Anthony Clarke Books, 1977), 55–6.

Page 242: "'a continuous, desperate attempt to vomit'": Chadwick, *History of the Popes*, 357.

Page 242: "two devastating encyclicals": Pius X, *Lamentabili Sane* (1907), *Pascendi Dominici Gregis* (1907).

Page 242: "'They should be beaten with fists'": C. Falconi, *Popes in the Twentieth Century* (London: Weidenfeld and Nicolson, 1967), 54.

Page 242: "The foremost English-speaking so-called modernist was George Tyrrell": The key works of George Tyrrell are *Lex Orandi: Or, Prayer and Creed* (London: Longmans, Green, 1903); *Lex Credendi: A Sequel to Lex Orandi* (London: Longmans, Green, 1906); *Through Scylla and Charybdis: Or, The Old Theology and the New* (London: Longmans, Green, 1907).

Page 243: "He wrote that he wanted to be clear": *The Joy of Love*, 3.

Page 244: "swear an anti-modernist oath": The anti-modernist oath was taken from 1907–1967 by all Catholic clergy and teachers in seminaries. A key passage: "I firmly hold, then, and shall hold to my dying breath the belief of the Fathers in the charism of truth, which certainly is, was, and always will be in the succession of the episcopacy from the apostles. The purpose of this is, then, not that dogma may be tailored according to what seems better and more suited to the culture of each age; rather, that the absolute and immutable truth preached by the apostles from the beginning may never be believed to be different, may never be understood in any other way. . . ."

Page 245: "as yet unpublished deposition": Chadwick, *History of the Popes*, 55.

Chapter Twenty-Four

Page 254: "quoting a Sufi poet": Ali al-Khawas, in *Laudato Si'*, 2233.

Page 254: "'doing theology on one's knees'": Address to students at Gregorian University, Rome, April 10, 2014.

Page 254: "'change is more consistent with one's scope": John O'Malley, *The First Jesuits* (Cambridge, MA: Harvard University Press, 1995), 367.

Page 255: "he taught for a number of years": Reno, "Failing Papacy," *First Things*.

Page 255: "'This is the first step named *unfreezing*'": Hugo Nelson Gomez-Sevilla, "Innovation and Change in Jesuit Education" (PhD dissertation, Loyola University, 2018).

INDEX

ABOUT THE AUTHOR

John Cornwell is an award-winning journalist and author. His books on Catholicism include the *New York Times* bestseller *Hitler's Pope* and the internationally acclaimed *A Thief in the Night: The Death of John Paul I*. He is author of *Pontiff in Winter*, a biography of John Paul II; and *Breaking Faith*, a survey of the Catholic Church at the millennium. His last book was *The Dark Box: A Secret History of Confession*.

Cornwell spent seven years studying for the priesthood and wrote a memoir of junior seminary life titled *Seminary Boy*. He later studied literature and philosophy at Oxford and Cambridge. He has written regularly about Catholicism for the *Financial Times* and the London *Sunday Times*. In 2019, he won the Wilbur Award for his profile of Popes Benedict and Francis in *Vanity Fair*. Since 1990, he has directed the Science & Human Dimension Project at Jesus College in the University of Cambridge. He is married with two children and lives in London.